ALSO BY ADAM FREEDMAN

★

The Naked Constitution
The Party of the First Part

A Less Perfect Union

A LESS PERFECT UNION

THE CASE FOR
STATES' RIGHTS

ADAM FREEDMAN

BROADSIDE BOOKS
An Imprint of HarperCollins*Publishers*

An earlier version of portions of the chapter "States' Rights and the Abolitionists" appeared in the Autumn 2014 issue of *City Journal*.

HarperCollins books may be purchased for educational, business, or sales promotional use. For information, please e-mail the Special Markets Department at SPsales@harpercollins.com.

Broadside Books™ and the Broadside logo are trademarks of HarperCollins Publishers.

FIRST EDITION

Designed by William Ruoto

Library of Congress Cataloging-in-Publication Data has been applied for.

ISBN 978-0-06-226994-2

15 16 17 18 19   OV/RRD   10 9 8 7 6 5 4 3 2 1

To Simon, Marion, Mark, and Paul

Contents

THE FUTURE: REVIVING STATES' RIGHTS

A Less Perfect Union

INTRODUCTION

The War Against the States

Falesha Augustus was at her wit's end.

Her ten-year-old son, Willie, was doing poorly at his local elementary school in Baton Rouge, Louisiana. He complained about being bullied, and he seemed to be overwhelmed by the large, unruly classes. When Falesha pleaded with school officials to teach her child the "fundamentals," they ignored her. When she came in person to seek the principal's help, the principal told her to stop hanging around the school.

Things finally began to change in 2012, when Willie qualified for a scholarship to attend the private school of his choice, or rather, his mother's choice. The scholarship was funded by the state of Louisiana, courtesy of a school voucher program aimed at low-income kids trapped in failing schools. Falesha promptly enrolled Willie in Hosanna Christian Academy in East Baton Rouge, a school known for small classes and a structured approach. Almost immediately, Willie began to thrive. "All I hear about is how he is eager to learn," Falesha said as Willie began fourth grade at his new school.[1]

The Louisiana voucher program has benefited thousands of families, 90 percent of whom are African American.[2] The scholarship students are doing better than they did at their old schools, with a marked improvement in math and reading test scores. Parents love the program, and so do the taxpayers—the vouchers save Louisiana millions of dollars, because private education is more cost-effective than public education.

Popular, effective, and inexpensive: Who could oppose the Louisiana scholarship program? Nobody—well, nobody except the federal government. In August 2013, Barack Obama's Department of Justice (DOJ) went to federal court to shut down the Louisiana scholarship program. Why? In theory, the DOJ was seeking to enforce school desegregation orders from the 1970s. But since the Louisiana program was helping black children get into largely white private schools, it was hard to argue that the program was harming African Americans. Instead, the government's lawyers were stuck complaining that the vouchers threatened to leave Louisiana's public schools excessively *white*. The administration did not deny that the scholarship kids might get a better education out of the deal, but it was more important for public schools to maintain "the desired degree of racial diversity."[3]

Under pressure from groups like the Black Alliance for Educational Options, the administration eventually dropped its demand that the state kill the program, but only on the condition that the federal government would get to make the final call on each and every scholarship application—a level of micromanagement that would effectively asphyxiate the whole initiative. The government's move prompted Lindsey Burke, a scholar at the Heritage Foundation, to marvel, "It's hard even to wrap your head around the audacity of Washington."[4]

The Taboo Doctrine

States' rights is all about liberating America's states to help kids like Willie Augustus without interference—or coercion—from Washington. That's not to say that every state should adopt a voucher program; rather, the point is that decisions about things like vouchers should be made in state capitals and school districts, not inside the Capital Beltway.

You may balk at the idea of "states' rights" as a force that can help America's minorities—that's okay, you've been conditioned to react that way. In newspapers and in classrooms, states' rights is endlessly characterized as a shorthand expression for slavery, Jim Crow, and other forms of institutionalized racism. According to the popular but, as we will see, misleading narrative, states' rights is a philosophy born in the American South and originally used to defend slavery, then to justify secession, and finally to resist racial integration. No political doctrine this side of fascism has been more thoroughly demonized than states' rights. A July 2013 *New York Times* essay by Michael C. Dawson, a professor at the University of Chicago, pretty much sums up the ivory tower's view of states' rights with his cocksure allegation that "since the nation's founding, 'states' rights' has been a rallying cry for those who wished to systematically disenfranchise and exploit large segments of their population."[5] Four months later, the Reverend Jesse Jackson chimed in over at the *Chicago Sun-Times*: "From the earliest days of the Republic, states' rights has always been the doctrine of reaction."[6]

Any politician who dares to breathe the words "states' rights" will be accused, in the shopworn metaphor, of sending out a "dog whistle" to stoke the racial fears of white voters. When Rick Perry, the governor of Texas, campaigned for president on an explicit states' rights platform, CNN's Rick Sanchez breezily dismissed him: "States' rights is . . . a racist term," he said.[7] When a Connecticut congressional candidate expressed support for "state sovereignty" in 2010, the far-left blog *Daily Kos* accused him of "nostalgia for the Confederacy."[8] Around the same time, the MSNBC host Chris Matthews asserted that no sane African American would support the Tea Party, because it is "a group that is basically pro-states' rights."[9] Even Republicans are afraid of states' rights. In January 2012, the Heritage Foundation's David Azerrad urged conservatives to "drop the term states' rights once and for all" because it "has more baggage than Samsonite and Louis Vuitton combined."[10] Mitt Romney's campaign dutifully followed this advice and, of course, sailed to victory in the 2012 general election.

The knee-jerk critique of states' rights is based largely on the politically convenient but mendacious attempt to link contemporary conservatives with old-time segregationists. I'll get to that in a moment, but the fact is that states' rights has historically been the rallying cry for just about every cause that progressives hold dear: the abolition of slavery, union rights, workplace safety, social welfare entitlements, and opposition to war. What, then, is states' rights?

Broadly speaking, states' rights is the right of every state to exercise all of the powers that have not been specifically entrusted to the federal government. States' rights is based on a fundamental individual right: the right of every American to enjoy local self-government. Like many of the rights we hold most dear, states' rights is a doctrine embedded in the Bill of Rights—that is, the first ten amendments to the United States Constitution. As I will argue in later chapters, the entire Bill of Rights was originally a charter of states' rights, because its purpose was to restrain the federal government from encroaching on state powers. But for now, it suffices to recall the final provision of the Bill of Rights, the Tenth Amendment:

> The powers not delegated to the United States by the Constitution, nor prohibited by it to the States, are reserved to the States respectively, or to the people.

Of course, the Constitution *does* delegate a number of important powers to "the United States" (i.e., the federal government). Those powers are set forth mainly in Article I, and they include things like national defense, interstate and international commerce, patents, and post offices. The Constitution also forbids the states from doing certain things like imposing tariffs or declaring war. But for the vast array of government functions that are not specifically withheld from the states—including things like health and safety, agriculture, education, and infrastructure—the Tenth Amendment makes it clear that the states remain in charge.

Washington's minions like to argue that states' rights is an unconstitutional doctrine, because our system makes the national government "supreme." That's just plain wrong. Under our system, it is the *Constitution*, not the national government, that is supreme. Federal statutes override state laws only to the extent the former conforms to our supreme law (see the Constitution, Article VI).

A Too-Perfect Union

Constitutionally speaking, states are independent sovereigns—in fact, they were sovereign states from the moment they declared independence in 1776. They later banded together under the Constitution not to form a single consolidated nation but to form "a more perfect union." To be sure, when the Constitution's framers said "more perfect," they meant a more centralized union than the "firm league of friendship" established by the Articles of Confederation in 1777. The exact degree of centralization, however, was a subject of heated debate; indeed, it was the primary issue dividing the delegates at the Philadelphia convention of 1787. On the one hand, there was a nationalist faction that pushed for a quasi-monarchical system (some wanted an actual monarchy) in which all government power resided in a single sovereign person or body.[11] On the other hand, there were Federalists who sought a stronger central government to coordinate certain issues of national scope, but who also wished to preserve the maximum degree of autonomy for the states.

In the end, the Federalists won: the Constitution that emerged from the convention created a federal union, not a national government; indeed, the word "nation" is nowhere to be seen in the document. That's why the faction that supported ratification of the Constitution became known as the Federalist Party. Rather than give the central government sweeping powers, as the nationalists had urged, the Constitution restricted Congress to a finite list of enumerated powers. The states were to retain sovereignty over the vast majority of domestic issues. Even before the addition of the Tenth Amendment, James Madison observed in *The Federalist Papers*—the collection of essays by Madison, Alexander Hamilton, and John Jay originally intended to win over the New York ratifying convention—that the Constitution gives states nearly complete power to pass and enforce laws touching on "the lives, liberties, and properties of the people, and the internal order, improvement, and prosperity of the State."

Despite such assurances, many of Madison's contemporaries accurately foresaw the danger of equating a "perfect" union with a strong central government. If a more "perfect" union is a more consolidated one, then what was to stop ambitious politicians from gathering up all the power at the national level in the name of yet-greater perfection? This was one of the central arguments of the Anti-Federalists (a somewhat inaccurate label, as I will explain later), who resisted the new Constitution because, among other things, "to make a union of this kind perfect, it is necessary to abolish all inferior governments and to give the general one compleat legislative, executive and judicial powers to every purpose."[12] The author of that sentence— Robert Yates, a judge from New York who wrote under the pseudonym Brutus—is rightly regarded as the most farsighted of the Anti-Federalists.[13]

Once the Constitution had been ratified, the Anti-Federalists accepted the outcome, but they successfully insisted on a Bill of Rights, including the Tenth Amendment, in the hopes of putting specific restraints on the central government. The Constitution plus the Bill of Rights strikes an exquisite balance between local self-government and centralized power; it remains the greatest charter of government devised by man. Alas, the temptation of Washington politicians to expand their power has proved to be more than the original parchment barriers could withstand. One by one, the restraints on federal power have withered away, leaving us perilously close to Brutus's nightmare vision of a completely "perfect" union—that is, an all-powerful national government.

Or perhaps we've already arrived at the ultimate in nationalist "perfection." In 2013, Eric Posner, a law professor at the University of Chicago, declared that "the idea of state sovereignty . . . is largely a joke these days. The federal government calls the shots and the states obey."[14] Note the word choice: the states "obey." He might as well have added "Resistance is futile!" A few years earlier, two Berkeley law professors belittled the states as "mere administrative units, rectangular swatches of the prairie with nothing but their legal definitions to distinguish them from one another." According to these two scholars, anyone deluded enough to think that the states represent "true political communities" is suffering from a "neurosis." Indeed, "federalism is America's neurosis" according to them.[15]

The purpose of this book is to explain how the process of perfecting our union went off the rails years ago, and how states' rights can get us back on track. My call for states' rights is neither nostalgic nor neurotic. Nor is it antigovernment. The government created by the Constitution is a wondrous thing, securing free movement of people and goods across an entire continent, protecting property rights, and providing a national defense. The federal government has been pivotal to America's success. But its popular support has plummeted precisely as it has grabbed more and more extraconstitutional powers. A revival of states' rights would actually increase Americans' trust in the federal government because the government would stick to its core competencies. And that's just the beginning. States' rights would also promote:

- Better schools, roads, and infrastructure, as states are freed from wasteful federal mandates;
- Lower taxes, as states engage in a virtuous competition for citizens and businesses;
- Improved stewardship of natural resources, as decisions reflect local priorities on land use;
- Less crowded prisons, by returning criminal jurisdiction to the states, where penal reform is light-years ahead of Washington; and
- An end to national gridlock, as the most divisive social issues devolve to state and local decision-makers.

Why Now?

The goals described in the previous section may sound great, but then, they may also sound impossibly ambitious. Not even Ronald Reagan succeeded in his goal to restore the proper balance between state and federal governments. Why should things be different now?

To halt, and reverse, the trend toward the centralization of power in Washington would require a cataclysmic shake-up of the political order. That's true, but it's also true that America is headed for such a shake-up whether we like it or not. When Ronald Reagan took office, the federal government's debt was only about 30 percent of the size of the economy (gross domestic product). Many Americans were receptive to Reagan's message of reining in federal spending, but there was little sense of urgency. Now there is. Since 2012, the national debt has exceeded 100 percent of GDP, basically, banana republic territory. As this book goes to press in 2015, the federal debt stands at just over

$18 trillion, having doubled in just six years. The Congressional Budget Office (CBO) predicts that another $9.4 trillion of debt will be piled on in the next decade. And, as the Cato Institute's Michael Tanner points out, these figures actually conceal the true size of America's public debt. When you include debt owed to government trust funds like Social Security and Medicare, and the future unfunded liabilities of such programs, it brings "our real indebtedness to over 480 percent of GDP."[16]

We haven't seen this kind of debt since the late 1940s, after the United States had racked up multiple annual budget deficits to fight World War II. But after the war was over, the government gradually paid down the debt to manageable levels. This time around, there's no world war to blame for our debt. Although the interventions in Iraq and Afghanistan surely contributed to our fiscal woes, America's debt has largely arisen from Congress's unconstitutional usurpation of power over policy areas like healthcare and education, and from the massive cash transfers from the federal government to state and local governments to create the illusion that everyone is better off with Washington in charge. The financial crisis of 2008 to 2009, however, shattered that illusion. The states, having been lured into massive overspending by decades of federal grants, now find themselves struggling to meet their financial commitments. Some of the biggest states—California, Illinois, New York—are tottering on the edge of insolvency, but the federal government lacks the wherewithal to bail them out. By the middle of the century, Tanner observes, "no one might be willing to buy U.S. government debt."[17]

Under President Obama, the federal government's response to the nation's fiscal hole has been to dig the hole deeper: creating new entitlements, expanding existing entitlements, and hobbling industry with punitive regulations. Both federal and state budgets are on an "unsustainable path," as Michael Greve, a professor at George Mason University, observes, and a "fiscal reckoning" is approaching.[18]

A fundamental reform of the political structure is long overdue, and a program that includes states' rights could very well succeed in today's political climate. There is a profound disconnect between how much power voters want the federal government to have and the amount of power that it actually wields. Recent polls have found that on a wide range of policies currently controlled by the federal government, a majority of Americans would prefer to see power returned to the states.[19] In 2013, Pew Research found that only 19 percent of Americans trust the federal government to do what is right all or even most of the time; 69 percent favor limiting the federal government's power. A Gallup poll taken around the same time found that 72 percent of Americans consider "big government" to be the biggest threat to the country's future, ahead of big business or big labor.[20] Americans believe that the federal government wastes 60 cents out of every dollar it spends.[21]

This gap between the actions of the political classes and the desires of the people creates the ideal condition for action. To most Americans, the federal government now stands for high taxes, perennial deficits, precarious entitlements, warrantless surveillance at home, and the aftermath of President Bush's foreign adventures abroad. With bipartisan disgust over Washington's wasteful and inefficient bureaucracy now evident, a principled campaign for states' rights can succeed where even Reagan failed.

Moreover, the price of inaction is unacceptably high. In their 2013 study of great powers from ancient Rome to modern America, the economists Glenn Hubbard and Tim Kane conclude that the "overcentralization of political power . . . is a common factor in imperial decline, usually a century or more after the centralization."[22] Under their analysis, America stands on the brink of such "imperial" decline. It was just over a century ago, in 1913, that the United States took a decisive turn toward centralization. That single year saw the introduction of the federal income tax and the federal corporate tax, and the establishment of the Federal Reserve. In that same year, the Seventeenth Amendment severed the link between state legislatures and the central government by requiring the direct election of US senators. In order to arrest the decline experienced by other great powers, Hubbard and Kane urge Americans to return to a system of autonomous states that are "allowed to experiment and even fail." In other words, states' rights.

What About Federalism?

Still, if "states' rights" is such a taboo phrase, why not just talk about "federalism" instead? Federalism refers to a system of government in which—in contrast to "nationalist" systems—sovereignty is divided between a central government and state or provincial governments. Federalism is not uniquely American; it exists in Canada, Mexico, Germany, Switzerland, and lots of other places that are nice to visit. The American version, which flows from the Constitution, guarantees to each state the right to self-government in all but a handful of areas entrusted to the central government. In theory, then, advocating federalism and advocating states' rights ought to amount to the same thing.

The problem is that the term "federalism" has come unmoored from the Constitution. In legal and academic circles, any recognition that states still deserve to exist alongside the federal government, even in a completely subservient capacity, counts as "federalism." In the spring of 2014, for example, the *Yale Law Journal* featured a symposium called, in wonderfully Orwellian terms, "Federalism as the New Nationalism" (*War as the New Peace! Hate as the New Love!*). The five contributors— all distinguished scholars—insisted that federalism is alive and well, but that it has "evolved" into "a form of nationalism." In the new federalism, states need not aspire to such outdated goals as autonomy or sovereignty; rather, states should relish their role as "the national government's agents"[23] or even as "co-administrators"[24] of federal programs. Some years earlier, Erwin Chemerinsky, the dean of the law school at the University of California, Irvine, wrote a book defining federalism as a doctrine that "empowers" rather than restrains government at all levels.[25] Poor Brutus must be turning in his grave.

It's not enough to promote "federalism." If what you mean is *constitutional* federalism, you need to talk about states' rights; it's the only way to make it clear that you believe in states as sovereign bodies. That said, I will of course refer to "federalism" throughout this book, since one cannot discuss states' rights without also discussing federalism. But when I talk about federalism, I mean genuine constitutional federalism, unless I'm criticizing some perversion, like "cooperative federalism" (more on that later).

Can States Have Rights?

One objection to states' rights is the notion that "rights" belong only to individuals, not states. But there's no reason why states cannot possess collective rights. For many of America's founders, states were "to be considered as moral persons, having a will of their own and equal rights—that these rights are freedom, sovereignty, and independence" as New York governor George Clinton put it in 1788.[26]

Even today, people talk about states' rights all the time in the international context: Israel has a right to exist, Ukraine has a right to defend itself, Bolivia has the right to its natural resources, and so on. Most important, all states—political communities—possess the right to self-government, or self-determination. In fact, self-determination is usually seen as the best guarantor of individual rights, since decisions made closer to home are more likely to reflect the will of the people. Again, this was conventional wisdom to America's founders: Thomas Jefferson's political ally John Taylor once observed that "states rights are rights of the people."[27]

If you drive around my neighborhood in Brooklyn, you're bound to see bumper stickers urging the Chinese to "Free Tibet." If you ask the driver, he or she will no doubt tell you that Tibet has a right to political autonomy. Forcing Tibet to live under Beijing's mandate violates the rights of Tibet and of all Tibetans. But just try asking the "Free Tibet" guy about Louisiana: Who gets to decide the state's K–12 education policy? You're unlikely to hear a robust defense of self-determination for Louisiana, even though the answer should be clear. The Constitution gives the central government no power whatsoever over education, and thus it is an area left entirely to the democratically elected leaders of the states.

To my liberal friends who think that's crazy Tea Party talk, all I can say is: how quickly you forget. When the shoe was on the other foot, and President George W. Bush imposed his educational priorities on local schools via the No Child Left Behind law, liberals howled in protest about the destruction of state autonomy. "The federal takeover of education is the last thing we need," declared liberal Democrat Howard Dean in 2004 when he was running for president. "I never understood why Washington politicians think they can design a cookie-cutter policy that works for all local schools."[28] I can't understand it, either. But that doesn't stop Washington from designing cookie-cutter policies for education. And transportation. And agriculture. And healthcare. And on, and on, and on.

Oh, Great and Powerful Uncle Sam

Notwithstanding Howard Dean's occasional flashes of common sense, American progressives are surprisingly comfortable with centralized power—surprising given the progressive commitment to community-based politics. But it's all part of a package: power abhors a vacuum, so if the states are bad, the federal government must be good. The irrational fear of states' rights and the irrational love of federal power are two sides of the same coin. To get an idea of liberal Washington's sense of its own virtue, look no further than Paul Begala, a former adviser to Bill Clinton and the consummate Beltway insider. In 2011, Begala made the following assertion in the pages of *Newsweek*:

> The U.S. federal government is the greatest force for good in human history. Period.[29]

Think about that for a moment. In the five thousand–odd years of recorded human history, nothing has done more good—not love, or faith, or science, or art—than the US federal government? Next time you're subjected to an airport search, just remember that the TSA guy snapping on his latex gloves outranks Mother Teresa on the Begala Scale.

The greatest force for good? Falesha Augustus would, I suspect, disagree with that. So would the slaves hunted down by federal marshals in the 1850s, the Japanese Americans interned in concentration camps in the 1940s, the suspected communists harassed by Congress in the 1950s, and the Tea Party activists targeted by IRS agents in the 2010s. Millions of people, in fact, who have had their lives destroyed by the federal government's kind attentions might just take issue with Begala's worship of Uncle Sam.

No doubt the federal government has done some extraordinarily good things—mainly because it has an extraordinary amount of *power*. The federal government commands an annual budget of over a trillion dollars and a workforce of over twelve million civilian employees, contractors, and grantees, not to mention 1.4 million uniformed servicemen, together with their tanks, planes, and aircraft carriers.[30] Washington owns some 640 million acres of land, or about 30 percent of the country's total landmass.[31] The federal government is *big*. And it's getting bigger. Over the last four decades, federal spending has grown 288 percent—nearly twelve times faster than the growth in Americans' income.

A Little History

To appreciate the magnitude of the federal power grab, it's important to see it in context. We'll return to this narrative throughout the book, but let me set the stage.

Political scientists divide American federalism into three eras: dual, cooperative, and coercive. Dual federalism, which lasted from the Constitution's ratification in 1789 until the New Deal, reflected the Founders' original understanding of the state and federal governments as joint sovereigns, each supreme within its own sphere. Realizing that individual liberty is at risk whenever political power becomes concentrated in one level or one branch of government, the Constitution's framers considered federalism, together with the separation of powers, to be the key safeguard of freedom.

During the era of dual federalism, the national government focused on its constitutional duties while the state and local governments tended to the safety and welfare of their residents. The debates of the time would seem quaint today, such as the controversy that raged over Congress's authority to subsidize infrastructure projects. Pre–Civil War presidents, including Madison, routinely vetoed bills providing for roads, canals, and other "internal improvements" as beyond the powers of the federal government. At the end of the nineteenth century, the British historian Lord Acton credited America's division of power with producing "a community more powerful, more prosperous, more intelligent, and more free than any other the world has seen."[32]

The early twentieth-century Progressives mounted the first serious attack on states' rights; this attack included the Sixteenth Amendment, which permitted a federal income tax, and the Seventeenth Amendment, which abolished the Constitution's original guarantee that state legislatures would select US senators. And yet, dual federalism limped along pretty well until Franklin D. Roosevelt's New Deal put an end to it. Despite some initial resistance from the Supreme Court, FDR

and his congressional allies managed to invert the constitutional order, making the states subordinate to the central government for the first time. The New Dealers did this through
a combination of aggressive interpretations of the Constitution
and conditional grant programs—the system of bribing states
to relinquish their independence. Thus was born the era of cooperative federalism, characterized by "a constantly increasing
concentration of power at Washington in the stimulation and
supervision of local policies," as Edward Corwin, a political
scientist and an adviser to FDR, put it.[33] Notwithstanding the
federal encroachment on their turf, states often welcomed the
new federal programs because they were accompanied by unprecedented grants.

But such a lopsided relationship couldn't stay "cooperative"
for very long. How does one state cooperate with the federal
leviathan? By the 1960s, Congress was piling on more and
more take-it-or-leave-it conditions to federal aid. The Highway Beautification Act of 1965, for example, told states to follow federal rules for regulating billboards or lose 10 percent of
their highway funding. By the 1970s, such conditional grants
combined with unfunded mandates—marching orders that
the federal government issues but doesn't pay for—created the
model that persists to this day: coercive federalism.

Just to be clear, the term "coercive federalism" is not conservative propaganda—rather, it is the accepted term in university political science departments, which are not exactly known
for their right-wing leanings. "Coercion" is no longer a point
of controversy; it has become a neutral label for what the federal government does every day of the week.

In the era of coercive federalism, no area of human activity
escapes federal control. Can your local high school hold a bake

sale? Don't bother asking the school board, or the teachers, or—heaven forbid—the parents. The ultimate decision rests with the US Department of Agriculture. In June 2013, the USDA issued fifty-three pages of regulations regarding school snacks (the USDA had tackled school lunches years earlier), including the conditions under which schools may allow students to sell cookies, brownies, and the like. Among other things, school bake sales must be "infrequent," they must not take place in the school cafeteria or during lunchtime, and the kids must not be allowed to eat the goodies on school premises.[34] Lest anyone be concerned about the constitutionality of federal bureaucrats dictating the manner and frequency of bake sales, the USDA has thoughtfully assured readers that "this rule does not have federalism implications." Phew!

The ever-increasing reach of federal power has not been popular. In 1973, a Harris poll found that majorities or near majorities of the American people favored federal control across a range of issues, including pollution control, drug reform, and health insurance. Forty years later, a survey asking the exact same questions found that public opinion had changed dramatically, with majorities favoring state and local control over the same issues.[35]

States' Rights and Racism

Even as ordinary Americans have lost faith in the federal government, political leaders have been reluctant to stand up for states' rights for fear of being labeled racist. There is, of course, nothing inherently racist about states' rights, but the doctrine remains unjustly tainted by association with those Southern politicians who used the language of "states' rights" to protect segregation in the 1950s and 1960s.

The notion that states' rights is hostile to civil rights arose from a rift within the Democratic Party in the mid-twentieth century. In 1947, Harry Truman angered the party's Southern base by establishing a commission on civil rights that would ultimately recommend legislation to end discrimination. The following year—a presidential election year—Senator Hubert Humphrey succeeded in getting the Democratic Party to adopt a civil rights agenda for the first time. Truman embraced the platform, but Strom Thurmond, then the Democratic governor of South Carolina, bolted from the party and created his own "States' Rights" ticket to run against Truman. Thurmond's party didn't last—he soon returned to the Democratic fold—but his campaign fostered the idea of states' rights as a philosophy inherently opposed to civil rights. That false dichotomy came to the fore a few years later in the battle over school desegregation.

In 1954, the Supreme Court ruled unanimously in *Brown v. Board of Education* that racial segregation in public schools is unconstitutional. In reaction to that ruling—which required states to open up white-only schools to all students—Virginia's Democratic senator Harry F. Byrd pushed the Old Dominion to adopt a policy of "massive resistance" to desegregation. The campaign of resistance resulted in small flurry of laws enacted by the Virginia legislature in 1956, notably, a statute requiring the governor to shut down any school facing a federal desegregation order. At the same time, the legislature created the Commission on Constitutional Government (CCG), a taxpayer-funded think tank that would publish papers on the virtues of limited government and states' rights.[36] Under the influence of its publications director, James J. Kilpatrick, the notoriously prosegregation editor of the *Richmond News Leader*, the CCG would publish tracts opposing federal involvement in racial matters. Other Southern Democrats like governors Ross Barnett of Mississippi and George Wallace of Alabama also used the language of states' rights to defy federal desegregation orders.

It is absolutely true, therefore, that many Southern politicians, journalists, and activists in the 1950s and 1960s claimed that segregation was a matter of states' rights. Kilpatrick himself clearly attempted to place the massive resistance movement in the tradition of Thomas Jefferson and James Madison by calling on states to exercise their right of "interposition"—a term originally associated with state-level resistance to the Sedition Act of 1798. But the segregationists' arguments were far removed from earlier assertions of states' rights. Before the 1950s, states' rights were typically invoked to enforce express constitutional limitations on the federal government. From the resistance to the Sedition Act to the battles over the New Deal, states' rights advocates were seeking to keep the federal government within its enumerated powers. The massive resistance movement, by contrast, represented an effort to ignore an express constitutional limitation on state power: the Fourteenth Amendment, which forbids states from denying "equal protection" to their residents. It is one thing to enforce provisions of the Constitution; it is something else altogether to defy the provisions you don't like.

Even if one ignores the Fourteenth Amendment, the argument for a state's right to segregation soon crumbled on its own terms. In 1959, the Virginia Supreme Court struck down the school closing legislation at the heart of massive resistance as a violation of the *Virginia constitution*. Shortly thereafter, the state's governor announced a retreat from the school closing strategy.[37] As a policy, therefore, massive resistance was over by 1959, but the CCG remained in operation for years, with Kilpatrick and others attacking federal civil rights legislation as a violation of state sovereignty. During its existence, the CCG distributed over two million copies of forty-nine booklets and pamphlets— and most of the distribution was outside the South.[38] The prolific activity of the CCG played a major role in cementing the popular perception of states' rights as a racist doctrine.

Principled supporters of states' rights soon recognized that the doctrine was being tarnished by association with the segregationists. In 1960, Senator Barry Goldwater, the future GOP presidential nominee, would criticize the "attempt to disparage the principle of States' Rights by equating it with defense of the South's position on racial integration."[39] As Goldwater pointed out, states' rights "affects Northerners as well as Southerners, and concerns many matters that have nothing to do with the race question." Throughout the 1960s, many Republicans embraced states' rights while also supporting federal civil rights legislation—indeed, the milestone laws of that era would not have passed without strong Republican support.[40]

Had the segregationists made peace with the Democratic Party, perhaps the academic and journalistic classes would now take a more nuanced view of states' rights. But in 1964 Strom Thurmond switched to the Republican Party, helping to establish a new GOP foothold in the South. In 1968, Richard Nixon's campaign pursued an aggressive "Southern Strategy" that emphasized "states' rights and limited government, fiscal conservatism, and a strong emphasis on law and order," according to the historian George Lewis.[41] Nixon did not seek to roll back any civil rights legislation, but because he advocated states' rights—just as the CCG had a decade earlier—the strategy has been described as an attempt to "play upon white constituents' racial fears," as Lewis put it.[42] From Nixon onward, it has become common practice to interpret any Republican reference to states' rights as a subliminal message to white racists.

The pivotal moment, according to the mainstream narrative, came in a single speech by Ronald Reagan during his presidential election campaign of 1980. In one of Reagan's first appearances after receiving the nomination, he spoke approvingly of states' rights at the Neshoba County Fair in Mississippi, a venue that is seven miles away from a town where three civil rights workers had been murdered sixteen years earlier. The location was unfortunate, but as law professor David Kopel points out, "It would be difficult to find many places in . . . Mississippi which are not within seven miles of the scene of some infamous past act of racial violence."[43] Indeed, the Democratic presidential candidate Michael Dukakis would speak at the same fair eight years later.

In any event, Reagan's choice of venue was considerably less provocative than Tuscumbia, Alabama: the headquarters of the Ku Klux Klan, where President Jimmy Carter decided to kick off his 1980 election campaign. But, unlike Carter's speech, Reagan's was considered racist because in the middle of a thirty-three-paragraph address devoted mainly to economics, Reagan made a single reference to states' rights. He said:

> I believe in state's rights; I believe in people doing as much as they can for themselves at the community level and at the private level. And I believe that we've distorted the balance of our government today by giving powers that were never

intended in the constitution to that federal establishment.
And if I do get the job I'm looking for, I'm going to devote
myself to trying to reorder those priorities and to restore
to the states and local communities those functions which
properly belong there.[44]

Not exactly incendiary language, but it would be hard to
overstate the importance of this speech in the conventional
narrative against states' rights. Reagan's invocation of states'
rights drew immediate coverage in the *New York Times* and
the *Washington Post*. In subsequent years more and more liberal commentators would incorrectly assert that Reagan's single reference to states' rights was intended "to send a signal
to white racists that he was on their side," as the columnist
David Brooks observed.[45] The historian Joseph Crespino, for
example, accuses Reagan of consciously repeating "a mantra
that had sustained a generation of Southern segregationists."[46]
Brooks rightly describes such simplistic attempts to equate
Reagan's lifelong belief in states' rights with racism as "a political nursery tale."[47]

Simplistic or not, the idea of states' rights as a racist tool
was essential to the broader agenda of academic historians who
were eager to explain the rise of the Republican Party, and
conservatism in general, as a product of American racism. In
their 1991 book *Chain Reaction*, Tom Edsall, a journalist and
academic, and his wife, Mary, argue that by 1980 party affilia-
tion was driven by racial politics, with racists aligning with the
Republicans.[48] Although neither Reagan nor any subsequent
Republican leader has opposed civil rights or endorsed racism,
any mention of big government, special interests, or high taxes
are code words of racial intolerance, according to the Edsalls.

In a 2007 *Slate* article, David Greenberg, a historian at Rutgers University, alleges that Reagan's ideas of small government and individual freedom "served to countenance racism"—although he never explains how.[49] No matter: Greenberg forges ahead, arguing that Reagan's message of states' rights and related doctrines carried "an unspoken subtext" of race, a "tacit" racial message, and an "implicit" revival of Southern segregation.

Greenberg and Co. have no evidence that Reagan or any other contemporary conservative has sought to use states' rights to achieve racist ends—if they had such evidence, there would be no need to resort to the endless litany of weasel words hinting at a sinister but purely telepathic racist conspiracy. Moreover, in the years since 1980, liberals have regularly advocated states' rights when it has suited their purposes. On at least three occasions since 2001, the liberal Massachusetts congressman Barney Frank introduced legislation calling for "states' rights to medical marijuana." An Obama administration official argued in 2010 that "states' rights are incredibly important"—at least in the context of tort law.[50] In 2013, an article in the *Atlantic* proclaimed "States' Rights Are for Liberals," citing issues such as gay marriage.[51] But when Ronald Reagan dared to use the same language, "everyone took [it] to be a coded declaration of support for segregationist sentiments," according to the *New York Times* columnist Paul Krugman.[52] For Krugman, this history still "matters" (he was writing in 2007), because it proves that the conservative movement is fueled by "white backlash against the civil rights movement," and therefore, as the country grows more racially diverse, the conservative base will naturally shrink.

Anyone who takes the time to look at history without wearing ideological blinders will appreciate that states' rights is a long-standing doctrine with no necessary connection to racial politics. The segregationists' cry of "states' rights" is a notable example of a sound doctrine being used to promote an evil end—something that happens all the time. Consider, for example, the considerable number of Americans who have invoked "patriotism" to justify anticommunist witch hunts or prohibitions on flag burning. Does this mean that "patriotism" must now be regarded as a code word for political suppression? One hopes not. Besides, if states' rights is forever tainted by association with segregationists, why not the Democratic Party? After all, virtually every leading Southern segregationist was a card-carrying Democrat.

The Progressive Police State

Remember when "making a federal case" out of something was a shorthand expression for treating something like a really big deal? The metaphor no longer works, because federal cases now arise from the most trivial "crimes" imaginable. As of 2008 (the last time that anybody tried to count), there were over 4,500 federal statutory crimes and some 300,000 regulatory crimes.

Most of these federal crimes have no constitutional basis. The Constitution gives Congress criminal jurisdiction over treason, piracy, counterfeiting, and offenses against the "laws of nations"—and that's about it. The Founding Fathers believed, as Hamilton put it in *Federalist* no. 17, that "the ordinary administration of criminal and civil justice" would be "the province of state governments." And yet—somehow—the federal government now manages to operate seventy-three distinct law enforcement agencies employing 120,000 full-time officers with the authority to make arrests and carry firearms. They range from the agents of the FBI to the Amtrak police, perhaps serving the national interest by arresting people who talk in the Quiet Car.

One of the great mysteries of American politics is why anyone—particularly progressives, with their hatred of the "police state"—should tolerate this massive concentration of power in the central government. It's not as though a centralized state is a more democratic state. To the contrary, it shifts power away from the approximately 513,000 elected officials at the state and local level and gives it to the 537 elected officials at the federal level: the members of Congress, the president, and the vice president.

Since the mid-1990s—as presidents Clinton, Bush, and Obama all pursued centralizing policies—the United States has slipped lower and lower in the World Bank's ranking for "voice and accountability," which measures the extent to which a country's citizens are able to participate in selecting their government representatives, as well as their freedom of expression, their freedom of association, and the freedom of the media. The United States has also experienced dramatic declines in its rankings for government effectiveness, regulatory quality, and control of corruption.[53]

The Tyranny of Bureaucrats

It's no surprise, then, that the main selling point for consolidating power in Washington has nothing to do with democracy, but rather with the supposed virtues of *unelected* officials. We are told that only the federal bureaucracy—with its agencies, commissions, and blue-ribbon panels—has the competence to deal with the Big Issues of the day. It's an old idea, dating at least from Woodrow Wilson's worshipful advocacy of European-style bureaucracy. In his 1887 article "The Study of Administration," Wilson laments that the majority of people are "selfish, ignorant, timid, stubborn, or foolish"—but rejoices that there are "hundreds who are wise."[54] The trick is to arrange things so that the wise ones wield all the power. One can almost see Wilson—collar starched and pince-nez glasses perched on his nose—as he complains that America's major problem is "the error of trying to do too much by vote."[55] Instead, America needed a class of expert administrators trained along German and French lines. Wilson grudgingly acknowledged that European centralization would have to be adapted to fit America's federal system, but called for the "interlacing" of bureaucracies at the state and federal levels. That may sound harmless, but why should a federal government of strictly limited powers be "interlaced" with the state governments? Here, as Wilson no doubt intended, was a first step toward a federal takeover of the states.

By the time of the New Deal, the champions of government by experts, like James Landis, the dean of Harvard Law School, were almost exclusively focused on concentrating expertise in the national government. The same mid-twentieth-century philosophy animates Barack Obama's seemingly unshakable faith that a smart, tech-savvy federal bureaucracy will "make government cool again."

Where to begin? How about with the rollout of the Affordable Care Act, in which the supercompetent federal government, with three years and hundreds of millions of dollars, could not manage to build a functioning website—a feat achieved by adolescents and small-business owners every day. In its first months of operation, the online health insurance exchange run by the federal government—open to citizens of thirty-six states—attracted fewer enrollees than the sites built by those incompetent rubes in the fourteen states that didn't throw in their lot with Uncle Sam. To be fair, however, the federal government did manage to arrange for millions of people to lose their health insurance policies, notwithstanding the president's ironclad pledge that "if you like your health plan, you can keep your health plan. Period."

Climate change—there's another Big Problem that only the federal government can be trusted with. The Environmental Protection Agency (EPA) took the issue so seriously that it assigned its highest-paid employee, John Beale, to the office responsible for directing policy on climate change. But it turned out that Beale knew nothing about climate change. In fact, Beale barely knew the address of the EPA, since he almost never showed up at the office, including one eighteen-month stretch during 2011 and 2012 when he did absolutely no work. In September 2013, Beale pleaded guilty to bilking taxpayers out of nearly $900,000 in pay and benefits.[56]

Big Government, Big Mistakes

On issue after issue, federal intervention has proved to be useless (John Beale) or positively harmful (ObamaCare). After all, only the federal government has the power to force bad ideas on the entire country. Universal healthcare for Massachusetts is an interesting experiment, something for other governors and state legislators to study. ObamaCare is a national disaster from which no escape is possible, save emigration. Or take housing policy: if one or two states pushed poor people to buy houses they couldn't afford, you'd get some local housing bubbles. When Congress decided to get into the act, the result was the 2008 housing meltdown and financial crisis.

When states are in charge, policy mistakes are localized and invariably corrected by popular pressure within the state, or competitive pressure from neighboring states, or both. When the federal government is in charge, all mistakes are Big Mistakes.

States' Rights: A Uniter, Not a Divider

States' rights is an issue—*the* issue—on which liberals actually agree with conservatives, if only they could acknowledge it. The presidency of George W. Bush saw a new resurgence of states' rights Democrats, and not only because of No Child Left Behind. By the time Bush left office, a majority of states had expressed opposition to the homeland security REAL ID measure—with at least seventeen states declaring nonacquiescence with the law.[57] That's a prime example of "nullification," a word that usually appears in liberals' dire critiques of conservative rule.

Distrust of centralized power cuts across the ideological spectrum.[58] Polls consistently show, as noted previously, that a majority of Americans have lost faith in the power of the federal government to do the right thing. On the flip side, surveys since the 1990s suggest that 60 to 70 percent of Americans favor transferring power from Washington to state and local governments.[59] In 2011, a unanimous Supreme Court—every justice from Ruth Bader Ginsburg to Clarence Thomas—held that the states' Tenth Amendment rights are a vital component of our constitutional order because, among other things, federalism "secures the freedom of the individual," and "allows local policies more sensitive to the diverse needs of a heterogeneous society," and "enables greater citizen involvement in democratic processes."[60]

Left, right, and center, we have all suffered for too long under the misguided policies of Washington. Reviving states' rights is the way for Americans to build smarter government, geared to the reality of our communities and responsive to the voters. Decentralized government makes more sense than ever, given today's technology. We don't need to gather together all our experts in one place. Knowledge is just a click away, whether you're in Washington, DC, or Lincoln, Nebraska. An American system that unleashes the creative energies of the fifty states in a virtuous competition for citizens and businesses might well be a less perfect union—if perfection means centralization—but it would be far better than the one we have now.

A few housekeeping matters before we move on. When I'm talking about the government in Washington, DC, I tend to use the terms "federal government" and "central government" interchangeably, even though, strictly speaking, "federal" ought to refer to the whole American system of state and federal sovereignty. But because most people (including me) are accustomed to thinking of the central government as *the* federal government, I adopt that usage. I also sometimes refer to the central government as the "national government," since it does possess certain national elements like a standing army and direct taxation.

The Past:

EVERYTHING
THEY TAUGHT YOU
IS WRONG

1

The Bill of (States') Rights

Only one of America's fifty state constitutions makes the startling claim that "the people of [this state] have the sole and exclusive right of governing themselves as a free, sovereign, and independent State." Which state is it? Which state would throw down the gauntlet of state sovereignty in this day and age? If you guessed Mississippi, or South Carolina, or some other former member of the Confederacy, you'd be wrong.

The answer is Massachusetts. In words written by John Adams in 1780 and never repealed, the Massachusetts Declaration of Rights positively forbids the commonwealth from relinquishing any state "right" that has not been "expressly delegated" to the central government.[1] It is as bold an assertion of states' rights as you'll find in any state constitution. And it has nothing to do with slavery, Jim Crow, or any of the other reactionary movements assumed to be lurking behind states' rights.

The key to understanding the history of states' rights is to disregard virtually everything you've read on the subject. Textbooks, newspapers, and magazines lazily perpetuate the myth that American history has been one long struggle between reactionary states and an enlightened federal government. According to this narrative, those who sought to expand the power of the central government "were fighting for progress and . . . a freer, stronger national government to cope with the problems of the time," as one professor put it.[2] States' rights, by contrast, is described as an idea that "took hold in the run-up to the Civil War in order for the South to preserve, among other things, the institution of slavery," according to a 2009 article in the *Christian Science Monitor*.[3] American history, like all history, "is written by the winners," as George Orwell famously observed.[4] And in its long-running campaign to usurp power from the states and the people, the federal government has—so far—been victorious.

An honest history of states' rights has to start with an acknowledgment that it is a doctrine dating back to long before the Civil War; in fact, to before the nation's founding. As we'll see in this chapter, nobody invented states' rights; rather, the idea flowed naturally from the distinct character of the original states and their colonial predecessors. When Americans started debating whether to ratify the Constitution, the defining issue was clearly the tension between states' rights and central power. That was the question that separated the "Federalists," who favored stronger central government, from the "Anti-Federalists," who argued for states' rights. Although the Federalists prevailed in their quest to ratify the Constitution, it was the Anti-Federalists—the states' rights faction—who insisted on a Bill of Rights, the part of the Constitution that we most revere today.[5]

The States Came First

The federal government opened its doors for business on March 4, 1789—the first session of the First Congress.[6] Eager to establish its reputation, Congress did nothing that first day. It would be another month before Congress could gather enough members for a voting quorum and before George Washington would be inaugurated as the first president.

While the federal government was still trying to establish its existence, the states were a fact of life for all Americans. By the time the new Congress passed its first law, the Virginia House of Burgesses had been meeting for 170 years; the Massachusetts General Court for 160. The Maryland Assembly, created in 1632, had enacted America's first Bill of Rights in 1639.[7] The states also had venerable cultural and religious traditions. New England Puritans had been sending their sons to Harvard since 1636, while the College of William and Mary had been educating High-Church Virginians since 1695. David Hackett Fischer's groundbreaking history *Albion's Seed* argues that the entire foundation of American culture was established by four waves of British immigrants, all of whom arrived *before* 1776. New England, for example, had a well-defined culture as early as 1641, according to Fischer.[8] And Akhil Reed Amar, a law professor at Yale, observes that "in the seventeenth century, British North America began not as a single continent-wide juridical entity but as a series of different and distinct colonies, each founded at a different moment with a distinct charter, a distinct history, a distinct immigration pattern, a distinct set of laws and legal institutions, and so on."[9]

The one and only common authority that the colonists had ever known was Great Britain—and that experience did not endear early Americans to the idea of central government. "No taxation without representation" is, after all, a plea for local self-government. If Parliament wanted money from America, it was supposed to ask the colonial legislatures— only the elected representatives of the Americans could legitimately impose taxes upon them. Or so the colonists thought. After nearly a century of relatively benign neglect from London, American leaders had come to believe, by the 1760s, that the British had essentially granted the colonies control over their own finances.[10] But after Britain's costly struggles in the Seven Years' War, Parliament dramatically escalated its top-down control over the colonies. Infamous measures such as the Stamp Act, the Tea Act, and the so-called Coercive Acts reminded the Americans that their rights—and property—were at the mercy of a distant legislature over which they had little influence.

When the break with England finally came, the Continental Congress did not declare independence on behalf of a single "United States." Rather, the Declaration of Independence asserts that the former colonies "are and of Right ought to be Free and Independent *States*"—plural. The Paris Peace Treaty of 1783, which formally ended the Revolutionary War, mirrors the language of the Declaration, recognizing each individual state to be "free, sovereign and independent." So limited was the power of Congress at that time, the American negotiators at the peace conference could not even commit to paying compensation to British loyalists whose property was confiscated during the war. Rather, the Americans simply agreed that Congress would "earnestly recommend" that the state legislatures provide such compensation.[11]

Federalists vs. Anti-Federalists

In the meantime, the newly independent states had formed a union under the Articles of Confederation. The Articles, adopted by the Continental Congress in 1777, clearly reflects the determination of the newly independent states to resist central control. After an introductory paragraph specifying that the name of the "confederacy" shall be the United States of America, the document gets down to business:

> Each state retains its sovereignty, freedom, and independence, and every power, jurisdiction, and right, which is not expressly delegated to the United States, in Congress assembled.

And those powers "expressly delegated" to Congress were few and far between. Congress had power over foreign affairs and defense—provided that the states supplied the money and the troops—and not much else. Referred to as a "firm league of friendship," the United States operated like an international organization, with each state having a single vote in Congress, and with any structural changes requiring unanimous consent by the states.

The Articles, like the later Constitution, assumes that the essential unit of American politics is the *state*, not the central government. The "United States" existed only at the pleasure of the states, not the other way around. To the extent that America's central government possessed any authority, it would have to be carved out of powers that would otherwise belong to the individual states. In 1883, Henry Adams—a Harvard historian and a descendant of presidents John Adams and John

Quincy Adams—would declare states' rights to be the "start-ing point of American history and constitutional law."[12]

That's not to say that the Articles of Confederation struck the right balance between the states and the Union. As Amer-icans learned in the years after 1777, certain hoped-for fea-tures of the Union—like a functioning internal market, and a strong defense—required a more robust central government. The Philadelphia convention of 1787 sought to address that problem. The convention itself, however, was a gathering of states—each state had one vote regardless of population—because only the states could grant additional powers to the central government.

While a few nationalists like Alexander Hamilton may have dreamed of a single, consolidated government on the European model, the Philadelphia delegates never seriously considered such an alternative. Instead, the convention would endorse James Madison's "Virginia Plan," which created the framework of the new constitution. But even parts of that plan went too far. Madison's initial proposal would have given the United States Congress a veto over state legislation. In attempting to sell this idea to skeptical delegates, Madison explained that the congressional "negative" would give Congress the same power over the states that the British Parliament had enjoyed "in Royal Colonies before the Revolution."[13]

The delegates were not comforted. Elbridge Gerry of Massa-chusetts warned that such a veto power "may enslave the states." Gerry and other delegates firmly held that the central government must not be allowed to usurp "powers the states had claimed ever since they were colonies chafing against parliamentary oversight," according to legal historian Alison LaCroix.[14] Maryland's Luther Martin put it a little more bluntly: the congressional negative would lead to "the destruction of the State governments, and the introduction of monarchy." The convention overwhelmingly rejected this part of Madison's plan.

Likewise, Madison's proposal to give Congress authority to legislate "in all cases to which the separate States are incompetent, or in which the harmony of the United States may be interrupted by the exercise of individual legislation" was greeted with outright skepticism and would ultimately fail to win over the delegates.

The Constitution that was adopted by the convention on September 17, 1787, was an elegant document that was "conspicuously hostile to centralized power," as the scholars Glenn Hubbard and Tim Kane observe.[15] The framers entrusted the central government with limited powers, mainly those concerning questions of defense, foreign affairs, and interstate and international commerce. The states, by contrast, retained power over "all the objects which, in the ordinary course of affairs, concern the lives, liberties, and properties of the people," as Madison observed in the *Federalist* no. 45.

The framers deliberately designed the Constitution to keep the federal government from overpowering the states. First, the federal government was granted only limited powers. Second, the Senate was originally elected by the legislatures of the states, and senators were considered "ambassadors" of their state governments.[16] Third, the national government itself was divided into three branches with checks and balances among them. Both federalism and separation of powers have the virtue of preventing too much power from being concentrated in too few hands. The combination of the two doctrines, as Madison wrote in the *Federalist* no. 51, creates "a double security . . . to the rights of the people."

The Bill of Rights

Nothing against Madison's "double security"—he was absolutely right about that. But since we're playing for high stakes, how about a triple security: a Bill of Rights? Unlike the state constitutions in existence in 1787, the proposed federal constitution contained no general declaration of rights, and almost no specific safeguards of rights apart from a few scattered provisions like those concerning habeas corpus and ex post facto laws. Nor did the Constitution have any affirmative guarantees of the retained rights of the states. The need to protect individual and states' rights against the new federal government was the major concern of those who initially opposed the ratification of the Constitution—individuals who were loosely grouped together as "Anti-Federalists."

Despite their label, the Anti-Federalists were not against *federalism*—that is, a system of decentralized government. To the contrary, that is precisely what they favored. The government under the Articles of Confederation was referred to at the time as a "federal" system, and both Federalists and Anti-Federalists wanted the United States to remain a federation. Most Anti-Federalists were willing to support some form of "national" (i.e., centralized) government overlaying the federal system—but they believed that the Philadelphia convention had gone too far.[17]

Given that most Americans favored a federal system, Madison, Hamilton, and their allies won a major rhetorical victory when they appropriated the title of "Federalists"—even though they were promoting a stronger *national* government—and to label the opposition as "Anti-Federalists."[18] The Anti-Federalists never accepted the designation; to them, *they* were the federalists and the other guys were "nationalists" or, worse, proponents of "consolidated" government, a radically unpopular concept during the founding era.

In the state ratifying conventions, the Anti-Federalists won support for the proposals that would eventually become the first ten amendments to the Constitution—that is, the Bill of Rights. Today, law professors and politicians talk about the Bill of Rights as if it were a gift from the federal government. Cass Sunstein, a Harvard professor and a former Obama administration official, for example, describes our individual rights as "a product of government."[19] Douglas J. Amy, a professor of politics at Mount Holyoke College, argues that "we only have the right of free speech because it is guaranteed in our constitution. If we didn't have our constitution, or if we didn't have government, our civil liberties would literally not exist."[20] But that's not how our Founders saw it. The Bill of Rights was not an assertion of government power; it was a restriction of such power. As Madison told Congress when he proposed the amendments, the Bill of Rights consists of "particular exceptions to the grant of power" to the general government.[21]

At the heart of the Bill of Rights is the preservation of states' rights. The Bill of Rights begins with the immortal words "*Congress* shall make no law"—abridging freedom of speech, and so forth. There are no limits put on the states; the first ten amendments are all about restraining the power of the federal government. It was not until the twentieth century—under the banner of the "Living Constitution"—that courts began to apply the Bill of Rights to state governments. As Professor Amar puts it, "The Bill of Rights protected the ability of local governments to monitor and deter federal abuse."[22]

The Anti-Federalists have been slandered by many histo-

as backward-looking sentimentalists; "provincial" and "agrarian" in the words of Richard E. Ellis, as distinct from the "cosmopolitan, commercial, and elite-minded" Federalists.[23] In reality, the Anti-Federalists included many sophisticated thinkers, including some like George Mason who had attended the Philadelphia convention.[24] The Anti-Federalists were correct about the need for a charter of rights, and for the right reasons—first and foremost, the preservation of liberty. Most Anti-Federalists acknowledged the advantages of a stronger central government, particularly in commercial and military matters. But for them, the primary purpose of government was neither commercial nor military; it was to secure the maximum amount of individual liberty.

Patrick Henry—of "Give me liberty or give me death" fame—acknowledged his devotion to the United States, but he felt that his liberty was safer in the hands of his fellow Virginians. In declaring his opposition to the new Constitution, he said, "The first thing I have at heart is American liberty, the second thing is American union." Surely that is the correct order of things: liberty first. If Americans had wanted nothing more than to be united under a strong central authority, there would have been no reason to break away from Britain. The point of the American federal union was—and should still be—to secure the rights of the people, including the right to local self-government.

The Anti-Federalists also understood that republican democracy works best on a small scale, with decisions being made as close to the people as possible. The larger the unit of government, the greater the risks of polarization and gridlock. Many delegates at the Constitutional Convention acknowledged this truth. A Connecticut delegate and future chief justice of the Supreme Court, Oliver Ellsworth, observed—in words that would not be amiss today—that "the largest states are the worst governed."[25] Think California, Illinois, and New York. The last thing the Anti-Federalists wanted was to have delicate local issues played out on a national stage.

The "cosmopolitan" Federalists, for all their sophistication, mostly opposed a Bill of Rights for reasons that seem strikingly naive today. Many of them argued that the Constitution's system of checks and balances alone would suffice to protect the people. Hamilton, for example, argued that the Constitution's mechanisms would render it "next to impossible that an impolitic or wicked measure should pass scrutiny with success."[26] Benjamin Rush denounced any bill of rights as an "idle and superfluous instrument" and rejoiced that the Constitution had not been "disgraced" by one.[27]

Incredibly, some Federalists insisted that the new government would attract such virtuous men that the people would have nothing to fear. The writer "Cassius" confidently predicted that the Congress would consist of men "of unsullied reputations . . . in whose bosoms the sacred principle of patriotism has, always, glowed in its utmost purity."[28] He must have been referring to a different Congress.

The Ninth and Tenth Amendments

In addition to the particular guarantees of state and individual rights, a majority of Anti-Federalists and state ratifying conventions also insisted on amendments to prevent federal judges and politicians from usurping states' rights. They settled on a two-track approach: an express reservation of state powers, but also a rule against expansive interpretation of federal powers.[29]

The first part of the equation became the Tenth Amendment, which provides that *"the powers not delegated to the United States [i.e., the federal government] by the Constitution, nor prohibited by it to the States, are reserved to the States, respectively, or to the people."* In other words, the federal government can exercise only those powers granted to it in the Constitution; all other powers belong to the states and the people.

Much has been made of the fact that the Tenth Amendment limits the federal government to those powers "delegated" to it, whereas the Articles of Confederation had limited the central government to those powers *"expressly* delegated" to it. The framers' decision not to add the word "expressly" to the text of what became the Tenth Amendment has been interpreted to mean that the Constitution gives Congress "implied powers," the limits of which are unknown.

But there is no evidence that any of the Founders thought that the omission of the word "expressly" was meant to open up new vistas of social engineering for Congress. Rather, "expressly" was left out of the Tenth Amendment to clarify that Congress could exercise narrow powers that were "incidental" to its enumerated powers. That point had to be emphasized because under the Articles of Confederation some had insisted that Congress could not exercise even perfunctory powers, like granting passports, because such functions were not "expressly" delegated. Even Chief Justice John Marshall, one of the most fervent nationalizers of the founding era, noted in *McCulloch v. Maryland* (1819) that the omission of the word "expressly" was simply meant to avoid the "embarrassments" suffered under the Articles of Confederation.

Anti-Federalists were wary of the power of judges to exploit ambiguities in the Constitution's text. Pamphleteers like

Brutus accurately predicted that the federal judiciary would end up determining "the nature and extent of the general government," which, in turn, would affect state powers.[30] In particular, Anti-Federalists worried about the provisions of Article I that would empower Congress to impose taxes "for the general Welfare," and to enact all laws that are "necessary and proper" for executing the government's enumerated powers. (Again, they were right: the general welfare clause and the necessary and proper clause would provide the main justifications for federal growth over the next two centuries.) In light of the broad wording of these provisions, judges could end up deciding that the national government's power is unlimited except in instances in which the Constitution imposes specific restrictions.

To address these concerns, the state conventions called for a "fixed rule" of interpretation that would restrain judges from creatively amending the Constitution; this "fixed rule" would ultimately become the Ninth Amendment. Typical of these calls was the resolution of the North Carolina convention that "those clauses which declare that Congress shall not exercise certain powers be not interpreted in any manner to extend the powers of Congress." In other words, just because the Constitution includes some express limits on Congress's power, that doesn't mean that everything else is fair game. You can't say, for example, that the *express* prohibitions against ex post facto laws and bills of attainder somehow *imply* that Congress is otherwise unrestricted in enacting criminal laws.[31]

The initial draft of what became the Ninth Amendment adopted the state conventions' language about limiting the "powers" of Congress. But in the final version of the amendment, the language of "powers" has turned to "rights."

The enumeration in the Constitution, of certain rights, shall not be construed to deny or disparage others retained by the people.

The change in terminology from "powers" to "rights" caused some hesitation. Edmund Randolph, the governor of Virginia, delayed the ratification of the Bill of Rights until he could be confident that it actually contained a proviso against expanded congressional "powers." Madison and his allies ultimately persuaded the Virginians that the rights of the people and the powers of the central government were two sides of the same coin. Any expansion of the powers of Congress would effectively be a contraction of the people's collective right to local self-government. That is what the Ninth Amendment protects.[32]

During the early years of the Republic, courts read the Ninth and Tenth Amendments as complementary provisions standing for the proposition that the federal government must stick to its delegated powers, and that those powers cannot be enlarged by creative interpretation. Although the Tenth Amendment was cited more frequently, courts would often read the Ninth Amendment's interpretive provisions into the Tenth. Nowadays, however, the idea of equating states' rights with the rights of the people has "long since fallen out of fashion," as the law professor Kurt Lash notes, requiring "a degree of intellectual effort to hear the words of the Ninth Amendment as they were heard by James Madison and the Founders."[33]

Once the Supreme Court buckled under the New Deal, it simply stopped enforcing the Ninth and Tenth Amendments, because there was no way to reconcile the Constitution's text with the rapidly expanding role of the central government.

The Tenth Amendment would be belittled as a "mere truism," while the Ninth would disappear completely, only to resurface in the court's 1965 decision in *Griswold v. Connecticut*. In *Griswold*, Justice Arthur Goldberg's concurring opinion famously revived the Ninth Amendment as a potential reason to strike down Connecticut's prohibition on contraceptives. The metamorphosis of the Ninth Amendment into a weapon to be used *against* the states is precisely the sort of interpretive latitude that the amendment's framers were trying to prevent.

But those developments lay in the future. With the Bill of Rights ratified, the Constitution was generally accepted by the former Anti-Federalists, many of whom coalesced around Thomas Jefferson's leadership as "strict constructionists"— that is, they sought to keep the federal government within the boundaries laid out by the enumerated powers on the one hand, and the Bill of Rights on the other.[34] In this way, they hoped to preserve the United States as a *federal* system and to prevent any slide toward a consolidated national system. Meanwhile, Hamilton and his cronies appropriated the term "Federalist" for the party favoring a loose construction of federal powers that would allow Congress to take over areas of state jurisdiction. Jefferson openly resented this use of the term "Federalist." Even as he neared the end of his life, Jefferson would lash out at "those who formerly usurped the name of federalists, which in fact, they never were."[35]

2

Free Speech, Free Trade, and Nullification

It didn't take long for the federal government to reveal its vast potential for benevolence. In the first decade of its existence, Congress passed a law making it a criminal offense to criticize . . . Congress. This was the infamous Sedition Act, signed into law by President John Adams on July 14, 1798. The act threatened fines and imprisonment against any person who dared to publish "scandalous" or "malicious" writings about either house of Congress or the president of the United States.

America had been engaged in an undeclared "Quasi-War" with France in which the French navy had seized American ships trading with the British. With the prospect of an all-out war brewing, the Sedition Act was part of a legislative package—the Alien and Sedition Acts—that was justified as a national security measure. But it is unlikely that anybody actually believed that criticism of the federal government would incite further French aggression. And although the act prohibited the defamation of Congress and the president, it offered no protection to the vice president, who happened to be Adams's archrival, Thomas Jefferson.

The Sedition Act was a political, not a military, weapon. As John Ferling notes in his biography of John Adams, its purpose was "to stifle domestic opposition to a war movement that many Federalists perceived as essential for the Party's salvation."[1] The Adams administration launched a witch hunt against opposition journalists and other rabble-rousers. At least twenty-five people were arrested and fourteen indicted under the Sedition Act. Matthew Lyon, a Vermont congressman and Revolutionary War veteran, was convicted for an article he published in the *Vermont Review* and served a four-month sentence in an unheated jail cell previously reserved for runaway slaves.[2]

Congress defended this tyrannical piece of legislation by citing the Constitution's two most elastic provisions, the general welfare clause and the necessary and proper clause— thus fulfilling the Anti-Federalists' dire warnings about those clauses. Ten years earlier, you'll recall, Federalists had argued that the national Congress would attract such virtuous office-holders that a Bill of Rights was unnecessary. Fortunately, they lost that argument and the Jeffersonian Republicans could point to the First Amendment's command that "Congress shall make no law . . . abridging the freedom of speech, or of the press." The Sedition Act also violated the Ninth and Tenth Amendments, because it exceeded Congress's enumerated powers. The states had never delegated to the central government any power to regulate the press; therefore, any such power was retained by the states.

The Virginia and Kentucky Resolutions

The Bill of Rights provided all the ammunition needed to defeat the Alien and Sedition Acts, but who would act at the national level? Neither Congress nor President Adams was inclined to reconsider the legislation, and the federal judiciary was stacked with Federalist sympathizers. Only the states could offer credible resistance to federal tyranny, and it was to the states that the opposition turned.

Before long, Thomas Jefferson had drafted legislation designed to express state opposition to the acts. The proposal made its way to John Breckinridge, a member of the Kentucky legislature. The "Kentucky Resolutions," as they became known, passed the legislature in November 1798, although Jefferson's authorship was kept secret. In the meantime, James Madison penned a similar series of resolutions that were introduced in the Virginia Assembly by his ally John Taylor. The "Virginia Resolutions" were adopted in December 1798.[3]

The Virginia and Kentucky Resolutions were the first post-Constitution documents to lay out the Jeffersonian principles that form the basis of states' rights. First, both documents refer to the Constitution as a "compact" by which (as the Kentucky version puts it) the states "constituted a general government for special purposes, delegating to that government certain definite powers."[4] Second, the parties to the compact—the states—must retain the power to determine whether the compact has been violated lest Congress be the sole judge of its own powers. Third, when the general government oversteps its bounds, the states have an inherent right to seek their own remedy.

According to the Kentucky legislature, the remedy was for a state to denounce unconstitutional laws as null and void. A year later, in a follow-up resolution, the legislature would dub this remedy "nullification." The original draft of the Virginia Resolutions also called for nullification, but in the final version this was changed to the right of a state to "interpose" its own authority "for arresting the progress of the evil." The resolutions were to be printed and distributed to the other state legislatures; both measures called on the other states to take action to protect the rights of their citizens.[5]

Contrary to the claims of their critics, the advocates of nullification and interposition never intended to suggest that a single state had the power to strike down a federal law. Madison's concept, *interposition*, describes a state legislature inserting ("interposing") its own authority between a federal law and the people of the state, not for the purpose of repealing federal law but for the purpose of "arresting the progress of the evil"— that is, the state legislatures have a duty to do what they can to block unconstitutional laws. In particular, each state could do what Virginia did: make a public declaration of its opinion that the Alien and Sedition Acts are unconstitutional.

In an age when legislative pronouncements were taken more seriously than they are today, this in itself was a significant assertion. In Federalist states like Rhode Island, the legislatures declared themselves legally unauthorized even to "consider" the constitutionality of the Alien and Sedition Acts. Virginia, by contrast, was asserting its sovereign right to assess whether a federal law was consistent with the Constitution.

Like Virginia, Kentucky viewed its resolutions as a "solemn protest," not as an effective repeal of the Alien and Sedition Acts. Although the term "nullification" would later take on the meaning of a state veto of federal law, nothing in Jefferson's resolutions implies such a veto. For one thing, the Kentucky

Resolutions call on the state's congressional delegation to work to repeal the hated acts, something that would be completely unnecessary if the legislature had been asserting a unilateral right to repeal federal laws. When the legislature declared nullification to be "the rightful remedy" to unconstitutional laws, it was referring to nullification by *all* the states, acting together. Accordingly, both the Virginia and Kentucky Resolutions were intended to inspire other state legislatures to put pressure on their congressional delegations as Kentucky had.[6] This was exactly the sort of coordinated state action that Madison, as well as Hamilton, had foreseen even before the Constitution was ratified. In the *Federalist* no. 46, for example, Madison had predicted that "ambitious encroachments of the federal government on the authority of the State governments" would provoke "plans of resistance" among the states.

The Virginia Resolutions also suggest that state legislatures could take other measures—beyond mere protest—to protect the rights of their citizens. But the legislatures could act only "within their respective limits" and their actions had to be "necessary and proper." Madison did not go into specifics, but later events would illustrate interposition in action. Shortly before the election of 1800, federal prosecutors brought a case against James Callender, an Anti-Federalist pamphleteer living in Virginia. Callender, a Scotsman who had earlier fled Edinburgh to escape sedition charges in Britain, had written a pamphlet heaping abuse on Adams as a "hoary headed incendiary," among other things.

Notwithstanding the Virginia legislature's denunciation of the Sedition Act, there was no attempt to block Callender's prosecution. Governor James Monroe made it clear—in a letter to Jefferson, no less—that he would not condone any interference with the prosecution, but in the very same letter he suggested that Virginia might pay for Callender's lawyer.[7] In fact, Callender's defense was underwritten by the state, as well as by private contributions. Here was a perfect example of constitutional interposition. The state did not attempt to preempt federal law or stop federal agents from doing their job, but the state did use its own money to pay lawyers who would make constitutional arguments against the Sedition Act.[8] Those arguments, unfortunately, made little difference. Callender's case was tried before Supreme Court Justice Samuel Chase—the "hanging judge," as he was known—who doggedly steered the jury to a conviction. Chase would later be impeached for his political use of judicial power.

In drafting the resolutions, both Jefferson and Madison were careful to emphasize the importance of fidelity to the Constitution and to the Union. Nullification and interposition were extreme remedies, not to be entered into lightly. In Madison's phrasing, interposition was the appropriate response to a "deliberate, palpable, and dangerous" exercise of unconstitutional powers. Jefferson reserved nullification for "momentous regulations . . . which so vitally wound the best rights of the citizen."[9]

Nearly a century later, Henry Adams would claim that the resolutions set forth ideas with a "character hardly less decisive than that of the Constitution itself." After all, Adams continued, "the hand which drafted the Declaration of Independence drafted the Kentucky Resolutions; the hand which had the most share in framing the Constitution of the United States framed . . . the Virginia Resolutions."[10] The "Principles of '98," as the two resolutions were collectively known, were highly influential throughout the nineteenth century.[11]

The Constitution as Compact

The Virginia and Kentucky Resolutions begin with the premise that the United States is a "compact" among states. The compact theory was uncontroversial during America's founding era. St. George Tucker, one of the most prominent of the early commentators on the Constitution, held that "the union is in fact, as well as in theory, an association of states."[12] In 1820, Supreme Court Justice Joseph Story, one of the founders of Harvard Law School, described the US Senate as a gathering of "sovereignties, co-ordinate and co-equal."[13] This straightforward idea—that a nation called the United *States* is, in fact, a union of *states*—is now regarded as hopelessly anachronistic. But what is the alternative? Opponents of the compact theory contend that the federal government was formed directly by "the people," in the sense of individual citizens. The evidence typically offered for this proposition is the Constitution's statement, in the Preamble, that "We the People of the United States . . . do ordain and establish this Constitution." But then, the Preamble also says that the purpose of the Constitution is to form "a more perfect Union."

States are the basic building blocks of our constitutional order. The Constitution itself was adopted by state conventions, not by a national plebiscite. Amending the Constitution requires the assent of three-fourths of the states—each state is equal, even though the framers clearly knew how to apportion votes by population, as they did for the House. Likewise, each state is equal in the US Senate. Congressional districts are drawn up by state legislatures, with each state getting at least one House member and no congressional district crossing state lines. Why would the framers have bothered with such convoluted rules if they intended to forge a consolidated nation rather than a union of states?

In fact, the first complete draft of the Constitution began with a roll call of the states: "We the people of the States of New Hampshire, Massachusetts . . ." and so on. But there was a practical problem with this wording. By its own terms, the Constitution would take effect upon ratification by nine states, but it was impossible to know in advance which states would ratify the document. It would have been presumptuous to list all thirteen states at the outset, so the "Committee of Stile" substituted a more generic reference to "the People."[14] But this was a matter of "stile," not substance. Certainly the author of the revised Preamble, Gouverneur Morris, had not intended to cut the states out of the picture—Morris would himself define the Constitution as "a compact, not between individuals, but between political societies."[15]

Note Morris's reference to "political societies." When the Founders spoke of a "compact" of states, they did not mean an agreement among state *governments* but rather among the *people* of the states. In his *Report of 1800* to the Virginia Assembly, James Madison clarified that the Constitution is a compact among the states in the sense of "the people composing those political societies . . . [I]n that sense, the Constitution was submitted to the 'states,' in that sense the 'states' ratified it."[16] This distinction matters because the purpose of American federalism is to preserve the people's right to local self-government— not to make state officials happy. States' rights is not a personal prerogative of a governor to disregard federal laws that he or she finds inconvenient. Rather, states' rights imposes a duty on state politicians: the duty to actually govern their states rather than abdicating that duty to Washington.

Revisionist History

Because the concepts of nullification and interposition would later be invoked by twentieth-century segregationists, historians and commentators have done their best to denigrate, or simply ignore, the Principles of '98. It appears to be beyond the capacity of today's opinion makers to grasp the concept of a legitimate idea being put to an illegitimate purpose. According to the *Economist* magazine, for example, nullification was born in the antebellum South as a theory to prevent the federal government from "regulat[ing] slavery"—an assertion that not only ignores the Resolutions but perpetuates the myth that states' rights was necessarily linked to slavery.[17] Sean Wilentz, a historian at Princeton University, acknowledges the Virginia and Kentucky Resolutions, but brushes them aside as having been written "in a panic."[18] There's no objective evidence for that assertion. The Alien and Sedition Acts were signed into law in July 1798; the resolutions were drafted, debated, and revised by the legislatures over a four-and-a-half-month period—as long as it took to draft the Constitution itself. Would Wilentz also say that the framers drafted the Constitution "in a panic"? In any event, the Kentucky legislature reaffirmed the Principles of '98 in a supplemental resolution the following year. In his *Report of 1800*, Madison offered an extended defense of the concept of interposition. If Jefferson, Madison, or any of their allies had been inclined to disown their "panicky" resolutions, one imagines they could have found the words to do so.

The other common line of attack against the Virginia and Kentucky Resolutions is that they were rejected by the other states as "affronts to the Constitution," as Wilentz puts it.[19] It is true that some Federalist-dominated legislatures denounced

the resolutions on party-line votes—no surprise there—but no
state, with the exception of Vermont, denied the underlying
compact theory of the resolutions.[20]

The real measure of popular support for nullification and
interposition came in the election of 1800. In what was widely
seen as a referendum on the Principles of '98, Thomas Jefferson
captured the presidency and his Republicans swept Congress.[21]
If Jefferson was seen as having "affronted" the Constitution,
why did he and his party win so decisively?

Northern States' Rights

Finding themselves out of power at the national level, the Federalists at the state level would soon discover the Principles of '98.
In 1807, with the Napoleonic Wars raging in Europe, Jefferson
instituted an embargo preventing American merchant ships from
traveling to any foreign port anywhere in the world. Ostensibly designed to punish Britain and France for harassing American shipping, the embargo wrecked havoc on New England's
maritime-based economy. In January 1809, the Massachusetts
legislature condemned the embargo as "unjust, oppressive and
unconstitutional, and"—wait for it—"not legally binding on the
citizens of this state."[22] Connecticut's governor called on legislators to "interpose their protecting shield" to defend the people
from "the assumed power of the General Government."[23] The
legislature obliged by forbidding state officials from "affording any
official aid or cooperation in the execution of the [embargo]."[24]
The Rhode Island legislature also exercised its right of interposition, recognizing that "the people of this State" were "one of the
parties to the Federal Compact."[25] State courts in New England

also allowed lawsuits against federal customs officers for violating citizens' rights while policing the embargo. By 1808, these court cases "were making a shambles of federal efforts to enforce the Embargo Law," according to one legal historian.[26]

The New England resolutions and court cases marked the beginning of a long, and largely forgotten, tradition of *Northern* states' rights—forgotten because it disrupts the comfortable narrative of states' rights as a Southern phenomenon. The next provocation came in 1812, when the Republican-led Congress declared war on Great Britain and President Madison called the state militias into federal service. The New England states refused to comply; the Supreme Court of Massachusetts even issued an advisory opinion assuring the governor that, as commander in chief of the militia, he had the power to determine whether the militia was required for federal service.[27] Constitutionally speaking, the question was more complex than that. Article I of the Constitution grants Congress the power to press the state militias into federal service to "repel Invasions" (and other purposes not relevant here), but there was no British invasion in 1812. That would not happen until 1814, when Napoleon's abdication allowed the British to send forces to America. The troop mobilization of 1812 was for the purpose of invading Canada; Americans initially thought they could seize a province or two to teach the British a lesson (for the record, the plan didn't work). The New England states, therefore, had a strong argument for keeping their militias at home. The more important point, however, is that this sort of state-level resistance to military adventures would be unthinkable today.

When the then secretary of war and future president James Monroe proposed conscription to raise a federal army, New Hampshire representative Daniel Webster vowed that his state would defy any draft. Although he would later gain fame in the

Senate as a foe of states' rights, in 1814 Webster argued that it would be the duty of state governments to "interpose" against "arbitrary power."

The war also led to another embargo. In 1813, Madison pushed an embargo bill through Congress, eliciting—like Jefferson's embargo—howls of protest from Federalist New England. The Massachusetts legislature announced its right "to protect its citizens from acts of violence by the United States . . . Whenever the national compact is violated . . . this legislature is bound to interpose its power." The Connecticut legislature declared that the United States "are a confederated and not a consolidated Republic."[28]

Northern resistance to the war culminated in the 1814 Hartford Convention, a gathering of leading Federalists that many predicted would lead to New England's secession. Instead, the convention issued a report in January 1815 that repeated, almost verbatim, Madison's principle that states have a right of interposition in the face of "deliberate, dangerous, and palpable infractions of the Constitution."[29] Shortly after the convention's declaration, news broke of Andrew Jackson's decisive victory over the British in the Battle of New Orleans and of the Treaty of Ghent concluding the war. In fact, the treaty had been signed before Jackson's victory, but Americans felt that their honor had been restored, and the Federalists suffered the taint of disloyalty for having opposed the war.

Deplorable Idiots and Unconstitutional Bastards

The New Englanders were using Madison's own words against him. Although the effort backfired, their cause was just: Madison had endorsed an unnecessary invasion of Canada, and he had forgotten many of the principles of limited government that had animated his political career. The dictum that power corrupts applies, unfortunately, even to our Founding Fathers.

The embarrassing experiences of the war—which had caught the American military ill-prepared and underfinanced[30]—led Madison to support greater centralization of power. In 1816, Madison supported a law establishing the Second Bank of the United States, even though he had earlier argued that the federal government had no authority to charter a bank (a function that was part of the reserved powers of the states).

As a congressman, Madison had been the leading critic of Alexander Hamilton's 1791 legislation creating the First Bank of the United States. At the time, Madison had ridiculed Hamilton's argument that the bank was authorized under the necessary and proper clause. If that's what "necessary" means, said Madison, then Congress's power could be expanded to "reach . . . every object within the whole compass of political economy."[31] Fifteen years later, Madison had "evolved"—to use the term now applied to anyone who gradually concedes more and more power to Congress—and suddenly the federal government was in the banking business.

The Supreme Court was called upon to decide the legitimacy of the bank in *McCulloch v. Maryland* (1819), a case involving Maryland's attempt to levy a state tax on the bank. Although the Principles of '98 had been endorsed by Republicans and Federalists alike during the first two decades of the nineteenth century, they held no attraction for the one person with the power to enforce those principles: Chief Justice John Marshall. Nominated by John Adams in the final days of his presidential administration, Marshall was a staunch Federalist who "revered Hamilton" (in the words of Hamilton's biographer Ron Chernow). He would serve on the court until his death in 1835—an astonishing thirty-four years—during which time he used judicial power to fulfill Hamilton's expansive vision of federal power.[32]

In *McCulloch*, Marshall granted Congress almost unlimited discretion in determining the scope of its own powers. Marshall began his analysis by drawing a valid distinction between the "ends" and the "means" of the central government. The enumerated powers of Article I constitute a complete list of the ends for which Congress can legislate, but the necessary and proper clause gives Congress the choice of means to achieve those ends. To take an example, the Constitution empowers Congress to "provide for the Punishment of counterfeiting" (Article I, Section 8) and to "declare the punishment for Treason" (Article III, Section 3). Even though the Constitution does not explicitly say how such punishments must be carried out, it is reasonable to assume that Congress can also hire prosecutors to secure convictions of those crimes, and to build prisons (or gallows) to deal with those found guilty.

In applying the abstract distinction between constitutional ends and means to the bank, however, the chief justice revealed his agenda to consolidate federal power. According to Marshall, the constitutional "end" of the bank was to aid the government "in prosecution of its fiscal powers"—a somewhat grandiose way of referring to Congress's power to impose certain kinds of taxes. But it was clearly not "necessary" for the federal government to own a bank in order to collect taxes: Congress had been making do without a bank ever since the First Bank's charter expired in 1811. And even if necessary, was it "proper"? At a minimum, a federal law can hardly be proper if it invades the powers reserved to the states under the Tenth Amendment, or if it relies on an expansive interpretation forbidden by the Ninth Amendment. Marshall ignored these principles and held that Congress could enact all means which are "appropriate"—rather than "necessary"—and which are "not prohibited" by the Constitution. In other words, Congress is theoretically limited to the "ends" that it may pursue (its enumerated powers), but it can use any "means" to achieve those ends. The bottom line—that Congress can do anything that is not expressly prohibited in the Constitution—is exactly what the Ninth Amendment was designed to avoid, as we saw in the previous chapter.

Critics immediately recognized that Marshall had effectively annulled the enumerated powers of Article I. Spencer Roane, a onetime Anti-Federalist and then the chief justice of the Virginia Supreme Court, wrote a scathing attack on Marshall in the *Richmond Enquirer*, arguing that "that man must be a deplorable idiot who does not see that there is no earthly difference between an unlimited grant of power, and a grant limited in its terms, but accompanied with unlimited means of carrying it into execution." Wisely, perhaps, Roane wrote under a pseudonym. Another Virginian, John Taylor, whom we last saw sponsoring Madison's resolutions of 1798, mocked Marshall's reasoning in which "ends may be made to beget means" and vice versa, "until the cohabitation shall rear a progeny of unconstitutional bastards."[33]

Five years later, in 1824, Marshall midwifed a new litter of unconstitutional bastards in the case of *Gibbons v. Ogden*. In *Gibbons*, the issue was whether the federal government had authority to regulate steamships going between New York and New Jersey. The court held that Congress did have such power under the commerce clause. That result was reasonable enough: steamboats ferrying people and goods from one state to another are part of "Commerce . . . among the several States." But Marshall went out of his way to describe Congress's commerce power in gratuitously broad terms. Commerce was more than merely trade, he declared, it was "intercourse," an ambiguous term potentially opening up Congress's power to other areas of interstate relations. Moreover, Marshall suggested that Congress could regulate any aspect of a state's internal commerce that might "*affect* other States" (emphasis mine).

This was an expansive reading of Congress's powers, but the chief justice insisted that there is not "one sentence" in the Constitution that could justify a strict construction of Congress's powers. To the contrary, the powers of the federal government must be construed as having no limits beyond those expressly "prescribed by the Constitution"—another example of Marshall's everything-not-prohibited-is-constitutional approach. According to the law professor Kurt T. Lash, Marshall *never* referred to the Ninth Amendment during his tenure as chief justice "despite repeated references to it by bench and bar as a rule prohibiting expansive readings of federal power."[34]

The Nullification Crisis

Four years after the fateful decision in *Gibbons*, Congress would use its (now) seemingly boundless power to spark a new constitutional crisis. At issue was the tariff of 1828—dubbed the "Tariff of Abominations" by critics—a measure that would lead to a showdown between the federal government and South Carolina.

Americans were deeply divided over what role, if any, Congress should play in promoting economic development. Since at least 1810, Kentucky congressman Henry Clay had been hawking his "American System," which included federally subsidized infrastructure projects and high tariffs to protect domestic industry. The infrastructure proposals—known then as "internal improvements"—clearly invaded an area reserved to the states. The states had not only the right but every incentive to ensure the maintenance and construction of decent infrastructure within their borders. During the first half of the nineteenth century, the states collectively spent some three hundred million dollars on projects such as New York's Erie Canal.[35] To his credit, President Madison vetoed an internal improvements bill as beyond Congress's enumerated powers. His successors, including Monroe, Jackson, and Polk, would also go on to reject infrastructure bills.

Tariffs were another matter. The Constitution *does* authorize Congress to impose import duties, and Congress had, in fact, already enacted protective tariffs in 1816 and 1824. On May 19, 1828, Congress passed a dramatically higher tariff, with rates of 62 to 92 percent on all goods entering the United States—the highest rates in American history. The tariff threatened to devastate the economy of the South, which depended on trading agricultural commodities for manufactured goods from Europe. The South would now lose much of its overseas export market, and would also be forced to "buy American" at higher prices.[36]

In theory, the tariff was meant to fend off foreign competition; in reality, it was designed to influence the presidential contest of 1828 between Andrew Jackson and John Quincy Adams. Jacksonian Democrats engineered the tariff to benefit mid-Atlantic and Western states—where Old Hickory needed the votes—at the expense of the South, which was bound to vote Democratic in any event.

Jackson handily won the election, but he then was stuck defending the Tariff of Abominations. At least five Southern legislatures passed resolutions condemning the tariff during the 1828–29 legislative session.[37] In South Carolina, the legislature published a document known as the "Exposition and Protest," warning that if Congress failed to repeal the law, the legislature would be forced to exercise its right of interposition. The author of the "Exposition and Protest" was not revealed at the time, because it happened to be the sitting vice president, John C. Calhoun.

In 1831, Calhoun resigned the vice presidency and went public with his opposition to the tariff. In his Fort Hill address, delivered in July of that year, Calhoun described the Constitution as a "compact" to which "the people of the several States" are parties. The right of each state to "interpose" against unconstitutional acts, said Calhoun, is "the fundamental principle of our system." The following year, Congress amended the tariff, slightly reducing the rates—but not enough to satisfy the South. South Carolina's governor called for a convention to consider the state's response to the tariff. The convention assembled on November 24, 1832, and within days adopted the Ordinance of Nullification, which declared any contracts or judgments made in pursuance of the tariff to be void. It also forbade federal officials from collecting customs duties within the Palmetto State.

In response, Jackson's allies introduced the "Force Bill," which gave the president the authority to use military force to coerce South Carolina into submission. In 1833, Congress passed the Force Bill, but on the same day it also passed a new tariff law repealing the punitive rates of the 1828 and 1832 measures. Jackson saved face, but in reality the threat of nullification had forced Congress to retreat.

Here, alas, revisionist history kicks into high gear. For post–New Deal historians, the nullification crisis is seldom about tariffs. Instead—and despite all evidence to the contrary—it's really about slavery. Because Calhoun supported slavery, historians portray his call for interposition as a thinly veiled move against abolition and a precursor to Southern secession. Thus, according to one high school textbook, nullification was a "dangerous assertion of states' rights" in which South Carolina was simply laying the groundwork for the day "when a northern-dominated federal government decided to end slavery."[38]

In the revisionist story, Calhoun was a closed-minded provincial who led his state into a position so extreme, it was rejected even by other Southern states. In reality, Calhoun was a sophisticated thinker who had been educated at Yale and at the Litchfield Law School in Connecticut. It is true that Calhoun supported slavery, but his objections to the tariff were based on serious constitutional concerns that had nothing to do with slavery. As Calhoun acknowledged, the Constitution grants Congress the power "to lay and collect taxes, duties, imposts and excises," but the Constitution also commands that those powers be used to promote "the general welfare," which was originally understood to mean that taxes cannot be used to benefit one state or one region. But that is precisely what Congress had done: it had imposed a tariff on the entire union to enrich the Northern and Western states. Moreover, Calhoun argued that, in order to be constitutional, a tax must have as its primary purpose the raising of revenue—a proposition that is still good law today. Calhoun did not advocate secession over the tariff; to the contrary, he urged interposition as a peaceful way to bring the federal government to the bargaining table.

Moreover, the notion that nullification was motivated by a desire to preempt future federal laws against slavery ignores one crucial point: there was no credible movement in Congress to abolish slavery in the South. One would have to believe that Calhoun willingly gave up the vice presidency for the sake of preventing a wholly hypothetical federal abolition law—a preposterous idea. Granted, one can find statements by some Southerners during the period complaining that *all* local institutions, including slavery, were at risk from federal interference. But at the same time, others, such as James Monroe, warned that nullification itself was a threat to slavery because it would encourage slave insurrection.[39]

Nor was South Carolina isolated during the nullification crisis, as some academics contend. The historian Richard E. Ellis points out that "there was considerable support among well-placed individuals throughout the South for the nullifiers."[40] Even in the North, Calhoun's arguments resonated. In 1829, the Maine legislature condemned the Tariff of Abominations, adopting exactly the same argument laid out in Calhoun's "Exposition and Protest," namely, that the tariff was unconstitutional because Congress had "abused [the taxing power] to accommodate sectional interests." In 1831, over two hundred delegates from fifteen states gathered at the Free Trade Convention in Philadelphia, the sole purpose of which was to persuade Congress to repeal the tariff. The convention's memorial to Congress, drafted by Albert Gallatin, a Pennsylvania statesman, branded the tariff as "at variance" with the Constitution because it "operates unequally and unjustly."[41]

To be sure, nullification remained a controversial doctrine, but South Carolina's stance had not tarnished the doctrine of states' rights. For the Jackson administration, the Force Bill had been a major setback, awakening many Americans to the coercive tendencies of federal power. In 1834—just one year after the crisis was resolved—Condy Raguet, a Philadelphia newspaper editor and political economist, asserted that "the doctrine of State sovereignty is, in truth, the basis of our whole republican theory."[42] The following year brought publication of the first volume of Alexis de Tocqueville's *Democracy in America*, widely hailed as one of the most insightful analyses of early American politics. Writing in the immediate aftermath of the nullification crisis, did Tocqueville warn against the dangerous assertion of states' rights? No: he repeatedly emphasized the genius of American federalism and warned against the dangers of centralization. Even if it could be proved that Americans would be more efficiently governed by a central authority, wrote Tocqueville, "still, the political advantages which the Americans derive from their decentralized system would induce me to prefer it."[43] Those "political advantages" included the promotion of liberty and resistance to tyranny. As Tocqueville put it, "What resistance can be offered to tyranny in a country where each individual is weak, and where the citizens are not united by any common interest? Those who dread the license of the mob, and those who fear absolute power, ought alike to desire the gradual development of provincial liberties."[44]

In asserting the Principles of '98, Calhoun had not retrieved some long-lost document from the dustbin of history. He was continuing a debate that was fresh in the minds of all the key players in the nullification crisis. It had been only fourteen years since the Hartford Convention had asserted the right of interposition on behalf of New England, and since Daniel Webster had pledged New Hampshire's nullification of any federal troop conscription. Webster, however, had reversed himself in order to support the tariff. In his famous 1830 debate against Senator Robert Hayne (Calhoun's ally), Webster sought to rebut the old Patrick Henry idea that, in the event of a conflict, liberty must trump union. Instead, Webster declared, "Liberty and Union [are] one and inseparable."[45] In other words, there can be no conflict between the two. Webster's rhetoric was effective, but illogical. As we shall see, the strengthening union did not necessarily promote liberty in the nineteenth century. Sometimes, it promoted slavery.

3

States' Rights and the Abolitionists

On March 24, 1859, a leading statesman who would soon find himself fighting in the Civil War gave a speech entitled "State Rights." In it, he warned of federal "usurpation" of state sovereignty on the issue of slavery, and he urged states to exercise their powers of nullification and interposition. He told his listeners to "stand firm" against federal power, declaring, "Here is the battlefield, every man to his gun!"[1]

The speaker was not—as you might be thinking—Stonewall Jackson or Robert E. Lee. Rather, it was Carl Schurz: one of the leading *abolitionists* of the nineteenth century. Schurz would go on to serve as a Union officer during the Civil War, after which he enjoyed a distinguished career as a journalist, a US senator, and the secretary of the interior. There is a park named after him on Manhattan's Upper East Side.

Schurz's speech was no aberration. Just one year earlier, another Northern politician had given a major speech warning that federal courts were threatening to deprive states of their right to regulate slavery within their own borders. That politician was Abraham Lincoln; the speech was his "house divided" address. In fact, as the law professor Paul Finkelman notes, in the years before the Civil War "the philosophy of states' rights or state sovereignty was adopted by many northerners" seeking to arrest the spread of slavery.[2]

How can this be true? If any proposition is sacred among educated Americans, it is that "states' rights" was the rallying cry of slave masters and federal power was the tool of abolitionists. The widely used textbook *Making a Nation* teaches college students that antebellum Southerners used the term "states' rights" as a euphemism for "the right of the states to maintain slavery and the right of individuals to hold property in slaves."[3] A plaque at the Smithsonian's National Portrait Gallery flatly refers to states' rights as a doctrine "which protected the institution of slavery." During a 2011 interview on National Public Radio, Adam Goodhart, the director of the Center for the Study of the American Experience at Washington College, asserted that "the only significant state right that people were arguing about in 1860 was the right to own what was known as slave property."[4] At this point, the interviewer, Terry Gross, compared Southern invocations of states' rights with the rhetoric of those opposing President Obama's healthcare law.[5]

This conventional history provides a handy rhetorical weapon for left-wing commentators who accuse states' rights conservatives of embracing a doctrine historically identified with "pro-slavery ideologies and . . . the disenfranchisement of African-Americans," as the *Nation* puts it.[6] But two things are missing from the conventional history: facts and logic. If states' rights was a doctrine that "protected" slavery, as the Smithsonian asserts, it's fair to ask: Protected it against what? Presumably against a federal law that would have imposed abolition on unwilling Southern states. But the federal government never came close to enacting such a law before the Civil War. What the federal government did was just the opposite—use its power to safeguard the institution of slavery and to protect the alleged property rights of slaveholders.

Before the Emancipation Proclamation (1863), the federal government posed little threat to slavery. Sporadic proposals by Northern congressmen to abolish slavery were purely symbolic; they had no chance of passing. Antislavery amendments introduced in the House of Representatives in 1818 and 1839 never made it to a full floor vote. An 1844 proposal to abolish representation of the slave population under the infamous three-fifths clause of the Constitution was overwhelmingly spurned by both houses of Congress.[7]

During the first half of the nineteenth century, proslavery politicians were much more likely to rely on federal power than on states' rights to protect the institution. The United States Constitution implicitly permitted slavery and even guaranteed the return of fugitive slaves to their masters. In the District of Columbia—over which the federal Congress had total authority—slavery remained legal until 1850, when it was finally abolished, but only in return for an expansion of slavery elsewhere. Congress did prohibit the international slave trade in 1808, but by that time every Southern state except South Carolina had already passed laws banning or restricting the slave trade.[8]

Henry Adams—Harvard historian, descendant of presidents John Adams and John Quincy Adams, and Boston Brahmin if ever there was one—defended states' rights as "a sound and true doctrine . . . as dear to New England as to Virginia."[9] Between slavery and states' rights there was, he wrote, "no necessary connection." To the contrary, "whenever a question arose of extending or protecting slavery, the slaveholders became friends of centralized power, and used that dangerous weapon with a kind of frenzy." In the 1830s, for example, proslavery politicians called on the federal government to use its postal powers to keep abolitionist pamphlets out of the mail. In 1835, President Andrew Jackson obliged by proposing to Congress legislation to prohibit the postal service from delivering "incendiary" literature that could provoke slave insurrection.

The postal-suppression legislation was referred to a committee chaired by John Calhoun, the most renowned states' rights advocate of the antebellum South. Calhoun objected to the proposal on the basis of state sovereignty: he could not abide federal meddling in a state-level debate. Calhoun watered down the administration's legislation, giving postmasters authority only to enforce state preferences: if South Carolina wanted to block abolitionist tracts, the post office would comply, but other states would be free to allow such materials. Calhoun's version was not exactly an enlightened piece of legislation, but it was considerably less oppressive than Jackson's original proposal. The bill, in any event, was defeated.[10]

Fugitive Slaves

The major states' rights issue leading up to the war was the right of free states and territories to exclude slavery within their own borders. This right was surprisingly (to modern eyes) tenuous, subject to various efforts to use federal power to coerce free states to recognize and enforce the "property" rights of slave masters.

The Constitution's fugitive slave clause was meant to give slave owners the right to capture runaway slaves. The clause, however, does not expressly require any state to participate in implementing its terms; rather, the clause speaks in the passive voice: the escaped slave "shall be delivered" to its owner. A slave owner had a federal right to regain his "property," but the Constitution provided no particular machinery for him to vindicate that right. In 1793, Congress filled in the details with the Fugitive Slave Act, which imposed an affirmative duty on both federal and state judges to enforce the claims of slave owners demanding the return of runaway slaves.

Notwithstanding the 1793 act, various Northern states passed "personal liberty laws" putting restrictions on the rendition of fugitive slaves and protecting free blacks from kidnapping. Pennsylvania, for example, created a presumption of freedom for black residents that could not be defeated unless a slave owner had registered his slave with state authorities within a certain time frame. Thus, even if a slave owner seized an escaped slave pursuant to federal law, he might be engaged in kidnapping as far as Pennsylvania law was concerned.[11]

A classic example of proslave interests using federal power to trump the rights of free states arose in the 1842 Supreme Court case of *Prigg v. Pennsylvania*. Edward Prigg, a Maryland slave catcher, had been convicted for removing a black woman and her children from Pennsylvania without complying with the provisions of Pennsylvania's personal liberty law. Prigg appealed his conviction to the Supreme Court on the grounds that he had complied with the federal Fugitive Slave Act, and that was enough. The Supreme Court agreed, upholding the constitutionality of the federal act, and striking down the conflicting provisions of Pennsylvania's law. Moreover, the court laid down the broad dictum that states could not interfere with federal officials charged with implementing federal law, including the Fugitive Slave Act.[12]

For all of its flaws, the *Prigg* decision did advance states' rights in one respect: the court said that Pennsylvania itself had no obligation to assist the central government in carrying out the Fugitive Slave Act. Thus, although a state could not stop federal agents from enforcing the act, it could stop its own officials from doing so. In essence the court had endorsed the principle of interposition first laid out in the Virginia and Kentucky Resolutions of 1798.

The nonslave states quickly took advantage of this one glimmer of states' rights. In 1847, Pennsylvania adopted a new personal liberty law withdrawing all state support for the Fugitive Slave Act. Under this law, state judges could not lift a finger to enforce the federal law and state jails could not hold runaway slaves. Other states followed with stronger personal liberty laws that greatly complicated the ability of slave owners to recapture fugitive slaves.[13]

The Southern states did not celebrate these assertions of states' rights. To the contrary, they called on the federal government to use its power to crack down on the wayward states. The Georgia legislature, in a typical example, passed a resolution declaring it the "imperative duty of Congress" to enforce slave masters' rights.[14] The fugitive slave issue was folded into the broader question of the expansion of slavery into new states and territories. Under the Compromise of 1850, California was admitted as a free state while New Mexico and Utah were organized as slave territories. Slavery was abolished in the District of Columbia, and a new Fugitive Slave Act was agreed to.

The Fugitive Slave Act of 1850 called for the appointment of federal commissioners in every state with authority to issue and execute warrants for the capture of runaway slaves. The act empowered the commissioners to "command" all citizens in the area to join a *posse comitatus* (in English: a lynch mob); those who refused to join the posse faced fines or even jail time.[15] Captured blacks were denied the benefit of jury trials—commissioners and judges were ordered to try any fugitive slave case "in a summary manner." Commissioners were paid ten dollars if they ruled in favor of the slave owner, but only five dollars if they ruled against him. All in all, it was one of the most brutal laws of the antebellum period, enacted by the federal government at the behest of slave states to quash the rights of free states.[16]

Once its provisions began to bite, the Fugitive Slave Act led to greater calls for Northern states' rights. In 1854, a federal marshal seized Anthony Burns, a runaway slave working in Boston, and brought him before the fugitive slave commissioner. Although Burns was represented by the noted lawyer Richard Henry Dana—author of the seafaring classic *Two Years Before the Mast*—he was returned to slavery. Amid protests in the streets of Boston, the abolitionist preacher Theodore Parker called for "calm, deliberate, systematic action . . . for the defense of personal liberty and the State Rights of the North."[17]

After the Burns case, and the Kansas-Nebraska bill of 1854, which reopened the slavery issue in areas where it had been closed for years, at least seven Northern states enacted new personal liberty laws aimed at defeating the new Fugitive Slave Act.[18] One of those states was Wisconsin, where a local antislavery editor, Sherman Booth, had been arrested in 1854 for interfering with federal marshals attempting to capture an escaped slave named Joshua Glover. The Wisconsin Supreme Court ordered Booth to be released on the grounds that the Fugitive Slave Act was unconstitutional. The marshal appealed to the US Supreme Court and had Booth rearrested. Again the Wisconsin Supreme Court released Booth.

Abolitionists cheered the Wisconsin court's defiance of federal authority. Horace Greeley, the editor of the *New York Tribune*, urged other states to follow the Badger State's "refreshing" example: "By another year we expect to see Ohio holding the same noble course. After that we anticipate a race among the other Free States in the same direction till all have reached the goal of State independence."[19] Likewise, Benjamin Wade, an antislavery congressman from Ohio, praised "noble Wisconsin" because "a State, in the last resort, crowded to the wall by a General Government seeking by the strong arm of its power to take away *the rights of the State*, is to judge of whether she shall stand on her reserved rights" (emphasis mine).[20]

The proslavery majority on the US Supreme Court, however, was not so enthusiastic about state independence. On March 7, 1859, the court unanimously held that Wisconsin had no power to object to the conditions under which her citizens were imprisoned by federal authorities. This strongly pro-national decision was written by Chief Justice Roger Taney, the principal author of the *Dred Scott* decision (discussed later in this chapter).[21]

Carl Schurz's "State Rights" speech was an immediate reaction to the Booth decision; it was delivered in Milwaukee. The Wisconsin legislature would respond to the Booth case by adopting a set of resolutions nullifying the Fugitive Slave Act. In words borrowed from the Kentucky Resolutions of 1798 and 1799, the Wisconsin resolutions declared that each state had a sovereign right to judge for itself whether a federal law transgressed the Constitution. And when Congress did pass an unconstitutional law, the legislature called for "positive defiance"—in other words, nullification.

Slave Transit

A related issue was "slave transit"—that is, the ability of slave owners to visit, or travel through, free states and territories without fear of their slaves being emancipated. This was a critical issue because even temporary slavery was abhorrent to free states. Many Northern jurists cited the policy laid down by British courts in the eighteenth century that a slave is emancipated the moment he or she sets foot on free soil. Besides, there was the danger of a slippery slope. If a master could bring one slave into a free state, why not a hundred? If he could stay for one week, why not one year?

As with the fugitive slave issue, slave transit was initially a matter of state comity; free states adopted policies to accommodate slaveholders traveling through their territory. But in the mid-nineteenth century, comity began to break down amid the rising friction between the North and South. Beginning in the 1840s, most Northern states adopted increasingly restrictive rules on slave transit, some barring masters from bringing slaves into their territory for any length of time. The Northern states had every right to adopt such policies, but proslavery forces showed little regard for states' rights in this area. Instead, many slave masters asserted a federal right to travel with their slaves that would supersede conflicting state laws.[22]

The alleged federal right of slave transit was a stretch.

Southerners invoked various constitutional provisions, including Article IV's command to grant "full faith and credit" to each state's official acts as well as its guarantee of "privileges and immunities," but nothing in the text directly addresses the issue. Although the argument was weak, slave masters would exploit a sympathetic federal judiciary to establish a right to export slavery "temporarily" to other states.

The issue of slave transit took center stage in a high-profile case called *Strader v. Graham*. The question in *Strader* was whether three African Americans who had been enslaved under Kentucky law could still be held to servitude after they had been emancipated under Ohio and Indiana law (because they had made several trips to those states). Kentucky's highest court held that Ohio and Indiana law did not change the status of the three slaves. In 1850, the US Supreme Court affirmed the Kentucky court's decision ostensibly because the federal court could not interfere with a Kentucky court's decision on a matter of Kentucky law. That sounds like a victory for states' rights, except that *Strader* did not concern a conflict between state and federal law; it concerned a conflict between state laws. On the one hand, Kentucky law imputed a permanent slave status, even to slaves who had left the state; on the other hand, Ohio and Indiana asserted the right to emancipate slaves within their borders. The Supreme Court used its power to favor the Kentucky approach of forcing free states to recognize slavery. *Strader* was anything but a states' rights decision.

Dred Scott and the Color-Coded Constitution

Like the *Booth* case, *Strader* exemplifies Taney's agenda to use the power of the federal judiciary to entrench slavery. His crowning achievement in this regard was his 1857 opinion in *Dred Scott v. Sandford.*

Dred Scott had been the slave of John Emerson, an army surgeon. Over the years, Scott had lived with Dr. Emerson in the free state of Illinois and in the territory of Upper Louisiana (now Minnesota), in which slavery had been "forever prohibited" under the Missouri Compromise of 1820. After Emerson's death, Scott sued the administrator of Emerson's estate, John Sandford, to gain his freedom based on his prolonged residence on free soil. Having been legally free in those places, the argument went, Scott could not be forced back to his former status. After losing in the Missouri Supreme Court and a lower federal court, Scott appealed to the US Supreme Court with the help of an antislavery lawyer who agreed to take on the case pro bono. Despite being well represented, Scott lost.

Writing for a 7–2 majority, Taney held that Scott had no legal right to sue for his freedom; indeed, as a black man, Scott had no right to bring any suit in federal court. According to Taney, the right to sue was a privilege of citizenship, and it was legally impossible for African Americans to become citizens. Even if some misguided states thought they could confer citizenship on emancipated slaves, not even free blacks could become "citizens of the United States."

Before *Dred Scott*, few people thought that there was a distinct status of federal citizenship. Rather, the conventional view was that if a person was a citizen under state law, he would also be a citizen under federal law.[23] Taney's decision imposed a uniform rule of white-only citizenship, completely undercutting the long-standing Northern-state tradition of free black citizens. While an African American might be entitled to freedom under state law, he could not assert that right in federal court or vote in federal elections, or exercise any other federal right.

With Taney's new definition of federal citizenship established, the case should have been over. But the majority went on to hold that, even if Scott had a right to bring his suit, he would lose anyway. First, Scott could not rely on Illinois law because, under *Strader v. Graham*, the Missouri courts had no obligation to recognize the emancipation laws of sister states. Secondly, Taney rejected Scott's claim that he had gained his freedom in the Louisiana Territory under the terms of the Missouri Compromise. To reach that result, Taney held that the Missouri Compromise was unconstitutional—a startling development that upset over thirty years of fragile equilibrium between North and South. Strictly speaking, the court was opining only on the validity of a *federal* law, but the court's rationale—that the emancipation of a sojourning slave amounted to an unconstitutional deprivation of "property rights"—could be equally applied to *state* laws purporting to liberate slaves in transit. One of Taney's associate justices, Samuel Nelson, vaguely asserted that the states' power to legislate on the topic of slavery was "restrained by the Federal Constitution." What had Nelson meant by that? It was far from an abstract question, as Northern states had continued to restrict the ability of slave masters to bring their "property" into their jurisdiction. In New York, for example, the highest court had held that, under state law, a group of Virginia slaves had gained their freedom the minute they entered the Empire State.

The Supreme Court had produced the staunchest possible defense of slavery, but it was not a defense of states' rights. To the contrary, the court's decision was openly hostile to such rights, given its rule of federal citizenship and its implicit warning against state attempts to emancipate slaves. A day after the decision was announced, the *New-York Daily Times* lamented that "slavery is no longer local, it is national."[24] The fear of nationalized slavery lies at the heart of Lincoln's "house divided" speech, with which he launched his 1858 bid for election to the US Senate. The speech is an indictment of the court, to be sure, but it is also a bracing defense of states' rights, specifically the right of free states to remain free. Seizing on Justice Nelson's dictum that the US Constitution might "restrain" states from regulating the status of African Americans within their borders, Lincoln warned that the Supreme Court would soon hold that the Constitution "does not permit a state to exclude slavery from its limits."

"We shall *lie down* pleasantly dreaming that the people of *Missouri* are on the verge of making their state *free*," said Lincoln, "and we shall *awake* to the reality, instead, that the *Supreme* Court has made *Illinois* a *slave* state."[25] Lincoln was not alone in his defense of state sovereignty against encroachments by the central government. The Republican Party itself had been "organized to protest against the invasion of State rights," as the journalist Edward Payson Powell wrote in 1897.[26] Specifically, the party was galvanized by the outrage caused by the use of federal troops in the new state of Kansas to enforce a proslavery constitution against the wishes of many Kansans. In light of *Dred Scott*, Republicans feared a conspiracy among the branches of the federal government to allow the "slaveocracy" to extend slavery into the states and territories.[27]

Lincoln lost his Senate bid to Stephen Douglas, after which he immediately launched a national speaking tour. Lincoln stayed relentlessly on message—and the message was not a call for the federal government to abolish slavery. Rather, it was a warning *against* the use of federal power to nationalize slavery. In at least sixteen public addresses, Lincoln predicted the eventual "nationalization of slavery" if Chief Justice Taney and his coconspirators were not checked by the Republican Party.[28]

Contrary to all these historical facts, *Dred Scott* is often portrayed as a states' rights decision. A victory for "the most radical states' rights Democrats"—that's how the law professor Jeffrey Rosen describes the case in an essay for PBS.[29] Meanwhile, *Exploring Constitutional Law*, a website run by the law school of the University of Missouri–Kansas City, describes *Dred Scott* as an "extreme example" of a "conservative court" promoting states' rights.[30] That's a little like calling *Roe v. Wade* an extreme example of pro-life jurisprudence.

Most Likely to Secede

Mainstream commentators who draw a straight line between South Carolina's support of nullification in 1832 and Southern secession in 1860 have turned history upside down. The Civil War was precipitated not by Southern nullification—there was no antislavery law for the South to nullify—but by the persistent efforts of Northern states to nullify proslavery federal laws.

Threats of secession were bandied about in the decades running up to the war—but the threats were as likely to come from Northern abolitionists as from Southern slaveholders. Many Americans shared Lincoln's view that the Union could not "endure, permanently, half slave and half free." One way to address this issue was to break up the Union, and for a while it looked like the momentum for secession was stronger in the

North. The abolitionist William Lloyd Garrison, for example, used his position as the editor of the *Liberator* to call for "the repeal of the Union between North and South," as he wrote in 1842. Two years later, the American Anti-Slavery Society passed a resolution at its annual meeting stating that "secession from the present United States Government is the duty of every Abolitionist." A few weeks later the Massachusetts Anti-Slavery Society adopted a similar resolution.[31] The logic of Northern secession was twofold. The free North could disassociate itself from the slave South, but also a hypothetical Northern republic would have no Fugitive Slave Clause, and thus it would be a safe haven for escaped slaves. According to the political commentator Bill Kauffman, abolitionists viewed secession as "the instrument by which slavery was not preserved but *abolished*, as border states, one by retreating one, emancipated their fast-disappearing slaves" (emphasis his).[32]

Meanwhile, in the South, those who wanted to break up the Union, known as "fire-eaters," were a distinct minority. In 1850, the fire-eaters pushed for popularly elected state conventions to consider secession, only to retreat after the Georgia and Mississippi conventions voted overwhelmingly to stay in the Union; Mississippi (Jefferson Davis's home) declared that secession "is utterly unsanctioned by the Federal Constitution."[33]

Up until the first shots were fired at Fort Sumter, the defenders of slavery were not known for resisting federal power. To the contrary, they had been exploiting federal power: to expand the reach of slavery, to enforce alleged federal rights to travel with or capture slaves, and to silence abolitionists. For decades, the slave interests had dominated Congress and the Supreme Court—the last thing they wanted was states' rights. As late as February 1861—when Virginia called a convention to consider secession—the "great majority" of delegates arrived in Richmond expecting the commonwealth to stay in the Union, according to the historian Edward L. Ayers.[34]

When the South did embrace secession, it was not because the federal government had done anything to abolish slavery; rather, the election of Abraham Lincoln and the rise of the Republicans meant that Northern states would be permitted to get away with what the South considered to be illegal nullification. Consider Mississippi's declaration of secession, which argues that Mississippi was forced to leave the Union because the Northern states had "*nullified* the Fugitive Slave Law" (emphasis mine). Likewise, South Carolina's declaration complains that Northern states "have enacted laws which either *nullify* the Acts of Congress [such as the Fugitive Slave Act] or render useless any attempt to execute them" (emphasis mine). Georgia's declaration rebuked Congress for failing to suppress antislavery speech, even though freedom of speech was thought to be a matter of state jurisdiction, because abolitionists were committing "offenses against the laws of nations."[35]

Secession, when it came, was not an expression of states' rights but something different altogether. States' rights is an aspect of federalism, the system of dual sovereignty created by the Founding Fathers to govern the relations between state and central governments. A state that secedes from the Union is not participating in federal-state relations—it is opting out of the system entirely. Secession is a rejection of federalism.

Even in the Confederacy itself, states' rights were seen as a potential threat to slavery. The Confederate constitution was a nearly verbatim copy of the US Constitution—except that, when it came to slavery, it gave more power to the central government and less to the states. On the issue of slave transit, for example, the Southern document "severely limited state power in an explicit attempt to create a more unified Confederacy," according to Finkelman.[36] Slaveholders were given an absolute right to bring their slaves into other states for indefinite periods—even if the host state wanted to abolish or limit slavery. The Confederate constitution also included an expanded fugitive slave clause that gave masters additional rights to capture slaves, even those who had become free under the laws of a sister state.

The Civil War was fought over the issue of slavery; nothing in this chapter is meant to cast doubt on that. But the war was not sparked by federal efforts to abolish slavery; there were no such efforts before the South seceded. To the extent states' rights contributed to the outbreak of war, they were Northern assertions of states' rights, and the South's frustration at the failure of the federal government to rein in those assertions.

After the war, however, federal politicians—eager to justify an expanded role for the national government—found it irresistible to associate states' rights with the Confederacy and, therefore, with slavery. By 1909, the journalist Herbert Croly could assert—with little fear of contradiction—that the growth of federal power since Reconstruction was necessary to slay "the double-headed problem of slavery and states' rights."[37] The stage was set for a federal coup against the states, under the banner of "progressivism."

4

Progressives Give Birth to a Nation

Americans rang in the new year of 1913 with customary exuberance. In big cities and small towns, they treated themselves to fancy dinners, a few drinks, and a bracing round of "Auld Lang Syne." In Indianapolis, leading citizens gathered at the Claypool Hotel, where the menu called for *crabes farcies* and *perdreau grille*, washed down with fine wines. In New Orleans, an eleven-year-old boy named Louis Armstrong—yes, *that* Louis Armstrong—got caught up in the revelry and fired a celebratory shot from his father's pistol into the air. (He ended up in a juvenile detention home, where he took up music to pass the time.)

One can forgive young Satchmo for his enthusiasm. At the dawn of 1913, the average American had reason to celebrate: he enjoyed a political liberty unknown to most other people on the planet. The great decisions that affected his life were made close to home—either literally *in* his home, or by state and local representatives. Taxing, spending, schools, roads, business regulation, and social issues—these were largely confined to the town hall, and never farther away than the state capitol. The average American knew his local representatives, and could vote them out of office if they failed to deliver.

In 1913, total government spending in the United States equaled 8 percent of gross national product (it's around 40 percent today)—and 70 percent of that spending took place at the state and local level.[1] The national government was funded mainly through tariffs on imports, and it confined itself largely to its constitutional duties. The White House was occupied by President William Howard Taft, a staunch defender of constitutional federalism. The prerogatives of state government were defended by the Senate, whose members were still selected by the state legislatures. There was no Federal Reserve Bank, and the US Supreme Court had only limited rights to review the decisions of state supreme courts.

All of that would begin to change before the next New Year's Eve. Within a year, the federal government would gain the power to tax the incomes of individuals and corporations. Taft would be replaced by Woodrow Wilson, who had built his career belittling the Constitution as an outdated drag on the forces of centralization. The Senate would change to a system of direct election, thus breaking the link between state and national governments that was so essential to the framers' plan. Congress would pass the Federal Reserve Act, setting the stage for centralized control—and manipulation—of credit, inflation, and housing markets. Political scientists would openly call on the federal government to use its treaty power to override the states' reserved powers.

In retrospect, it is clear that 1913 was the decisive turning point in American federalism. The victories won by the so-called Progressives in that year signaled a permanent move away from states' rights and toward federal power. World War I and Prohibition would accelerate this trend, which culminated in the New Deal's consolidation of federal power under the guise of "cooperative federalism." Americans began 1913 as citizens of their states; by the end of the year, they were well on their way to becoming subjects of a national government.

Welcome to the Progressive Era

The Progressives were self-proclaimed legal and social reformers who often dominated American politics during the period from the late nineteenth century until the New Deal. Across many different fronts, they campaigned for a larger and more active government to address the perceived problems of the industrial age.[2]

Conventional wisdom teaches that the centralization of power in Washington—particularly post-1913—was an unalloyed good because Wilson and other Progressives were able to harness the power of the federal government to achieve "social justice." According to the high school text *Making a Nation*, the Progressives were all about making "modern institutions" that were "more humane, responsive and moral."[3] Another popular textbook, *Nation of Nations*, tells us that Woodrow Wilson "believed he was meant to achieve great things, and he did. Under him, progressivism peaked."[4]

What did the "peak" of progressivism look like? Consider Wilson's record on race. Whereas his stodgy predecessor, Taft, appointed thirty-one African Americans to federal office, Wilson appointed only nine—eight of whom were carryovers from Taft. Within six months of Wilson's inauguration, the Treasury and the Postal Service would be ordered segregated; other parts of the civil service would soon follow. One black clerk had to work in a specially constructed cage to avoid contact with white colleagues.[5] Wilson also approved the introduction of Jim Crow laws in the District of Columbia. In 1914, a delegation of black leaders headed by Monroe Trotter, a Harvard graduate, visited the White House to protest Wilson's segregationist policies, only to be told by the president that "segregation is not humiliating, but a benefit." Minutes later, Wilson dismissed the delegation because he found Trotter's manner "offensive."[6] If this was the peak of progressivism, I'd hate to see the valleys.

Wilson's racism was not an exception to his avowed progressivism; it was part and parcel of his vision of "progress." He believed that the central government must lead the nation in applying scientific principles to government—and Wilson accepted the pseudoscientific assertion that blacks carried contagious diseases and therefore needed to be quarantined.[7]

What about economic and social reforms? Yes, these were at the heart of the Progressive movement, but it was the *states*, not the federal government, that pioneered reform. Under reformers like Wisconsin's Robert "Fighting Bob" La Follette, the states enacted workplace safety laws, wage and hour regulations, and consumer protection measures. As the historian Gary Gerstle noted in the liberal magazine *Dissent*, "In the Progressive Era, the states were in the vanguard of reform efforts to assert the priority of the 'people' over the 'interests.'"[8] The federal government—in particular, the US Supreme Court—did what it could to block these efforts, striking down state reform laws on the basis of a strained reading of the due process clause. When Congress did get around to enacting progressive reforms, it invariably lagged behind the states.

A Union or a Nation?

Before the Civil War, advocates of consolidated national government had been strikingly unsuccessful: the grand designs of Alexander Hamilton and the American System of Henry Clay, for example, remained largely unfulfilled. Federal infrastructure projects were vetoed, fugitive slave laws resisted, abusive tariffs nullified. America was still seen as a *union* of sovereign states; her citizens owed their first loyalty to their states. In 1860, Wendell Phillips—a Boston lawyer and one of those Northern advocates of breaking up the Union—contrasted "homogenous nations like France [which] tend to centralization" with "confederacies like ours."[9]

Once the North mobilized for war, "centralization was the order of the day," observed the Progressive Era historian William Archibald Dunning—and he meant that approvingly.[10] The federal government, for example, created a national system of banking and currency, and took the first steps toward nationalizing the independent state militias. Dunning conceded that the constitutional objections to such power grabs were "unassailable," but "the territorial unity of the nation was held to outweigh all other considerations."

Having exercised unprecedented power during the war, Northern Republicans were not apt to give it up—notwithstanding their recent championship of states' rights against a national government they believed to be controlled by the "slaveocracy." Besides, many Republicans were former members of Clay's Whig Party, and thus inherited that party's enthusiasm for national projects.

America as a *union*—once so dear to New Englanders and Southerners alike—now gave way to the idea of America as a *nation*. After all, if we are a union of states, then the Constitution must be viewed as a compact among the states. The parties to that compact must retain the sovereign power to define the areas of reserved powers that the central government cannot invade. The unacceptable result would be that the former Confederate States would regain their sovereign powers. In 1865, the *Nation* magazine was founded in New York and quickly established itself as a platform for Northern opinion leaders.

In 1867, the Massachusetts Republican senator Charles Sumner set off on a lecture tour entitled "Are We a Nation?" The answer to that question was meant to be a resounding yes. The upshot of being a nation is that "we must have . . . all those central pervasive powers which minister to the national life." And when Sumner says "we," he doesn't mean "we the people." He means the politicians in Washington must have "all those central and pervasive powers." Nice work.

"I have never reconciled myself," said Sumner, "to the use of the word 'Federal' instead of 'National.' To my mind . . . our Constitution is not Federal, but National." An odd observation indeed from a man who had once fought against the Fugitive Slave Act as an offense to his native Massachusetts. The doctrine of states' rights threatened "incalculable mischief," according to Sumner. Such rights would reduce America to the "barbarous independence" of the Indian tribes or the chronic "chaos" of Mexico.

Sumner's worries about states' rights were, in fact, already being addressed by constitutional amendments. The Thirteenth Amendment had abolished slavery as of 1865; by 1868, the Fourteenth and Fifteenth Amendments had created an array of federally protected rights including due process and universal male suffrage. These amendments arguably divested states of certain powers they would otherwise have had, but this was not unprecedented. The original text of the Constitution had forbidden states from passing ex post facto laws, bills of attainder, or laws interfering with private contracts, and had guaranteed to the people of each state a republican form of government. The post–Civil War amendments expanded the list of federal guarantees, but they did not fundamentally change the design of the federal system: Congress remained bound by its enumerated powers on one side and the Tenth Amendment on the other. The evil of slavery, in short, had been stamped out, constitutionally, by the action of three-fourths of the states, acting as a union.

Lincoln, it was said, had "preserved the Union." But his successors got to work transforming the Union into a nation. The wartime forces of centralization continued right into the Reconstruction era. In 1870, the Supreme Court upheld Congress's power to issue paper money—a Civil War innovation—based on the most expansive reading yet of federal power. Writing for the court's majority, Justice William Strong stated that the powers of Congress need *not* be "specified in the words of the Constitution." Instead, the federal government can exercise any power that was not expressly denied by the Bill of Rights. This was the sort of interpretation that the Ninth Amendment was meant to prevent—the notion that the federal government could get away with anything that was not expressly prohibited. Like Justice Marshall before him, Strong simply ignored the Ninth Amendment.[11]

Not only had Congress assumed the power to create a national currency, it had taxed out of existence the paper currency previously circulated by state banks. A simple 10 percent tax did the trick; overnight, the federal government gained a monopoly on banknotes. The Supreme Court upheld that exercise of power in *Veazie Bank v. Fenno* (1869). During the same period, the court curtailed the taxing power of the states, holding that states could not tax items in interstate commerce, or patent rights, or corporate franchises granted by the United States.

The battle between an American *nation* versus a *union* raged on throughout the late nineteenth century. In 1876, the House of Representatives defeated a resolution declaring that "the people of the United States constitute one nation" and approved a competing resolution affirming that "the Government of the United States is a Federal Union and was formed by the people of the several States in their sovereign capacity." Four years later, the Bostonian Edward Hamilton published the book *A Federal Union, Not a Nation* to combat the idea that the United States was a centralized republic like France. Hamilton found it surprising that any American could believe that "the Federal Government can of right interfere with the management of the local affairs of the people of the States."[12]

Progressive Nationalism

The great project of the Progressive Era was to stamp out all memory of a "union of states" and instill in every American the idea of the United States as a consolidated nation. The Progressives were so successful that now—a century later—we hardly notice the difference. While today's liberals denounce the scourge of "nationalism" in other parts of the globe, they are the heirs to one of the most aggressive nationalist campaigns in history. Take another look at those politically correct history textbooks we saw earlier: *Making a* Nation, a *Nation of* Nations; to which one might add such titles as *The American* Nation, *A People and a* Nation, and *Unfinished* Nation, from the American Textbook Council's list of "widely adopted" history books. Notice something?

In February 1880, the *Atlantic Monthly* extolled "the development of the national idea" and a "strong" national government. The notion that the United States is a compact of sovereign states had been "wholly discarded," according to the magazine.[13] Eight years later, Edward Bellamy proposed an extreme version of nationalism in his utopian novel *Looking Backward*. In this smash bestseller, Bellamy depicts a hypothetical America, circa 2000, in which all power is vested in an "industrial army" that controls all aspects of life. The states have been abolished, because "state governments would have interfered with the control and discipline of the industrial army."[14] This was the Progressive idea of heaven on earth.

By the end of the century, *Looking Backward* had sold more copies than any other American book except *Uncle Tom's Cabin*, and had spawned 165 "Nationalist Clubs," originally founded by former military officers enchanted by the idea of transforming the United States into a permanent industrial army. As a leader in the People's Party (which later merged with the Democratic Party), Bellamy called for the nationalization of telephones, telegraphs, railroads, coal, and all public utilities as "first steps" toward nationalism. Bellamy's agenda was "an historical precursor of totalitarian collectivist ideological currents," according to the historian Arthur Lipow.[15]

It was Bellamy's cousin, Francis Bellamy, who penned the Pledge of Allegiance in 1892.[16] In recent years, the only controversial aspect of the pledge has been the Cold War addition of the words "under God," which sparked a series of (ultimately unsuccessful) lawsuits based on the establishment clause. But to focus on those two words is truly to miss the forest for the trees. The pledge involves daily worship, not of any deity, but of a flag. The American flag, once regarded as "the Union flag" is described as the flag of "one nation, indivisible." As far as the pledge is concerned, the states don't exist at all.

The desire for nationalism reached a fever pitch in the opening years of the twentieth century. The intellectual backbone of the movement was provided by writers like Herbert Croly, the editor of the *New Republic*, who in 1909 published *The Promise of American Life*, an extended argument for reviving Alexander Hamilton's vision of a consolidated republic under the banner of a "new Nationalism." Croly's book, which would go on to shape much of the New Deal agenda, argued that the success of state government was "a popular but ill-founded American political illusion."[17]

The Commerce Power

And yet, the nationalist project kept running up against the plain text of the Constitution. Some creative interpretation was needed, and the raw materials had been supplied by Justice Marshall long ago; namely, the commerce clause and the necessary and proper clause.

In 1890, Congress passed the Sherman Anti-Trust Act, a law aimed at monopolies but broadly worded to prohibit all "contracts in restraint of trade." The Sherman Act looms large in the standard tale of American history. Famously wielded by the trustbuster Teddy Roosevelt, the Sherman Act is credited with reining in corporations, or "business trusts," that had been terrorizing the country. But in reality the Sherman Act added little to existing law. Monopolistic contracts were already unlawful under state common law, and at least twenty-seven states had constitutional or statutory provisions against "trusts" by the time the Sherman Act was passed. By 1899, the number was thirty-eight. Roosevelt was not, in fact, much of a trustbuster; state governors and state judges were.[18]

The groundbreaking aspect of the Sherman Act was its assertion of *federal* power over contracts that did not actually involve interstate commerce—that is, the sale of goods and services across state lines. In the 1895 "Sugar Trust" case, however, the Supreme Court rejected that congressional assertion, holding that the Sherman Act could not be used to regulate purely intrastate activities. The court drew a distinction between manufacturing activities like sugar refining, which occur within the borders of a particular state, and "commerce," which takes place among the states. Congress has authority under the commerce clause to regulate the sale of sugar across state lines, but it cannot regulate the manufacture of sugar.

The Sugar Trust distinction between manufacturing and commerce—between that which is truly local and that which is truly national—was faithful to the Constitution's original meaning. In the founding era, the word "commerce" was understood to mean "trade"—that is, the buying and selling of goods and services. The commerce clause, therefore, gave Congress power over trade only among the states and with foreign nations. In fact, at the Philadelphia convention, the delegates rejected a proposal that would have given Congress the power "to establish public institutions, rewards, and immunities for the promotion of agriculture, commerce, trades, and manufactures."[19] Not only does the wording show that the framers distinguished "commerce" from "manufactures," but the defeat of the proposal also reflects the convention's opposition to giving Congress power over the general economy.

The Sugar Trust case presented a major obstacle to the Progressive campaign to centralize control over all economic activity. In *The Promise of American Life*, Croly argued that a constitutional amendment to give the federal government power over intrastate commerce was "indispensible" to achieve the Progressive agenda.[20] Croly's goal was ultimately achieved, but through judicial activism, not a constitutional amendment. In the meantime, the Progressives developed alternative strategies to evade the Constitution.

Birth of the Administrative State

Congress's effort to expand its power under the commerce clause actually began three years before the Sherman Act, with the passage of the Interstate Commerce Act (ICA) in 1887. The ICA regulated railroads—the economic powerhouse of the day—including the rates they charged. This was an unprecedented assertion of federal power, but Congress at least respected the federal structure by regulating rates only on interstate routes.

But—and speaking of unconstitutional bastards—the ICA gave birth to a new creature: the "independent agency." In drafting the ICA, Congress had not specified acceptable rates for interstate railroads; instead, Congress created a new executive department to do the heavy lifting. The Interstate Commerce Commission was granted broad authority to remove "undue, unreasonable, or unjust discrimination" against interstate commerce. This was a violation, not of federalism, but of separation of powers. Article I of the Constitution vests Congress with "all legislative powers granted herein." Nothing in the Constitution gives Congress power to delegate its legislative power to unelected bureaucrats. But the constitutional objections to the ICC "fell on deaf ears," according to the Progressive journalist Henry Litchfield West. According to West, who was writing from the perspective of 1918, the "danger" posed by the wicked railroads "was so imminent that there was no patience with those who would split hairs over a technical construction of the Constitution."[21]

West's comment perfectly captures Wilsonian progressivism, right down to the contempt for those pettifogging hairsplitters who insist on following the actual text of the Constitution. Progressives justified the consolidation of power by insisting that government had become too complicated for the local yokels to handle. As Croly put it, "The average American individual is morally and intellectually inadequate to a serious and consistent conception of his responsibilities as a democrat."[22] Democracy was all well and good in olden times, but in the age of motorcars and telegraphs, political power had to be transferred from locally elected officials to experts insulated from popular pressure.

"Science" was the buzzword of the new century, and scientific principles had to be applied to the messy business of government. Social science textbooks included such popular titles as *Applied Eugenics*—that is, the science by which government could control human breeding so that only those with the "best" genes would reproduce. After all, if government experts can manage the economy, why not the gene pool? As governor of New Jersey, Wilson had signed a eugenics law for the Garden State.

Independent agencies like the ICC furthered the Progressive ideal of government by experts—scientists!—far removed from the masses. By the early years of the new century, the ICC had interpreted its power over interstate rail traffic as a mandate to regulate all railroad rates, even for routes entirely within a single state. In one famous case, the ICC declared that Texas railroads had to charge higher rates on intrastate routes to avoid "undue" competition against interstate railroads. In other words, the ICC's mandate to prevent *discrimination against* interstate commerce had become a mandate to insulate national carriers from local competitors who were charging unduly *low* rates. This will come as no surprise to students of "agency capture"—the near-universal tendency of federal regulatory agencies to end up protecting the industries they were meant to regulate. It is, of course, possible for state regulators to be captured by industry, but the bracing reality of interstate competition naturally restrains how far state officials can go in coddling local businesses.

A Texas railroad company challenged the ICC's rate-raising order, and the case went all the way to the Supreme Court. In the "Shreveport Rate Case" (*Houston E. & W. T. Ry. Co. v. United States*, 1914), the court upheld the federal government's power to regulate purely intrastate traffic because of its competitive effect on interstate commerce. In fact, the court said that Congress's power over commerce extended to "all matters" having a "close and substantial" relation to interstate commerce. The Shreveport decision seemed to resurrect Chief Justice John Marshall's expansive reading of the commerce clause in the 1824 case of *Gibbons v. Ogden*, under which Congress could regulate purely intrastate commerce that might "affect other States."

John Marshall was all the rage in those days—he was the only major founding-era jurist who could lend a veneer of originalist credibility to the Progressive agenda. The exaltation of Marshall became a critical project of the Progressive movement. The American Bar Association organized a national "John Marshall Day" in 1901 to celebrate the centennial of Marshall's appointment as chief justice. Law schools named after Marshall were founded in Chicago, Cleveland, Atlanta, and Jersey City during this era, not to mention the countless John Marshall High Schools that popped up all over America.

Progressive scholars reinvented Marshall as a secular saint who had protected the nation from "those disintegrating influences . . . masked under the patriotic title of 'States' Rights,'" according to Wharton professor James T. Young's *The New American Government and Its Work.*[23] Likewise, political scientist Edward Corwin's 1913 book, *National Supremacy*, lionizes "the great Marshall" who had "manipulated the engines of constitutional exegesis . . . in light of his own statesmanlike perception of the needs of a growing nation."[24] In plain English: Marshall was "great" because he twisted the Constitution to fit his own idea of what the country needed. Corwin would later publish a worshipful biography of Marshall, including an entire chapter devoted to Marshall's battles against the "Menace of States' Rights."[25]

What Police Power?

The Shreveport decision did not overturn the Sugar Trust case, but it created a huge loophole in the court's previously clear division between intrastate and interstate activity. In Shreveport, the court essentially blessed Congress's growing tendency to interfere with the internal affairs of the states, provided there was some alleged connection with interstate commerce, however tenuous.

In addition to the Sherman Act and the ICA, Congress had, by 1914, stretched its commerce power to regulate lottery tickets, prostitution, and the purity of food and drugs. These laws marked the beginning of a federal criminal code—something the Constitution's framers had never envisaged. In 1903, the Progressives unveiled the first federal prison in Fort Leavenworth, Kansas. Back then, there were only a few hundred federal prisoners; today, there are over two hundred thousand.

Contemporary observers acknowledged that the invocation of the commerce clause to regulate intrastate behavior was a pretense.[26] The real purpose was to extend Congress's control over what is known as state "police powers"—a term that does not refer specifically to cops but encompasses all the sovereign powers retained by the states.[27] In the nineteenth century, scholars understood police power to mean that states had control over internal transportation, labor law, business practices, education, public health, safety, and morals. The federal government was not necessarily *incompetent* in those areas (although it usually was), but the federal government was legally *impotent*: it had no constitutional power to meddle with state police powers.

Think about it this way: the enumerated powers of the federal government are a subset of the powers that would otherwise belong to the states. By ratifying the Constitution, the states delegated those powers to the central government. To be sure, the federal government is supreme within its enumerated powers, but the Ninth and Tenth Amendments make it crystal clear that all other powers are retained by the states. The Progressive nationalists turned this understanding upside down. Corwin, for example, would argue that states' rights are carved out of Congress's otherwise limitless powers.[28]

The Progressives believed that only the federal government could effectively regulate an economy that had grown increasingly interdependent. "State regulation means conflict and confusion," cried Young in *The New American Government*—and this was a textbook (one of the student assignments: "Prepare an essay on 'The Need for and Results of Federal Railway Regulation'"). Federal regulation was needed to achieve coordination; this became a standard argument of Progressives.

Although the Progressives convinced themselves that they lived in a brave new world, economic interdependence had been a fact of American life since the beginning. The Founding Fathers knew all about it—the Constitution was largely motivated by the desire to create a single market, free from internal barriers. To that end, the framers adopted the commerce clause, which empowers Congress to strike down the sort of protectionist barriers that had bedeviled the Union under the Articles of Confederation. But they did not believe that an interdependent economy meant that Congress had to control every aspect of the American economy—which is essentially what the commerce clause has come to mean.

The Progressives could not point to any particular breakdown in America's economic life that had resulted from a lack of federal regulation over economic actors. Rather, they relied on the noticeably unscientific theory of the "race to the bottom." According to this thesis, unless the federal government imposes minimum standards, democratically elected state lawmakers will turn their states into dog-eat-dog social Darwinist hellholes. Makes sense, right?

Mainstream historians have rewritten the past to conform to the Progressive narrative. A classic example is the story of Congress's decision to regulate food and drugs. Here's a version taken from an American history study guide developed by the Monterey Institute for Technology and Education (part of the University of California system):

> In the early 1900s, there was little regulation of the food or drugs that were available to the public. In 1906, Upton Sinclair published a book called *The Jungle* [describing unsanitary conditions in the meatpacking industry] . . . After much pressure from [Teddy] Roosevelt, Congress reluctantly agreed to pass the Meat Inspection Act and the Pure Food and Drug Act of 1906.[29]

In reality, by the time Congress passed the Pure Food and Drug Act, virtually every state in the Union had adopted laws prohibiting adulterated food and drugs. Portions of the 1906 federal law were lifted directly from uniform statutory language that had already been enacted by dozens of states.[30] Even the bit about Congress being "reluctant" is flatly inaccurate, given that the Pure Food and Drug Act passed the House by a vote of 247–17, and the Senate by a vote of 63–4.[31] But facts can't be allowed to interfere with a good story—in this case, the tale of a Progressive president hectoring a "reluctant" Congress to step in where the states had failed to act.

The race-to-the-bottom argument was a myth from the get-go. Virtually every important progressive reform began at the state level, as we've already seen with the Pure Food and

Drug Act and the Sherman Act. Nor were the states shy about regulating railroads. In the years before the ICA, states had enacted numerous taxes and regulations on railroads, but were often rebuffed by federal courts.

By the time the Supreme Court upheld the federal lottery statute in 1902, every state had its own law condemning the operation of lotteries and the sale of lottery tickets. In 1910, when Congress enacted the Mann Act, targeting the "white slave" trade, at least two-thirds of the states had already adopted similar laws against trafficking in prostitutes, as well as laws against procuring or soliciting prostitutes.[32]

The convergence of state laws was not a lucky coincidence. Rather, it arose from various efforts among the states to achieve harmony, most notably the uniform law movement, which culminated in the launch of the Uniform Law Commission in 1892. The commission was, and still is, an entirely voluntary effort among the states to identify policy areas where uniformity is desirable. The movement's crowning achievement is the Uniform Commercial Code, which standardizes the law of business contracts across all states without any federal assistance. Over the years, the commission has proposed over three hundred uniform laws, many of which have been adopted by all fifty states or by a sizable chunk of them.[33]

Federal legislation may not have been needed to avert a race to the bottom, but it did allow the national government to take credit for the steady improvements happening in the states. As Henry Litchfield West enthusiastically observed, the Pure Food and Drug Act meant that "nearly every manufactured article of food which now enters the household bears the magic legend 'Guaranteed under the US Pure Food Law,' while the advertisements in newspapers and streetcars assure the would-be purchaser that pickles and shrimps and catsup and herring bear the seal of Federal approval."[34]

Aside from the odd food choices—I wouldn't want to have dinner *chez* West—there can be no doubt that the "magic legend" played some role in conditioning people to think of the federal government as their protector. It may be superficially comforting, but, of course, if Big Brother has the power to watch out for you, then he also has the power to watch you.

The Supreme Court's Nationalism

The Supreme Court itself had become partially caught up in the nationalist fervor of the age. Decisions like the Shreveport case invited Congress to expand its turf, but the turf was already littered with state laws. The court then hit on several strategies to mow down state laws.

First, there was "substantive due process," a doctrine that allows federal courts to strike down state laws for violating the Fourteenth Amendment, which prohibits states from depriving any person of life, liberty, or property "without due process of law." It is a powerful doctrine, but blatantly unfaithful to the text of the due process clause, which was originally understood to be a guarantee of traditional common law procedures protecting criminal defendants.[35] The framers' understanding, as best we can reconstruct it, was that appellate courts would use the due process clause to evaluate the fairness of criminal proceedings—not to evaluate the substantive merits of legislation. But by the end of the nineteenth century, the clause became a roving license for courts to strike down state laws they found to be unwise. In 1897, for example, a unanimous

Supreme Court struck down a Louisiana insurance regulation on the basis that it invaded the "liberty of contract" of those trying to break into the Louisiana insurance market.

The court's willingness to strike down state business regulations on due process grounds is most famously associated with the 1905 decision in *Lochner v. New York*. In that case, the court overturned a New York law setting maximum working hours for all bakery employees. Once again, the court construed the Fourteenth Amendment as protecting the individual's "power to contract in relation to his own labor." For the next three decades, the US Supreme Court struck down "over two hundred state statutes regulating 'local' economic activity . . . mainly in the areas of labor legislation, regulation of prices, and restrictions on entry into businesses," according to law professor Stephen Gardbaum.[36] Mainstream scholars routinely criticize the *"Lochner* era" of the Supreme Court, typically portraying the justices as activists bent on imposing laissez-faire economics on poor Americans. Well, maybe, but the relevant point for our purposes is that the *Lochner* era was characterized by the use of federal judicial power to squelch progressive state laws. If today's liberals want to avoid a return to the *Lochner* era, there's an easy solution: give states the freedom to design their own reforms without the threat of federal veto.

The Federal Rule of Corporate Personhood

Secondly, there was the expansion of "corporate personhood." These days, the notion that corporations possess constitutional rights infuriates liberals. Much of the furor is misdirected at the Supreme Court's campaign finance decision in *Citizens*

United v. Federal Election Commission, which actually held that *individuals* don't forfeit their constitutional rights when acting through a corporation. In any event, corporate personhood has been a prime target of the Occupy Wall Street movement, and even the subject of a constitutional amendment proposed by Vermont's (self-described) socialist senator, Bernie Sanders, who thinks that Congress must intervene to put corporations in their place.

What Comrade Sanders never mentions is that corporate personhood was an invention of the very federal government that he would like to expand. In *Santa Clara County v. Southern Pacific Railroad Co.* (1886), the US Supreme Court announced the rule that corporations are "persons" for purposes of the equal protection clause of the Fourteenth Amendment. That clause forbids the states from "deny[ing] to any person within its jurisdiction the equal protection of the laws." The result of the *Santa Clara* rule of corporate personhood was a flood of cases in which railroads and other businesses successfully challenged state railroad regulations and taxes that applied "unequally" to corporations and human beings. Once again, we see the use of *federal* judicial power to defeat *state* reforms.

A third strategy used against the states involved a doctrine called "field preemption." In 1912, the Supreme Court struck down a North Carolina statute concerning railroad freight traffic even though the law did not conflict directly with the ICA (*Southern Ry. v. Reid*). The court held that Congress had "taken possession of the field" of railroad rate regulation when it passed the ICA. This was a remarkable discovery, since the ICA had been around for twenty-five years and nobody had previously suggested that the federal law ousted *all* state power to deal with railroad rates. Certainly Congress had said no such thing in 1887. But field preemption quickly became an irresistible tool for federal judges. It allows them to exercise veto power over virtually any state law that intersects with a federal law, even if the state law is designed to reinforce federal law. In the decade after *Reid*, the Supreme Court "overturned many state regulations explicitly on the ground of the newly recognized power" of field preemption, according to Gardbaum.[37]

Finally, federal courts also overturned state laws as violations of the so-called dormant commerce clause—a clause that exists only in the imagination of judges and law professors. The general idea is that the Constitution implicitly forbids states from passing internal regulations that might affect interstate commerce, even when there is no conflicting federal law.

Many experts wish the Constitution contained a dormant commerce clause, but wishing doesn't make it so. The Constitution does have a supremacy clause, which empowers a judge to strike down a state law if it directly conflicts with a valid federal regulation of interstate commerce. But it is something else altogether to say that because Congress *could* exercise its commerce power to trump a particular state law, the federal judiciary should step in and save Congress the trouble.

Before the Progressive Era, the Supreme Court largely refused to apply the dormant commerce clause. In the leading case of *Cooley v. Board of Wardens* (1851), the court upheld a Pennsylvania law requiring all ships in the port of Philadelphia— including ships involved in interstate commerce—to use local pilots. In the absence of a federal law to the contrary, Pennsylvania had the right to regulate pilotage in its own waters. The *Cooley* decision, however, gave credence to the dormant commerce clause theory by stating that Congress has an exclusive right to legislate on subjects that are "inherently national." Beginning in the 1880s, the Progressive court picked up on this dictum, but with an expanded view of what was "inherently national."

I'll Drink to That. Or Not.

Nothing stimulated the expansion of the commerce clause—both the real one and the dormant version—quite like alcohol. The temperance movement led to various state prohibition statutes, like Iowa's 1886 law forbidding the importation of "intoxicating liquors" into the state. In *Bowman v. Chicago and Northwestern Railway Co.* (1888), the Supreme Court held that such a ban violates the dormant commerce clause, since Congress might someday enact its own laws about interstate commerce in booze. Iowa then passed another law prohibiting the sale of all liquor, whether domestically produced or imported. Again the court struck down this law, now holding that states could not regulate liquor imported from another state so long as the liquor remains in its "original package" (*Leisy v. Hardin*, 1890).

There was a certain absurdity about the "original package doctrine," which rested on the idea that goods shipped across state lines retain some metaphysical "interstate" quality until they are removed from their packaging. But the *Leisy* decision went even further, holding that federal courts should strike down any state law that "inhibits, directly or indirectly, the receipt of an imported commodity" from any other state. That doctrine completely undercut Iowa's expressed preference for prohibition, since the state was powerless to stop people from buying kegs of beer off railway cars. Not that alcohol prohibition is a wise policy—I for one wouldn't vote for it—but it is surely part of state's police power to decide whether to allow, or prohibit, liquor.

In response to the outcry over *Leisy*, Congress passed the Wilson Act of 1890, giving federal blessing to state laws regulating imported liquor, even in the original packaging. In 1912, Congress adopted an express federal prohibition against shipping alcohol into any state in violation of that state's own police laws. So far, so good: Congress was using its commerce clause power to preserve state police powers over liquor. But then Congress overplayed its hand. In 1917, it passed the Reed Amendment, which banned the shipment of alcohol into any state that prohibits the manufacture or sale of liquor—even if that state would otherwise accept imported liquor.

The perversity of the Reed Amendment became clear in *United States v. Hill* (1919). In that case, the Supreme Court upheld the federal conviction of Dan Hill, who had carried a bottle of beer with him from Kentucky to West Virginia. It is true that West Virginia did not allow the manufacture of alcohol, but it did allow people to bring up to a quart of booze into the state, which is what Hill had done.

In a short space of time, Congress and the Supreme Court had gone from protecting state autonomy to forcing states into a more extreme version of prohibition than they would choose for themselves. In 1938, law professor Frank Strong would refer to *Hill* as the "Magna Charta" of Congress's drive for greater commerce clause powers.[38]

The Hammer Falls

Progressives like Henry Litchfield West argued that the need for federal intervention applied "with especial force in the matter of child labor" and that the primary opposition to federal legislation in this area arose from the South, where "states' rights is finding its last citadel."[39] Actually, reformers had been working since the nineteenth century to limit child labor— and they had been doing so at the state level. The first law limiting child labor was enacted in Massachusetts in 1842; other states soon followed suit.[40] Congress did not take action on child labor in the nineteenth century, not because of indifference, but because labor law was an area entrusted to the states. Constitutional scruples, however, were cast aside in 1916 when Congress passed the first federal regulation of child labor, the Keating-Owen Child Labor Act. To achieve its end, Congress relied on the trusty commerce power: the Keating-Owen Act prohibited manufacturers from shipping their products across state lines unless they conformed to federal child labor laws. Technically, the law did not force companies to adopt federal standards, but no rational manufacturer would voluntarily opt out of interstate commerce.

Unlike laws concerning interstate commerce in booze, lottery tickets, or adulterated food, the Keating-Owen Act did not pretend that goods made with child labor were intrinsically harmful; rather, Congress just did not like the way they were made. This was too much, even for a nationalistic Supreme Court. The court struck down the Keating-Owen Act in the 1918 case of *Hammer v. Dagenhart*. In the conventional telling, *Hammer* was a disastrous decision, consigning untold millions of children to toil away in Dickensian workhouses. According to a middle school study guide published by the Yale–New Haven Teachers Institute, *Hammer* was followed by twenty years of "hard work, pain, suffering and even death."[41] In reality, on the day *Hammer* was decided, every state in the Union had child labor legislation on its books, and virtually all of those laws had been enacted before the Keating-Owen Act.

It's true that the state laws varied, but that variation stemmed from the differences among local labor markets. Child labor was a complex local issue. Congress itself did not attempt to ban child labor but only to regulate it: the Keating-Owen Act allowed children as young as fourteen to work eight hours a day, six days a week. The goal of federal regulation was not to abolish child labor; rather, it was an effort by politicians in high-wage states to minimize the competitive advantage enjoyed by lower-wage states.[42] A national standard would allow state politicians to appear "tough" on child labor without having to worry about competition from sister states. A federal law also allowed Congress to take credit for the ongoing decline in child labor that was really due to state legislation.

The Flexible Taxing Power

Within six months of the *Hammer* decision, Congress tried another subterfuge. The 1919 Child Labor Tax Law slapped a 10 percent tax on the sale of goods made in factories that did not meet federal standards for child labor. Theoretically, this law was based on Congress's power to levy taxes "for the General Welfare"—one of the clauses that the Anti-Federalists had warned about. Once again, the Supreme Court struck down the law as a back-door attempt to regulate state labor practices (*Bailey v. Drexel Furniture Co.*, 1922).

Progressives exploited the *Hammer* and *Drexel* decisions to rally support for national child labor legislation and, more broadly, for federal intervention in the economy.[43] In 1922,

Charles Pierson, a lawyer and constitutional scholar, observed unhappily that "it is popular nowadays to apply the term 'forward looking' to people who would make the National Government an agency for social welfare work," whereas those who supported states' rights were "lacking in vision."[44]

Although the Supreme Court came under attack from the Progressives for thwarting federal child labor reform, the justices were hardly consistent in their support for states' rights—remember the *Lochner* cases in which the court overturned state regulations on the basis of made-up federal rights. In 1919, the court upheld a federal tax on "narcotics," even though the tax was nominal and served merely as a pretext to impose a national prohibition on certain drugs. According to the court, Congress could use its taxing power to criminalize supplying individuals with prohibited drugs—even if the recipient had a valid prescription under state law. Some years earlier, the court upheld a federal tax on colored margarine, a blatant piece of special-interest legislation on behalf of the butter industry (*McCray v. United States*, 1904).

In all these cases, the tax at issue was a sham. Heaven knows, the central government didn't need the extra revenue after 1913, when Congress imposed the first national corporate franchise tax and the Sixteenth Amendment cleared the way for a national income tax. The federal government, which had previously relied on tariff revenues, had a vast stream of new revenues at its disposal.

What progressive causes did all that money support? War, for starters. In 1917, Woodrow Wilson led the country into its first European war, an undertaking that did not come cheaply. Moreover, the Wilson administration used the war as an excuse to remove the last vestiges of independence that the state militias enjoyed. With federal funding as an inducement, the states had gradually been coerced into sacrificing control over their own militias, now known as the *National* Guard (there's that word again). By 1916, guardsmen were required to take a dual oath, one state and one federal. This allowed the federal government to call up state troops directly without going through the governors. Gone were the days when the states could protest Washington's war fever by refusing troop requisitions, as the New England states had done in 1812. Over 20 percent of the expeditionary force that Wilson sent to Europe was made up of state guardsmen, who had theoretically signed up for only defensive wars.

The Even More Flexible Spending Power

The use of federal funds to bribe states into accepting federal policies did not stop with the National Guard. The first national program for funding highway construction began in 1916. It had little demonstrable effect on roads, since the federal dollars accounted for only 2 percent of overall road construction.[45] But it taught Congress that state autonomy could be purchased relatively cheaply. More conditional funding programs followed.

The 1921 Maternity Act, which promised federal funding to states that agreed to participate in a national maternal health program, provoked a court challenge from Massachusetts, of all places. The Bay State, which would later produce so many fervent nationalizers, argued that the Maternity Act coerced the states into compliance. The Supreme Court disagreed, breezily asserting in *Massachusetts v. Mellon* that Massachusetts was "free to accept or reject" the money. But of course the state was not really "free" to turn down federal grants: their residents had already been taxed for the program, leaving state politicians a choice between taking the money or subsidizing the other states. The idea that conditional funding programs are voluntary is the legal fiction that ultimately cleared the way for Congress to dictate state and local policies through the power of the purse.

The addictive quality of federal funding helps explain why *Massachusetts v. Mellon* is one of the relatively few examples of a state government challenging such a program. In fact, federal grant programs tend to be popular with state politicians who can take credit for grand projects without having to foot the entire bill. But such programs still violate states' rights. Recall Madison's words that the federal union is a compact among the *people* of the states, not the *governments* of the states.

Federalism was not designed for the benefit of state politicians. For over a century, states' rights had protected individual liberty by preventing excessive centralization of power. But the Progressives were strikingly successful in dismantling the key structural limits on federal power. Through a combination of war, constitutional amendment, judicial activism, and an expanded commerce clause, America's political classes had, by the 1920s, achieved a radically more centralized union. And they were just warming up.

5

FDR Creates Satellite States

On March 2, 1930, a state governor took to the radio to warn citizens that politicians in Washington were intent on destroying the "individual sovereignty of our States." The national government's desire to seize "practically all authority and control," predicted the governor, would cause the United States "to drift insensibly toward . . . autocracy."

The most outrageous thing, according to this governor, was Congress's usurping of the traditional police powers of the state. Under the Constitution, Congress had no right to legislate on "the conduct of public utilities, of banks, of insurance, of business, of agriculture, of education, of social welfare and of a dozen other important features. In these, Washington must not be encouraged to interfere."

Who was this archconservative, constitutional fundamentalist? Actually, it was Franklin Delano Roosevelt—then the chief executive of New York State—and his target was the supposedly nationalistic tendencies of Republicans in Congress and in the Herbert Hoover administration. In the same radio address, FDR argued that Congress had clearly exceeded its enumerated powers by building a federal government that cost taxpayers $3.5 billion annually. Unless Americans acted to "halt this steady process of building commissions and regulatory bodies and special legislation . . . we shall soon be spending many billions more."[1]

Uncanny: How did FDR know? Oh, wait, it's because *he* was the one who ended up spending "many billions more." Two and half years after his states' rights speech, FDR would win the presidency by promising to use the power of the federal government to lift Americans out of the Great Depression. In the first fiscal year of his administration, FDR—the guy who had complained about a $3.5 billion federal government—would spend $2 billion on antipoverty programs alone. In his administration's first seven years, federal government outlays exceeded Hoover-era spending by over $21 billion—and that was before America's entry into World War II. *President* Roosevelt and his allies would deploy that money in an effort to wipe out the very state sovereignty that had been so precious to *Governor* Roosevelt.

Even judged by the low standards of politics, Roosevelt's about-face on states' rights reveals a staggering degree of hypocrisy. As president, FDR would work to tear down every constitutional limitation on the power of the national government—he would mock those who adhered to the constitution as reactionaries, stuck in the "horse and buggy" era. The "individual sovereignty of our States" would become, under Roosevelt, a dead letter.

A Highly Successful Flop

Most historians insist that FDR had no choice but to expand the federal government because the Depression required national action. The same American history study guide that we saw in the previous chapter declares that in the 1930s "it became apparent that no entity except the federal government had the resources to address the profound suffering of the Great Depression." Note the passive voice: it wasn't that anyone made a conscious decision to jettison the Tenth Amendment, it just "became apparent" that it didn't apply anymore. In reality, the federal government's role was hotly debated. Even the progressive jurist Louis Brandeis reportedly told FDR's aides in 1935 "I want you to go back and tell the president that we're not going to let this government centralize everything."[2] In addition to the tendency to gloss over the disagreements among FDR's contemporaries, the standard history is wrong on many fronts.

First, the Great Depression was primarily *caused* by the federal government. What made the Depression "great" was a one-third contraction in the nation's money supply between 1929 and 1933, a phenomenon driven largely by wrongheaded policies of the Federal Reserve: the central banker created by the Progressives in that fateful year of 1913. The initial federal response to the crisis—which included massive tax hikes and protectionist tariffs—compounded the economic contraction.

Second, New Deal policies did not bring about an economic recovery. Although mainstream accounts, like Ken Burns's worshipful 2014 documentary *The Roosevelts*, credit FDR with "expertly managing" the Depression, FDR's policies in fact prolonged the crisis for a decade—longer than any economic crisis before or since.[3] Under the New Deal, economic growth languished—briefly reaching pre-Depression levels in 1936, only to slump again in 1938. Real recovery would not come until World War II. Unemployment averaged 18.6 percent from 1933 to 1940, and it never went below 14 percent.[4]

In previous depressions (or "panics," as they used to be called), economic recovery came swiftly without federal intervention. In 1921, for example, economic output fell by 9 percent and unemployment soared to 11.7 percent. Rather than shredding the Constitution, the Harding administration allowed the market to work. Within a year, unemployment was plummeting; within two years, it was down to 2.4 percent.

The Panic of 1893, likewise, was on a par with the Great Depression. A quarter of the nation's railroads went bankrupt, and unemployment among industrial workers exceeded 20 percent in some cities. Nobody in Congress considered it "apparent" that the federal government should attempt to tackle unemployment.[5] Within five years, the economy was back to its earlier prosperity. By comparison, in 1938—after five years of New Deal programs—unemployment was *still* near 20 percent.

And while market forces did their thing, government stood idly by, allowing widows and orphans to starve, right? Actually, in America, relief for the poor had always been a joint effort of charitable organizations and government—local government. "Counties, cities, and townships administered relief to their residents—usually through their township supervisors or superintendents of the poor—using local tax revenue," according to the historian Susan Stein-Roggenbuck.[6]

Economically, the New Deal was a flop. Politically, it was a roaring success. It ushered in a massive expansion of government, aggrandizing politicians not only at the federal level but at the state level as well. That's right: state governments grew during the New Deal. It isn't that the New Deal led to smaller state governments; rather, the New Deal led to larger, but more subservient, state governments. Size is a matter of dollars, not autonomy. The two don't always go together. Like the satellite states of the Soviet era, the American states of the 1930s were getting bigger, but they were losing their autonomy.

FDR *and* Il Duce

The intellectual framework for the New Deal—particularly the contempt for constitutional limitations—had already been erected by the Progressives. The New Dealers shared the Progressives' faith in government by experts, even though FDR had once scoffed at Hoover's reliance on "master minds" (as he derisively referred to them), arguing that truly objective government experts do not exist. But lo, just two years later, with FDR in the White House, we find the president surrounded by his own collection of masterminds, the "Brain Trust" drawn largely from academia.

FDR's experts were not content to rely exclusively on American progressivism, which, after thirty-odd years, was beginning to look a little frumpy and Midwestern. Instead, as the historian Ira Katznelson observes, "the core policymakers in this initial phase of the New Deal . . . were drawn to Mussolini's Italy."[7] In 1933, Roosevelt expressed his admiration for Benito Mussolini in a letter to an American envoy and confided that "I am keeping in fairly close touch with the admirable Italian gentleman."[8] Yes, bringing fascism to America was the explicit goal of many of the early New Dealers. In those years before Pearl Harbor, "fascism"—in short, an authoritarian system of centralized national control over business and labor—was not yet a bad word. To the contrary, it had positive connotations for most Progressives, promising an efficient integration of government and private sector.

On March 4, 1933, almost three years to the day after his paean to states' rights, FDR's first inaugural address foreshadowed the authoritarian impulses behind the New Deal. Roosevelt described the president's job as leading "this great army of our people"—shades of Edward Bellamy's "industrial army"—"dedicated to a disciplined attack upon our common problems."[9] The president kindly paid his respects to the Constitution, but then breezily observed that the economic crisis "may call for a temporary departure" from constitutional procedures. In particular, if Congress failed to do his bidding, FDR declared that he would seek "broad Executive power to wage a war against the Emergency."

This was war, all right, but the enemy was not "our common problems." The enemy was the entrepreneur and the consumer. In June 1933, FDR signed into law the National Industrial Recovery Act (NIRA), under which the president could unilaterally impose "codes of fair competition" on virtually every American industry. The codes would force businesses to conform to top-down mandates on wages, hours, and countless other details of business conduct. When he was briefed on NIRA, Mussolini reportedly exclaimed *"Ecco un ditatore!"*—"Behold a dictator!"[10] Within two years, that admirable American gentleman FDR had ordered 557 basic codes and 189 supplementary codes designed by the National Recovery Administration and backed by over ten thousand pages of administrative orders.[11]

And that was just the tip of the iceberg. During his tenure in office, Roosevelt issued 3,723 executive orders, more than all subsequent presidents from Truman to Obama combined. Not only did he impose business "codes" by executive fiat, but he used executive orders to seize private businesses from their owners during strikes. In 1933, FDR ordered Americans to surrender any personally owned gold to the federal government. During World War II, he would order 112,000 Japanese Americans to be put into "relocation centers," which, as Supreme Court Justice Owen Roberts explained, is "a euphemism for concentration camps."[12]

NIRA was just one part of a package of "reforms" pushed through during FDR's first hundred days. This package also included the Agricultural Adjustment Act, which was, essentially, a mini-NIRA for the agricultural sector. Under the AAA, the federal government restricted farm output in order to keep agricultural prices high. As the Cato Institute's Chris Edwards points out, "While millions of Americans were out of work and going hungry, the federal government plowed under 10 million acres of crops, slaughtered 6 million pigs, and left fruit to rot."[13] Yes, only the federal government could take on such a big job.

Another early New Deal program was the Federal Emergency Relief Administration (FERA)—actually, an expanded version of a Hoover experiment—which made grants to state governments. In theory, the states were free to spend the money as they saw fit. In reality, FERA's enabling legislation gave the agency's administrator discretion to withhold up to half of the grant money unless states conformed their relief efforts to federal dictates. When a state refused to cooperate, FERA could simply take over that state's relief programs. On at least seven occasions, FERA's administrator, Harry Hopkins, did in fact "federalize" state relief efforts and—according to Professor James Patterson—would have federalized many other state programs had he not been anxious to avoid the "appearance of federal dictation."[14]

Intellectuals cheered the consolidation of power in Washington as the first step to a fascist makeover of the United

States. One of the chief architects of NIRA, Hugh Johnson (also *Time* magazine's man of the year for 1933), kept a portrait of Mussolini hanging in his office and distributed fascist literature to his colleagues in the cabinet.[15] In 1934, Lorena Hickok, a former journalist who toured the country for FERA, wrote wistfully to Hopkins that "if I were twenty years younger . . . I think I'd start out to be the Joan of Arc of the Fascist movement in the United States."[16] As late as 1936, FDR's Committee on Administrative Management sent two academics to Italy to study Mussolini's "modern" administrative methods. This was a year after Italy's bloody conquest of Ethiopia.

And the states? They were obsolete, according to opinion leaders like the *New York Times Magazine*, which, in early 1935, reported on a "growing sentiment . . . among certain members of Congress with advanced social views" to abolish the states altogether. As evidence, the *Times* pointed to a proposed plan—but without naming any of its proponents—to replace the forty-eight states with nine administrative "departments." Each department would have its own elected governor, but he or she would be answerable to the president because each department would simply be a subdivision of the national government. "There would still be that system of [constitutional] checks," explained the *Times*, "the whole federal process remaining the same, except that State governments as such would cease to exist."[17]

FDR vs. the Constitution

With its first hundred days behind it, the Roosevelt administration got down to the hard work of arresting and prosecuting citizens who dared to work long hours or produce abundant crops. There was just one problem: the Constitution. The federal government had no enumerated power to regulate business practices, or agricultural production, or labor practices; therefore, it clearly had no business imposing fines or jail time on people who failed to follow the new mandates.

In 1935, the US Supreme Court killed NIRA in the case of *ALA Schechter Poultry Corp. v. United States.* In *Schechter,* lawyers from the National Recovery Administration sought to put some Brooklyn-based chicken butchers in jail for violating the "Live Poultry Code." The butchers were convicted, but the Supreme Court overturned the convictions, holding that the code, and therefore NIRA itself, exceeded Congress's power under the commerce clause. As in the Sugar Trust case, the court reaffirmed the original understanding of "commerce" as referring to trade across state lines, and not as an all-purpose synonym for economic activity. Chief Justice Charles Evans Hughes observed that the code did not actually regulate the interstate sale of chickens, but instead regulated the business practices of butchers who might handle chickens that had crossed state lines. The court was willing to allow regulation of intrastate activities that had a "direct effect" on interstate commerce, but here the connection to interstate commerce was too tenuous.

Hughes conceded that there might be cases where the line between "direct" and "indirect" effects might be ambiguous—courts exist to deal with gray areas—but that was no reason to abandon the distinction. Without some line between interstate and intrastate affairs, "there would be virtually no limit to the federal power and for all practical purposes we should have a completely centralized government."

FDR immediately convened a White House press conference in which he compared the *Schechter* decision to the proslavery ruling in *Dred Scott*. It was in this presser that Roosevelt lambasted the court for its "horse and buggy" understanding of interstate commerce. He stoutly announced that the administration would find some way to invest the federal government with "the powers which exist in the national governments of every nation of the world." Like Italy!

The following year, 1936, the Supreme Court struck down a separate New Deal law that had established yet another industry code: the Bituminous Coal Code ("bituminous" being a fancy word for black coal). The country was divided into twenty-three "coal districts," each with its own unelected board responsible for implementing the code. The boards were empowered to determine the maximum hours and wages in coal mines, and to set prices for the local coal industry. Labor disputes would be resolved by a panel of arbitrators appointed by the president. Coal producers that failed to subscribe to the supposedly voluntary code would have to pay a punitive 15 percent tax on their gross sales.

The court held that Congress had no constitutional authority to turn the coal industry into a government utility (*Carter v. Carter Coal Co.*). Such a power, if it exists, was reserved to the states and never delegated to the national government. Writing for a near-unanimous court (only Justice Benjamin Cardozo dissented, in part), Justice George Sutherland demolished the argument that the state governments had authorized the federal power grab by their failure to object. The right to "complete and unimpaired state self-government" belongs to the people, not state officials. In other words, state politicians cannot "abdicate" their powers, even if doing so would provide welcome relief from their responsibilities.

In a somewhat curious detour, Sutherland stressed that "the Constitution itself is, in every real sense, a law." The fact that he felt compelled to point this out reveals less about Sutherland than it does about the New Dealers who treated the Constitution as an archaic cultural tradition—sort of like quilting—that can be put aside when there is important work to be done.

This was a tough year for the New Dealers. A few months earlier, the court had also struck down the AAA in *United States v. Butler*. The court's decision was based on the fairly obvious— one would think—fact that Congress's power to regulate commerce does not include the power to coerce farmers to produce less food. One of FDR's top advisers, Edward Corwin, a professor and once a leading Progressive scholar, proposed that the president silence his critics on the bench by adding six new justices who would guarantee pro-administration decisions.[18]

In February 1937, Roosevelt unveiled his infamous court-packing scheme, provoking a national debate. The scheme was never enacted but the threat worked. Later in 1937, the court blessed the National Labor Relations Act (NLRA) as a proper exercise of Congress's commerce power, even though the act regulated purely intrastate labor practices (*NLRB v. Jones and Laughlin Steel Corp.*). Not only did NLRA invade states' rights, but it did so unnecessarily. The centerpiece of the act—the promotion of collective bargaining—had already been embraced by thirty-two states before Congress got involved. As we saw in the last chapter, states consistently beat the federal government to the punch when it came to progressive legislation.

But in *Jones and Laughlin*, Justice Roberts, who had previously opposed the New Deal's expansion of federal power, now abandoned the Sugar Trust distinction between commerce and manufacturing. Instead, he joined a new majority that resurrected the Shreveport Rate decision that Congress's power over commerce extended to "all matters" having a "close and substantial" relation to interstate commerce.

In theory, the "close and substantial" test means that certain activities must, logically, have such a "distant and insubstantial" relation to interstate commerce that Congress could not legitimately assert power over them. But for the remainder of the New Deal, and for decades thereafter, the court would uphold every congressional assertion of commerce power no matter how tenuous the connection to interstate commerce. In two cases from the 1940s, the court upheld Congress's power to regulate purely intrastate activities of building maintenance workers and elevator operators. Why? Because they worked in buildings where some of the tenants produced goods destined for interstate commerce.

In 1942, the court upheld Congress's power to dictate how much food a private citizen could grow on his own land for his own consumption. The case of *Wickard v. Filburn* involved an Ohio farmer (Roscoe Filburn) who cultivated eleven acres of wheat more than was allowed under the (now revised) AAA. Mr. Filburn did not sell the excess wheat; rather, he used it on his own farm, to feed livestock and make flour for his family. As punishment for growing too much food, the Department of Agriculture fined Filburn forty-nine cents a bushel. Instead of paying the fine, however, Filburn filed suit in federal court, arguing that his constitutional rights were being infringed.

After Filburn won a partial victory in the district court, which reduced the amount of his fine, the secretary of agriculture, Claude Wickard, appealed to the Supreme Court, seeking to vindicate the federal government's power to control agricultural production—even when the produce never crosses state lines. The court obliged. Applying "the principles first enunciated by Chief Justice Marshall in *Gibbons v. Ogden*," the court held that the commerce power "is not confined in its exercise to the regulation of commerce among the States"— even though that's precisely what the text says ("to regulate Commerce . . . among the several States"). The invocation of John Marshall, as we saw in the previous chapter, was a reliable indicator that the court was playing fast and loose with the Constitution's language.

New Deal lawyers were a new breed who portrayed their constitutional infidelity as a positive virtue. They weren't disregarding the text; they were expounding the "Living Constitution"—a theory that had been promoted by Progressive politicians and academics since the 1920s.[19] According to this doctrine—which still holds sway in most law schools—you don't need the consent of three-fourths of the states to amend the Constitution, as the text says. Instead, judges and politicians can creatively reinterpret the text to remove any constitutional barriers to their preferred policies.

As a practical matter, the Living Constitution is a disaster for states' rights. The Constitution and the Bill of Rights are devoted largely to defining the limits of the central government's power. Because the Living Constitution liberates judges to disregard those parchment barriers, it naturally leads to federal judges' aggrandizing the federal government at the expense of the states.

Wickard was a breathtaking example of this federal power grab. One can read the Constitution backward and forward but one will never find a provision empowering Congress to regulate agricultural production at all, much less to dictate the amount of wheat a farmer can grow for his own consumption. For a state to pass such a law would be foolish and counter-productive, but it would be constitutional. For Congress to do so—and for the Supreme Court to bless it—is essentially a declaration that the Constitution is dead. Long live the Living Constitution!

To justify the result in *Wickard*, the court applied its "living" interpretation not only to the commerce clause but also to the necessary and proper clause of Article I, Section 8. As previously noted, the latter provision empowers Congress to "make all laws which shall be necessary and proper for carrying into Execution the [enumerated] Powers." The assumption in cases like *Wickard*—and now the conventional wisdom—is that the necessary and proper clause "is an enlargement . . . of the powers expressly granted to Congress," to quote a website devoted to legal education.[20] The truth is the reverse—the necessary and proper clause was inserted to emphasize Congress's duty to adhere strictly to its enumerated powers.[21] But from the earliest days, the Anti-Federalists had predicted that the clause would be exploited to usurp power from the states. That is what Congress and the court were now doing.

The Second New Deal

Before he had completely subdued the Supreme Court, FDR did make superficial concessions to states' rights by retreating from the extreme centralization of his first hundred days. In 1935, Roosevelt launched what came to be known as the "Second New Deal," a policy shift that would ostensibly involve paying more respect to the states.

Declaring that the central government "must and will quit this business of relief," FDR proposed a scheme of unemployment insurance that would be administered by the states, although funded by federal tax credits. He also unveiled a new system of matching grants to states that provided federally recognized "categorical assistance"—that is, welfare relief for certain categories of needy persons, such as widows or the blind. "Returning relief to the states" was the administration's theme for 1935—much to the chagrin of a professional social work establishment that was just getting used to the convenience of one huge money spigot in DC.[22]

Roosevelt had not rediscovered the virtues of states' rights. Even in the midst of the "Second New Deal," he centralized policies when he could get away with it. Old-age pensions, for example, emerged in 1935 as an entirely national program with no state participation. In 1938, FDR would secure passage of the Emergency Relief Appropriations Act, which gave the president unilateral power to disburse $4.8 billion of federal money. Among other things, FDR used the money to create the Works Progress Administration (WPA), of which he put Harry Hopkins in charge.

But FDR did begin to harness state governments in 1935, partly because of the need to give local bosses patronage, but also because of the "lack of bureaucratic and administrative capacity at the federal level," as the historian Gary Gerstle has observed.[23] In other words, the *state* governments had the knowledge and the manpower needed to implement FDR's grandiose schemes. But the central government did have the uncommonly useful power to print money and then spread it around.

Consider, for example, how the New Deal Congress

co-opted the states with respect to unemployment insurance. Part of the Social Security Act imposed a federal tax—rising to 3 percent—on the gross payroll of every company with eight or more employees. Companies based in states that had adopted federally approved unemployment insurance laws would get a 90 percent rebate on the tax. Any state politician who failed to secure that 90 percent rebate was asking for trouble. Not surprisingly, the states fell in line.

Was the tax-and-rebate scheme constitutional? The issue came before the Supreme Court when an Alabama corporation challenged the law as (among other things) an invasion of state sovereignty. From 1789 to 1935, relief of the unemployed was one of those topics squarely within the police powers of the state—that is, it was one of those powers reserved to states under the Ninth and Tenth Amendments. After the passage of the Social Security Act, each state not only had to enact an unemployment insurance program, but the program had to be approved by the unelected members of the Social Security Board.

Unfortunately, in *Charles Steward Machine Co. v. Davis* (1937), five justices of the Supreme Court rejected the Alabama corporation's challenge. Writing for the majority, Justice Cardozo insisted that Congress had to have the power to nationalize unemployment relief, not because the Constitution says so, but because it is "too late today for the argument to be heard with tolerance that in a crisis so extreme the use of the moneys of the nation to relieve the unemployed and their dependents" is beyond the powers of Congress. This is the argument—as old as the Alien and Sedition Acts—that constitutional limitations can be disregarded whenever Congress decides there is an "emergency." Why not just say that the Constitution applies except when it doesn't? Cardozo then rhetorically asked, "Who then is coerced through operation of this statute? . . . Not the state," he answered. "For all appearances," said Cardozo, "she is satisfied with her choice, and would be sorely disappointed if it were now to be annulled."

This is what's known as pulling yourself up by your own bootstraps: since Alabama enacted a federally compliant law and hasn't seen fit to repeal it, the state must be acting voluntarily. Ergo, no federal coercion! "Alabama is still free" to repeal its unemployment law at any time, declared Cardozo. The fact that Alabama could not exercise its "freedom" without subjecting its citizens to a punitive tax was simply ignored.

But even if Cardozo's ivory tower fantasy was correct—even if Alabama's politicians were perfectly content to go along with the federal mandates—it doesn't change the constitutional equation. As James Madison observed during Virginia's struggle against the Sedition Act, the word "state" stands for a political community; it is not a shorthand expression for the politicians who happen to hold state office at any given time. By equating "state" with "state politicians," Cardozo rejected the key insight that the court had recognized just one year earlier in the *Carter Coal* case: the right to local self-government is not something that belongs to state politicians to waive at their convenience.

On the same day as the *Charles Steward* decision, the court also upheld the Social Security Act's old-age pension scheme. In *Helvering v. Davis*, the court held that the creation of a national pension plan—although beyond any of Article I's enumerated powers—was nonetheless authorized under the general welfare clause. Justice Cardozo announced that "the conception of the spending power advocated by Hamilton and strongly reinforced by [Justice] Story has prevailed over that of Madison."

Well, there you have it. It's not as though Cardozo him-self were rewriting the Constitution. It's just that the whole Hamilton vs. Madison thing had gone into double overtime, and Hamilton had scored the tie-breaking goal, allowing him to posthumously define the scope of the "spending power" (as Cardozo described it) under the general welfare clause. Except that there is no spending power in the general welfare clause. That clause, which is at the very beginning of Article I, Section 8, provides that "the Congress shall have Power to lay and col-lect Taxes, Duties, Imposts and Excises, to pay the Debts and provide for the common Defence and General Welfare of the United States"; enumerated powers follow.

The entire provision is about taxing, not spending. It gives Congress the power to tax—a controversial power in 1789, and one that Congress had lacked under the Articles of Confeder-ation. But the clause restrains this fearful power by specifying that any taxes must be justified in the name of (1) paying down the debt; (2) defense; or (3) the "general welfare." As originally understood, the general welfare clause was not a grant of extra powers to Congress; rather, it was an additional constraint on those powers. Congress was to be limited to its enumerated powers—that is the main thrust of Article I—but Congress also had to ensure that it did not use its taxing power to favor any particular region or faction. That is why the Constitution mandates that tax revenues be used only to pay the debt (which is owed by the entire union), or to provide for the *common* de-fense or *general* welfare.

With *Helvering*, Cardozo and his allies turned the general welfare clause into a loophole giving Congress nearly complete discretion to spend the money that it collects without regard to enumerated powers. Imagine the Constitution's framers painstakingly spelling out the specific powers of Congress—and then deciding that Congress could ignore those limitations as long as it was spending taxpayer money. What else does Congress do?

Good-bye, Tenth Amendment

Having abdicated its responsibility to set limits on congressional power, the Supreme Court also abandoned any attempt to protect states' rights. After the disastrous decisions of 1937—*Jones and Laughlin*, *Charles Steward*, and *Helvering*—it would be thirty years before any litigant could successfully invoke either the Ninth or Tenth Amendment in any federal court. Here at last was the full flowering of the changes that had begun to take hold in 1913: a radically transformed Union in which the states are subservient to the central government. By 1941, the Supreme Court would brush aside objections to the federalization of employment law—long the exclusive province of state law—asserting that the Tenth Amendment is "but a truism" that does not in any way limit the scope of Congress's powers (*United States v. Darby*).

The new measure of federal power was to be the consent of the states. Not real consent, but the phony consent of the *Charles Steward* opinion, and of the *Massachusetts v. Mellon* opinion of the previous generation. States would be deemed to consent to national policies provided they accept whatever carrots, and avoid whatever sticks, Congress may brandish. The old idea of "dual federalism" was officially dead. In its place, as the law professor Frank Strong observed in 1938, there was a "new brand of federalism" that involved "expanding federal power through the *implied* consent on the part of the states" (emphasis mine).[24]

This new brand of federalism was called "cooperative federalism," a feel-good label that obscures the coercive reality of federal power. "Cooperation" was not hard to come by, now that Congress had unfettered "general welfare" power to—how shall I put this?—*persuade* the states to sign up for national programs. Under the cooperative system, the national government grew by throwing money at the states. Between 1932 and 1940, federal outlays for cooperative programs grew from $250 million a year to nearly $4 billion.

This infusion of government money "created the possibility of unprecedented political patronage for the politicians in control of the money."[25] Mainstream commentators—eager to preserve FDR's iconic status—would like us to believe that Roosevelt and his allies resisted the temptation to use relief money for political purposes. The *New York Times*' Paul Krugman, for example, wrote in 2008 that FDR had made big government "clean" by steering clear of pork barrel legislation.[26] Krugman's version of history is pure fantasy. In reality, the New Deal led to political corruption on a vast scale.

Throughout the New Deal, the Roosevelt administration systematically diverted funds from Southern states—which were the poorest, but also safely Democratic—to Northern "swing states" that FDR needed in order to win reelection. Under Hopkins's leadership, the WPA channeled money to projects that would benefit pro-FDR politicians. According to an analysis by Gavin Wright, an economic historian at Stanford University, roughly 80 percent of the state-by-state variation in per-person New Deal spending can be explained by politics rather than real differences in need.[27] At one point, FDR threatened to cut off every penny of infrastructure spending for New York City unless Mayor Fiorello La Guardia fired Robert Moses, a municipal planner who happened to be a political foe of Roosevelt's.[28]

None of this should come as a surprise to progressives who consistently rail against politicians being "bought and paid for." If money from Wall Street can corrupt a politician, why not money from Washington?

Good for States, Bad for People

Thanks largely to cooperative fiscal programs, which often required states not only to comply with federal conditions but also to match federal grants, state governments grew during the New Deal. In 1913, the states accounted for 9.3 percent of all government expenditures in the United States. By 1940, that figure had grown to 17.5 percent—nearly double. Moreover, the states were allowed to exercise regulatory powers concurrently with the federal government. That had not been the case under the system of "dual federalism," in which state and federal powers were mutually exclusive. The nice thing about that system—aside from being faithful to the Constitution—was that any particular activity was regulated by, at most, one level of government. But in the New Deal, as Michael S. Greve, a professor at George Mason University School of Law, observes, "not a single [federal] regulatory regime unambiguously trumped or displaced the states."[29] For example, Congress created the Securities and Exchange Commission to regulate stock and bond trading—but without eliminating the state regulators who covered the same turf. As political scientists often put it, dual federalism is like a layer cake, with clearly delineated levels of government, while cooperative federalism is a marble cake, with overlapping state and federal roles.

The growth of *state government* does not equal an expansion of *states' rights*. Remember: states' rights belong to the people of each state, not to the politicians. By creating a system of autonomous states locked in a virtuous competition for citizens and tax revenues, American federalism had been maximizing individual liberty since 1789. For politicians, however, the New Deal grant programs offered a tempting way out of the rigors of competition. Federal grants allowed them to take credit for expanded services "without resort to the politically embarrassing expedient of state taxation," as New Dealer Jane Perry Clark conceded in 1938.[30] The money came with strings attached, but those strings would apply to all states, and thus would not put any particular state at a competitive disadvantage. State politicians, in short, sacrificed autonomy for money and protection from competition.[31]

As a result of federal-state collusion, state politicians took on redistributive programs far beyond anything their constituents had actually asked for—a fact that eventually caught up with the politicians. In Michigan, for example, a popular referendum in 1936 overturned the state legislature's attempt to create a centralized welfare system so that the state could qualify for Social Security funds.[32] That's right: in the midst of the Depression, voters in Michigan opted to retain local control over poor relief, even though that meant sacrificing federal dollars. Two years later, the 1938 midterm elections delivered a national repudiation of the New Deal. Republicans and anti–New Deal Democrats captured governorships across the country, even in progressive bastions like Minnesota and

Wisconsin. A Republican won the Pennsylvania gubernatorial race partly on the strength of his campaign pledge to burn all three thousand pages of regulatory legislation signed by the Democratic incumbent. The GOP picked up eighty-one seats in the House of Representatives and six in the Senate.[33] Politically, 1938 might have been the beginning of the end for FDR, but he would soon be reborn as a wartime leader.

The Death of Local Government

The growth of state governments did not come at the expense of the federal government, which also exploded during the 1930s and 1940s. Rather, the big loser in the New Deal was local government. In 1913, local governments represented over 60 percent of total government expenditures. By 1952, that figure was 20 percent, and it has never since exceeded 30 percent. Local government—rule by people who know their constituents personally, who are readily accessible, and who are directly accountable at the ballot box—had been the basis of American civics before the New Deal.

But local governments were largely powerless to arrest the centralizing tendencies of the New Deal. Although voters occasionally rebelled against federal-state collusion—as occurred in Michigan's 1936 referendum—the only institution that could have enforced the Constitution's structural provisions was the Supreme Court. Unfortunately, the New Deal court abdicated its traditional role as a "structure court"—an enforcer of the Constitution's organizing principles—and instead became a "rights court."[34] After the late 1930s, Congress would be allowed to centralize as much power as it wanted, unless it intruded on certain rights that the court deemed worthy of protection (local self-government not being one of those rights).

As for state laws, the court had no hesitation about striking them down under the "substantive due process" technique we saw in the previous chapter. What was changing, however, was the scope of substantive due process. Since the Progressive Era, the Fourteenth Amendment had been expanded to "incorporate" certain parts of the Bill of Rights—so that, under the guise of "due process," federal courts could now veto any state law for violating provisions that were originally intended to serve as a restraint on the federal government. And even that was not enough: the court went on to assert that the Fourteenth Amendment gave it authority to punish states for violating any other right that the court deems to be "so rooted in the traditions and conscience of our people" that it must be enforced by the judiciary (*Snyder v. Massachusetts*, 1934).

The Supreme Court had now set itself up as the national arbiter of acceptable policy. It would take a couple of decades and some ill-considered judicial nominations, but the Supreme Court would come to pose the greatest threat to states' rights during the postwar era, as we will see in the next chapter.

Big Brother Comes of Age

Billboards don't usually make the news, but on November 4, 2011, the *Boston Globe* reported that a large Bud Light billboard on the north side of Boston's TD Garden sports arena would be taken down and replaced with a smaller sign.

This was news because it meant that the Garden's management had finally surrendered after an eight-month-long battle with government officials over the fate of the billboard. The government in question was not, as you might be thinking, the mayor or city council of Boston. Nor was it the governor of Massachusetts. No, the mandate to change the Bud Light billboard came straight from Washington, DC, because the big sign was spoiling the view from a federally subsidized highway.[1]

It's good to know—isn't it?—that in 2011, while the federal government was busy *not* passing a budget, *not* planning for the ObamaCare rollout, and *not* blocking Iran's nuclear program, it did find time to dispatch a team of inspectors to Boston to check compliance with federal "highway beautification" standards. In March 2011, inspectors from the Northeast Right of Way Team (that's ROWT in federalspeak) of the Office of Outdoor Advertising (OOA) of the Federal Highway Administration (FHA) of the US Department of Transportation (USDOT) issued a report finding that no fewer than forty-two Boston-area billboards violated federal standards. The report is not for the faint of heart: aside from the Bud Light monstrosity, there was a Dunkin' Donuts sign defacing Terminal A at Logan Airport, and at least one Chipotle sign violating the pristine beauty of a city "T" stop.[2]

Let's stipulate that some of the billboards probably were, in fact, tacky. Perhaps Boston would look nicer without them. But the decision to remove, or shrink, a billboard is not a pure aesthetic decision; it's a decision to seize someone else's property. Each billboard represents a valuable stream of income for the owner. If anyone is going to have the power to decide whether a particular billboard is too big, or too ugly, or whatever, shouldn't it be the representatives of the people who actually have to live with the billboards? Or should it be the anonymous civil servants of the ROWT of the OOA of the FHA of the USDOT?

From Cooperation to Coercion

The story of how petty federal bureaucrats came to have veto power over roadside billboards is pretty much the story of postwar America's descent into coercive federalism. After the New Deal spending binge and World War II were over, Congress needed something else to throw money at, so it returned to one of the original federal grant programs: highways. There was still no legitimate constitutional basis for the federal government to get into the business of road building, which may explain why President Eisenhower and his congressional allies sold the interstate highway system partly as a matter of national defense—it would help evacuate the cities in the event of nuclear attack.[3] Thus the new federal road network was known as the "Interstate *and Defense* Highways." No wonder we won the Cold War.

From 1952 to 1962, federal grants for highway construction rose from $415 million to $2.75 billion.[4] Wherever federal money flows, of course, conditions will follow. By 1958, Congress had established national standards for the control of outdoor advertising near highways. An absurd thing for Congress to do, but at least the federal pressure on the states was mild. States that voluntarily agreed to adopt the federal standards for any particular highway would receive a "bonus" payment equal to one half of 1 percent of the highway's cost of construction. Twenty-three states adopted the federal standards, while the rest decided it wasn't worth the bonus payment.

Under the bonus system, states still had a meaningful choice—half of them simply opted out of the federal standards. Obviously, that wouldn't do. During the presidency of Lyndon Johnson—whose wife had made highway beautification a pet project—Congress passed the Highway Beautification Act of 1965, which required states to comply with federal billboard standards. Rather than paying a "bonus" to states that adopted federal standards, Congress would now exact a penalty—10 percent of annual federal highway aid—from any state that failed to embrace the federal act. Compliance with federal highway standards went from twenty-three states to all fifty states.[5]

There you have it—that is how cooperative federal programs became coercive. Political scientists refer to this phenomenon as the rise of federal "sanctions"—that is, the growing tendency of Congress to force states to adopt national policies by threatening to withhold federal aid. Federal highway funds were used not only to impose highway standards but also to require states to hide junkyards along roads and to adopt certain personnel policies, among other things. The rise of such coercive conditions was the logical outgrowth of New Deal precedents like the *Charles Steward* decision that allowed Congress to economically pressure states to adopt federal programs. Eventually, Congress also developed the technique of "crossover sanctions" in which federal money in one area is used to put pressure on states in other areas—for example, the threat to withhold highway construction funds to force states to adopt a uniform national drinking age or the use of sewage treatment grants as an inducement to comply with the Clean Air Act.[6]

Another Annus Horribilis

If federal coercion ended with highway billboards, one could just about put up with it. But highways were just the beginning. In 1965, the same year as the Highway Beautification Act, Congress got its hooks into K–12 education for the first time with the Elementary and Secondary Education Act. Originally billed as a modest effort to provide "assistance" to states, it has grown into the No Child Left Behind/Race to the Top juggernaut in which federal officials dictate curriculum and testing standards.[7]

The 1965 amendments to the Social Security Act created

Medicaid: a system of nationalized medical assistance for the poor. Like the New Deal programs, Medicaid provided billions in "free money" to the states. But unlike those initiatives, Medicaid did not even give states the theoretical choice of opting out of the program. Thus, even though the transformation that began in 1913 was largely complete, the legislation of 1965 represented a significant ratcheting up of federal power: the dawn of coercive federalism. According to some commentators, the central government first unambiguously overtook the states in sheer political power in this period.[8] Conditional grants were the main engine of this shift in power: more federal grant programs were enacted during the Johnson administration (1963–69) than in all previous years of US history combined.[9]

Free to Choose!

By the mid-1970s, there were over forty federal grant programs in the healthcare field alone. The laws governing the eligibility for these grants made little accommodation for state sovereignty. North Carolina, for example, was told it would have to amend its state constitution or forfeit all federal healthcare grants. The state went to federal court, arguing that its sovereignty was being invaded, but without success. The judge emphasized that North Carolina was not being forced to do anything—the state could just as easily decide not to amend its constitution and thereby disentitle its citizens from over forty federal grant programs.[10]

The decision in that case—*North Carolina v. Califano*—perpetuated the legal fiction that federal grant programs do not infringe on state sovereignty because they are "voluntary." States are always free to liberate themselves from federal mandates—the theory goes—by simply rejecting the grants to which the mandates are attached.

Ronald Reagan was the only president to make a serious effort to cut federal grants—precisely because they blurred "the classic division of functions between the federal government and the states and localities," as he pointed out in his 1983 budget message. Between 1980 and 1985, Reagan cut federal intergovernmental grants by 15 percent; if you exclude the Medicare/Medicaid entitlements, the number is 21 percent. He also tempered the coercive effects of federal grants by consolidating narrow micromanaging programs into "block grants" with much looser conditions. In the 1981 budget, eighty programs were consolidated into nine block grants.[11]

Reagan's policies also produced—albeit belatedly—the block grants featured in the historic 1996 welfare reform. In 1987, Reagan launched an initiative to make it easier for states to experiment with different approaches to reducing welfare dependency. Previously, governors would have to navigate a maze of different bureaucratic agencies to get relief from federal mandates; Reagan created a single interagency task force that could approve state initiatives. This set off a wave of policy experimentation, including a Wisconsin reform law that implemented the first-ever work requirement for able-bodied welfare recipients—something that would not have been possible under the existing federal rules for Aid to Families with Dependent Children (AFDC). Within a few years, the AFDC caseload in Wisconsin declined 81 percent. As happens in a healthy federal system, other states took notice and tried to emulate Wisconsin's reforms.[12]

The state welfare reforms culminated in the federal Personal Responsibility and Work Opportunity Reconciliation Act, which was signed into law by President Clinton in 1996. Rather than dictating the precise contours of welfare eligibility, the law gives each state a block grant—based on its historic share of AFDC spending—to be used to create a new program called Temporary Assistance for Needy Families (TANF). Each state was largely free to create its own version of TANF, provided there was a mandatory work requirement for able-bodied welfare recipients. Unlike the New Deal–era AFDC, TANF grants were fixed amounts—not "matching" grants— thus eliminating the perverse incentive of states to spend more than they needed in order to maximize federal aid.

Establishment liberals balked at the idea of giving states such freedom. New York senator Daniel Patrick Moynihan—who would later come to advocate devolving more power to the states—predicted that the reform would unleash the dreaded "race to the bottom." He called the legislation "the most brutal act of social policy since Reconstruction."[13] Supposed experts predicted that, within a year, a million children would be starving in the streets.

You probably don't remember the misery, starvation, and squalor caused by the 1996 welfare reform. That's because it didn't happen. Instead, the state TANF programs were a roaring success, reducing the old AFDC caseload by two-thirds nationwide. More important, the TANF block grants didn't just reduce *welfare*, they reduced *poverty*. Beginning in 1994, when the state-level precursors of TANF began to take effect, poverty rates in America plummeted. In *Work over Welfare*, Ron Haskins of the left-leaning Brookings Institution reports that between 1994 and 2000 "child poverty fell every year and reached levels not seen since 1978. . . . The poverty rate of black children was the lowest it had ever been." The decline in poverty was "widespread across demographic groups," according to Haskins, and it was "caused by increased employment and earnings of female headed families."[14] The states—liberated by the flexibility of block grants—were able to do something that the federal government had failed to do for half a century: move welfare recipients into work.

Coercion Continues

Notwithstanding Reagan's efforts, Congress kept piling on new grant conditions whenever it found a new way to score political points. There was, for example, the crossover sanction in the National Minimum Legal Drinking Age Act of 1984: states had to adopt a twenty-one-year-old drinking age or forfeit 10 percent of their federal highway construction funds. A legal challenge to the act made it to the Supreme Court, giving it a golden opportunity to revisit the issue of federal compulsion. In a 1987 decision (*South Dakota v. Dole*) the Supreme Court upheld the drinking age law by a vote of 7–2—in other words, not even close. The justices ruled that Congress could impose just about any condition on a federal grant, provided the condition is "not unrelated" to the purpose of the grant. The drinking age, for example, is "not unrelated" to highway construction because some of the young people who drink alcohol will end up driving on federally subsidized highways. By that logic, it's hard to think of anything that is wholly *unrelated* to highway construction. Why not make highway funding contingent on a state's education policy? After all, the actuarial tables tell us that better-educated drivers get into fewer accidents. As the

Brookings Institution has noted, there is "virtually no intelligible rationale" for making the drinking age a matter of federal law.[15]

The *Dole* decision conceded that, at some hypothetical point, federal pressure might "turn into compulsion," but a threatened loss of 10 percent of highway funds didn't cut it. With that kind of direction from the high court, lower courts were not exactly eager to go out on a limb and accuse the federal government of crossing the line into compulsion. In 2000, for example, an appellate court held that the potential loss of 12 percent of a state's education budget may be "politically painful," but it wasn't coercive.[16] For over twenty years, not a single federal court dared to strike down a conditional federal grant as being unduly coercive.

It was not until Congress did something really beyond the pale—ObamaCare, to be precise—that the Supreme Court finally found a federal condition that it didn't like. Under the Affordable Care Act as originally passed, states that refused to expand Medicaid eligibility according to federal guidelines risked losing 100 percent of their funding for Medicaid, which is by far the largest federal grant program. The Supreme Court held for the first time that Congress had crossed the frontier from pressure to compulsion. The court's decision striking down that aspect of ObamaCare was "historic," according to John Kincaid, a federalism expert at Lafayette College, but unlikely to be repeated.[17]

More Conditions—Hold the Grants

From Congress's point of view, there is just one drawback to conditional grants: they cost money. As federal budget deficits began to restrain Congress's ability to create new grant programs, the federal government turned to the use of *unfunded mandates*—that is, telling the states what to do without picking up the tab. Thus, Congress and federal regulators began issuing direct orders to state governments to comply with federal mandates under the threat of civil or criminal penalties.[18] Such mandates also allowed national politicians to take credit for popular reforms without being blamed for corresponding tax increases.[19]

In 1970, there were only nine significant unfunded mandates. By 1980, there would be thirty-four; by 1995, over one hundred. There are now hundreds of unfunded mandates costing untold billions of dollars—untold because there is no official tally of federally imposed costs on state and local governments. According to a 2005 study, thirty cities (mostly small and midsize) spent an aggregate of $548 million in annual costs to comply with just eleven major federal mandates. These ultraexpensive mandates include such national priorities as historic preservation guidelines (heavens, we mustn't leave *that* up to the states!), sewer overflow rules, and lead paint regulations.

The one-size-fits-all nature of federal mandates is the stuff of legend. For years, the EPA required that all local water sources be tested for a pesticide that was used only in Hawaii to protect pineapples.[20] As long ago as 1980, Ed Koch, then the mayor of New York City, criticized the "maze of complex statutory and administrative directives" coming from Washington, which "threaten both the initiative and the financial health of local governments across the country."[21] Koch conceded that he had supported such mandates as a congressman, but as mayor had come to realize the folly of Washington bureaucrats trying to micromanage local affairs.

Congress eventually got around to responding to criticism from people like Ed Koch by adopting the Unfunded Mandates

Reform Act (UMRA) in 1995. President Clinton hailed the law as a "historic" effort to shift more decision-making authority to state and local governments.[22] This was slightly out of character, since Clinton was no great supporter of states' rights. But in the case of UMRA, Clinton was savvy enough to understand that the law had been carefully designed to achieve . . . absolutely nothing. For starters, the act excluded about two-thirds of all mandates, including the real big-ticket items like Medicaid, from the technical definition of "unfunded mandates." As for the remaining mandates, UMRA does not abolish all of them. It does not abolish some of them. It does not gradually phase them out, either.

So, how exactly did Congress rein in unfunded mandates? In a classic display of bipartisan courage, UMRA requires the CBO to estimate the cost of any new unfunded mandates. If the CBO thinks that a particular mandate will impose more than $50 million of costs on state or local governments, then any member of Congress can—and I hope you're sitting down for this—*raise a point of order.* This parliamentary procedure will temporarily halt the mandate, but it is easily overridden by a majority vote (presumably, the same majority that voted for the mandate in the first place). Between 1996 and 2012, there were a grand total of three points of order that achieved any success.[23]

UMRA is not just ineffective, it's positively nonsensical. The point of the law was to relieve the states from burdensome regulations, but it contains no provision for Congress to get input from the states themselves. Instead, UMRA relies on the classic Beltway philosophy that Washington knows what's best for the states. In short, Congress would sort out the bad mandates from the good ones, not through consultation with the states, but through the voluntary exercise of congressional restraint. Once you see "Congress" and "restraint" in the same sentence, you know a law is doomed to failure.

As a sop to those who wanted greater input from the states, UMRA provided for a single study to be prepared by the Advisory Commission on Intergovernmental Relations (ACIR), a somewhat obscure but useful commission with a majority of its members being elected officials from state and local governments. The ACIR report, which recommended the repeal of various mandates (including a federal metrification initiative), proved to be so controversial that Congress defunded ACIR entirely.[24] That's the reality of all federal mandates: they are backed by such entrenched interests that you cannot seriously challenge any of them—not even metrification!—without provoking swift payback from Congress.

Earth Day

One of the early drivers of unfunded mandates was environmental law, particularly the Clean Air Act of 1970 and the Clean Water Act of 1972. Technically, the Clean Air Act does not require states to implement the Environmental Protection Agency's regulations; rather, it merely *allows* states to do so. States that fail to come up with a federally approved State Implementation Plan, however, will be forced to follow a Washington-designed Federal Implementation Plan (FIP). The federal government's FIPs are intended to punish states and their local industries; indeed, one EPA administrator boasted that the agency's tactics resembled those of the ancient Romans: "They'd go into a little Turkish town somewhere and they'd find the first five guys they saw and crucify them."[25]

Defenders of these latter-day Caligulas argue that their tactics are necessary to protect the environment from the callous indifference of the states. According to conventional history, the Clean Water Act rescued America from the brink of environmental apocalypse. Before the federal government acted, according to the *New York Times,* "the nation's waters were in terrible shape . . . Lake Erie on its deathbed, Ohio's Cuyahoga River bursting into flames."[26] In reality, the states were actively working to protect the environment well before the federal government got involved. By 1966—six years before the federal Clean Water Act—every state had enacted water pollution legislation and had empowered one or more state agencies to enforce environmental standards. In Cleveland, the citizens knew about pollution on the Cuyahoga long before Washington took notice. In 1968, the city's voters approved a $100 million bond issue to finance river cleanup, whereas Congress allocated nothing to Cleveland. As for Lake Erie, if it was on its "deathbed," as the *New York Times* says, it was partly due to the fact that the federal government (the Army Corps of Engineers) was busy dumping over a million cubic yards of contaminated material into the lake each year in the late 1960s.[27]

A similar mythology surrounds the Clean Air Act, a law that was actually modeled on legislation already passed at the state level. Studies have shown that, nationwide, air pollution declined at the same rate in the years before the Clean Air Act (when states were still regulating air pollution) as afterward.[28] Or consider wetlands. The states began adopting legislation to protect wetlands in 1963—long before the federal government began taking action in 1975. By the time Uncle Sam stepped in, all but one of the fifteen states with 10 percent or more of land area in wetlands had passed wetlands protection statutes. Strange as it may seem to nationalists, the people who actually lived near wetlands understood their importance and took action to protect them without being told to do so by Washington.[29]

Judicial Activism

The term "judicial activism" was coined in 1947 to describe how the New Deal–era Supreme Court effectively rewrote the Constitution to suit its own policy preferences. Typically this involved the court's giving its blessing to Congress's unceasing efforts to transfer power from the states to Washington. The only problem with that kind of activism is that the court had to wait for Congress to act first, which hardly seemed fair. The Supreme Court, after all, has nine very talented lawyers. Why not let them dictate policy directly to the states?

Why not, indeed? That seemed to be the philosophy of Earl Warren, who took the helm as chief justice in 1954. A popular ex-governor of California, Warren had little interest in the dreary task of interpreting the law; he preferred to make law. From 1954 to 1969, the Warren court graciously supplied all sorts of new laws to the state governments, thus relieving legislators of the bother and inconvenience of writing bills.

The court achieved its newfound power over the states by conjuring up phony constitutional rights to trump state law. The main source of these rights was the doctrine known as "substantive due process," which, as we've seen in the previous two chapters, empowers federal courts to strike down state laws for violating the Bill of Rights—or other unspecified rights that courts consider "fundamental."

In the early twentieth century, federal judges invoking due process were the enemy of progressive legislation. But as New Deal justices filled the high court, it became clear that substantive due process was an empty vessel that could be used to promote any agenda. Justice William O. Douglas—one of FDR's appointees—once referred to the due process clause as "the wildcard to be put to such use as the judges choose."[30]

Douglas got to use his "wildcard" in the court's 1965 decision *Griswold v. Connecticut*. In that case, Planned Parenthood challenged a Connecticut law forbidding the use of contraceptives, even by married couples. It may have been an archaic law, but it was not unconstitutional. The framers did not see fit to mention contraceptives in the Constitution; nor is the topic implicated by any fair reading of the text. Thus, the question of whether to get rid of the law is one that was left up to the voters of Connecticut and their state representatives. But the Warren court took it upon themselves to act as a mini–state legislature, voting seven to two to overturn the law, with Douglas given the task to make up a reason.

In *Griswold*, Douglas swept aside the lack of any constitutional provision dealing with contraception, because "specific guarantees in the Bill of Rights have penumbras, formed by emanations from those guarantees that help give them life and substance." Douglas goes on to say that the right to use contraceptives is found within a "zone of privacy" based on "emanations" from the First, Third, Fourth, and Fifth Amendments.

Eight years after *Griswold*, the Supreme Court used the same substantive due process razzle-dazzle to declare a constitutional right to abortion on demand (*Roe v. Wade*). The court had never before ruled on the constitutionality of abortion laws for one blindingly obvious reason: the Constitution says absolutely nothing about abortion. It is one of those innumerable issues "reserved to the States . . . or the people" under the Tenth Amendment. At the time of the nation's founding, nobody would have dreamed that the document conferred a federal right to abortion, particularly since the common law (which all the states embraced) treated abortion as a crime. Up until January 1973, abortion remained a matter of state law, with most states treating the procedure as a felony.[31]

All of that changed with a stroke of Justice Harry Blackmun's pen. No longer would elected state legislatures be entrusted with this delicate issue. Instead, the federal judiciary would be the national arbiter of abortion policy, with all lower courts instructed to use a multifactor balancing test to evaluate the validity of state abortion laws by balancing such factors as the stage of pregnancy, the viability of the fetus, the life and health of the mother, and the existence of a "compelling state interest." All of this in aid of a constitutional "right to privacy" that no one had heard of eight years earlier.

The decision was an "exercise of raw judicial power," as Justice Byron White said in dissent, that "constitutionally disentitled" the people and the legislatures of the fifty states from weighing the pros and cons of abortion for themselves. It is a decision that continues to poison American politics. Judicial nominees are either pro-*Roe* or anti-*Roe*—nothing else matters. Antiabortion protestors are silenced by unprecedented restrictions on First Amendment rights—including the thirty-five-foot no-speech zone around abortion clinics in Massachusetts that was overturned by a unanimous Supreme Court in

2014 (*McCullen v. Coakley*). The national political parties have staked out opposing positions and have effectively purged dissenting voices from their ranks. None of these things would have happened if abortion had remained a matter of state law.

Other substantive rights have been shoehorned into the due process clause, such as the Eighth Amendment's prohibition on cruel and unusual punishments. Originally intended to reassure the states that the federal government would not institute a reign of terror with barbaric punishments, the Eighth Amendment now empowers federal judges to second-guess state prison administrators on issues ranging from the conditions of solitary confinement to the contents of the prison menu.

Our New Federal Overlords

The Warren court also discovered that the equal protection clause of the Fourteenth Amendment has vast potential as an engine of judicial empowerment. The clause holds that no state may "deny to any person within its jurisdiction the equal protection of the laws." The point of those words—ratified in the midst of Reconstruction—was to require that states treat blacks and whites equally. Once upon a time, the clause was understood to be so specific to race relations that it was rarely cited in federal court. Oliver Wendell Holmes once referred to it as the "last resort of constitutional arguments" (*Buck v. Bell*, 1927).

In the century after ratification of the Fourteenth Amendment, the Supreme Court turned the equal protection clause from a prohibition against state racism to a guaranty of it. That journey—like some others I can think of—was paved with good intentions.

It began with *Brown v. Board of Education* (1954), in which the Supreme Court struck down laws in four states that either mandated racial segregation of public schools or allowed local authorities to mandate such segregation. Notwithstanding some gauzy statements by the chief justice about how the Constitution must be interpreted in light of social science research, the rationale of *Brown* is pretty straightforward: state-sponsored segregation violates the equal protection clause. You don't need social sciences to tell you that mandatory apartheid violates the Fourteenth Amendment. That's no affront to states' rights, since the amendment had been adopted fair and square by three-fourths of all the states.

Brown mandated desegregation. States could no longer forcibly *segregate* African Americans based on the loophole of "separate but equal" that had been blessed by the court in *Plessy v. Ferguson*. But the court did not say that states had to, or even could, forcibly *integrate* African Americans into schools. The court was well aware of the distinction between desegregation and integration; it required only the former. In 1964, Congress passed the Civil Rights Act to codify *Brown*. The act requires "desegregation," which it defines as "assignment of students to public schools . . . without regard to race." And just to be clear, Congress specified that desegregation did *not* include race-based assignment of students designed "to overcome racial imbalances."[32]

In short order, the Supreme Court would ignore both *Brown* and the 1964 act by adopting its own agenda of mandatory integration. In 1968, the court held that the Civil Rights Act requires school districts not only to end segregation but to forcibly integrate their schools. In *Green v. School Board of New Kent County*, the court rejected as inadequate a Virginia school district's program to open the doors of its formerly white-only schools to black students. Rather, the district would have to adopt measures, such as zoning law changes, that would guarantee integrated schools. Even though the act had defined "desegregation" precisely to avoid that result, the court held that the statutory definition applied only to Northern schools.

By 1971, the Supreme Court had upheld a lower court's order against a Virginia school district that imposed a busing plan and racial targets for individual school populations (*Swann v. Charlotte-Mecklenburg Board of Education*). Shortly thereafter, the court approved the decision of a federal judge in Denver who found that the city's policy of building schools close to where children live—what were they thinking?—was unconstitutional because kids in predominately black neighborhoods would go to predominantly black schools. As a result, the judge had placed the entire Denver school system under his personal supervision (*Keyes v. School District No. One, Denver, Colorado*). That was just the beginning of a national wave of receiverships and decrees by which federal courts assumed control of schools. Even after states had eliminated all de facto and de jure discrimination, federal courts took over school districts in an effort to remove the perceived "vestiges" of discrimination. The problem with battling such subjective enemies as "vestiges" is that the fight can go on forever. In the Kansas City, Missouri, school district, for example, the first wave of federal integration orders caused white families to flee to the suburbs. So in 1977 a new lawsuit (*Missouri v. Jenkins*) alleged that the school district was violating the Fourteenth Amendment because it wasn't doing enough to lure white families back to the city. For over a decade a single federal judge ran the Kansas City school district as a personal fiefdom, mandating specific capital improvements to city schools and even imposing a local tax to pay for them. Things began to change only in 1995, when the Supreme Court held that the judge could not set salary levels for the city's teachers.

The specter of the federal courts mandating specific procedures for local schools was something new. In *Swann* (the Virginia case), Chief Justice Warren Burger argued that busing and other forced integration measures are within a federal court's power to craft "equitable remedies." The Constitution gives federal courts jurisdiction over "all Cases, in Law and *Equity*, arising under this Constitution" (Article III, Section 2; emphasis mine). "Equity" is a technical term for the branch of the law that permits judges to order individuals to do—or refrain from doing—a certain act.

But the Constitution's framers understood equitable powers to be strictly limited. In the *Federalist* no. 80, Alexander Hamilton assured readers that federal equity jurisdiction could be invoked only by allegations of "fraud, accident, trust or hardship." In such cases, it was thought that federal courts ought to have the power—just as state courts did—to craft narrow remedies where a simple money judgment wouldn't do the trick. Fast-forward to the 1970s, and equitable powers had evolved from a narrow remedy to the "structural injunction"—that is, a court order requiring state and local officials to transfer their executive functions to a federal judge, often for years on end. Moreover, because such equitable orders last for years, they can have unintended consequences. Consider the Obama administration's efforts—which I describe in the introduction—to use forty-year-old desegregation orders to stop Louisiana from issuing school vouchers, which predominately benefited poor African American families.

Unfortunately, because the federal courts developed this new version of "equitable powers" in the context of civil rights, those who raised concerns about federal usurpations of states' rights were smeared by association with those Southern politicians who defied *Brown*. There is, of course, an obvious difference between a court saying that each state must desegregate its schools (*Brown*) and a court requiring a state to implement a specific plan to guarantee racial integration (*Swann*, *Keyes*, *Jenkins*, etc.). But such subtleties no longer mattered. The school desegregation fights had convinced progressives that federalism—that is, our constitutional system of divided state and federal sovereignty—was a structure that necessarily furthered racial discrimination. As long ago as 1964, the political scientist William H. Riker could declare, "If in the United States one approves of southern white racists, then one should approve of American federalism."[33] Or take the *Jenkins* case. When the Supreme Court held that local officials in Kansas City, rather than a federal judge, should be allowed to determine teachers' salaries, the American Civil Liberties Union complained that the court had "turned a blind eye toward the intractable problem of racism and race discrimination and abandoned any pretense of judicial restraint."[34] It's an odd world when a decision that actually limits judicial control over local affairs is characterized as a lack of judicial restraint.

The visceral reaction of liberals against any assertion of states' rights is particularly tragic because it halted what had been a significant midcentury movement among progressives toward decentralization. In the 1950s and 1960s, a communitarian small-is-beautiful philosophy had been gathering force among the American left as an alternative to the nationalistic liberalism of the New Deal. The progressive Southern novelist William

Faulkner openly declared his belief in states' rights during the 1950s, but was uncomfortable associating himself with the racial agenda of most states' righters of the time.[35] In the 1960s, counterculture writers like Paul Goodman advocated local autonomy and community-based politics. In his essay "People or Personnel" Goodman argued that "overcentralization is an international disease of modern times"—a statement that was repeated in the 1962 Port Huron manifesto of Students for a Democratic Society, the flagship organization of sixties radicalism.[36] In more recent years, a number of left-leaning scholars, like Harvard's Robert Putnam (the author of *Bowling Alone*), have continued the critique of overcentralization, but they are invariably overshadowed by mainstream liberals who "came to believe that almost all doctrines emphasizing the value of local community were indistinguishable from the phony 'states' rights' arguments used by segregationists," as the *Washington Post's* E. J. Dionne put it.[37]

The Sainted Clause

Meanwhile, back in the halls of Congress, our nation's leaders continued to exploit the commerce clause, which had been transformed by the New Deal into a catchall justification to federalize issues that don't fit into Congress's other enumerated powers.

Granted, the big action had shifted to conditional grants under the general welfare clause, but the commerce clause still served as a handy tool for Congress to usurp various aspects of state police power—a trend with its origins in the Progressive Era regulation of lottery tickets and booze. A clause that was designed to maintain free trade among the states is now used as the basis for a national criminal code—a development that poses a serious threat to individual liberty.

Most of the federal crimes that rely on the commerce clause involve conduct with little or no bearing on interstate commerce at all. Consider the federal law against "loan sharking"— the lending of money at usurious interest rates, typically involving threats against the borrower. Congress made this a federal crime in the Consumer Credit Protection Act of 1968—a thoroughly unnecessary law, since every state had (and has) usury laws on the books. The Supreme Court upheld the federal loan-sharking law even in situations in which the lender and the borrower were residents of the same state and all the sharking took place within that state (*Perez v. United States*). There are now hundreds of thousands of federal laws and regulations that can be enforced criminally, covering everything from unauthorized copying of the Smokey the Bear logo to failure to pay child support.[38] The majority of these criminal provisions were enacted after 1970.[39]

In 1990, Congress made it a crime to bring a gun within a thousand feet of any school. Mind you, bringing a gun to school is generally against state and local law, not to mention school rules, and so the law accomplished nothing. Well, actually it did accomplish something: it shook the Supreme Court from its long slumber. In 1995, the court did something it hadn't done since 1937: it struck down a federal law as exceeding Congress's power. In *United States v. Lopez*, the court held that the Gun-Free School Zone Act had no particular connection with commerce and so failed to pass constitutional muster. (By the way, the defendant in *Lopez* was initially charged with violating state law but state prosecutors dropped the case once the feds came in. Once again, the federal law added nothing to existing state law, but it gave congressmen something nice to write in their constituent newsletters.)

The *Lopez* decision was actually quite modest. The court did not overrule *Wickard*, or any of the New Deal precedents; instead, the court simply pointed out that those earlier cases did not extend the commerce power to reach "noneconomic" activity. In effect, the court solidified *Wickard* by giving Congress a free pass to regulate any local activity that might, in the aggregate, have a "substantial effect" on the economy. And yet, even that wide berth was not enough for liberals. In dissent, Justice Stephen Breyer argued that Congress should be allowed to regulate any activity, provided that "scholars" and "society at large" can perceive a connection between the activity and "national economic well-being."

In his weekly radio address, President Clinton condemned the *Lopez* decision and called on Attorney General Janet Reno to find a way to circumvent the court's ruling—an odd assignment for the attorney general, one might think. But in the end, Congress spared Reno the hard work. Congress reenacted the law but with language limiting its scope to any "firearm that has moved in or that otherwise affects interstate or foreign commerce"—a legislative gimmick often used to invoke Congress's commerce power. The new version of the law was upheld by the courts.

In 2000 the Supreme Court struck again, correctly holding that the Violence Against Women Act—however laudable its purpose—could not be justified under the commerce clause (*United States v. Morrison*). In the same year, the court overturned a federal conviction for arson, a case in which the perpetrator had set fire to an owner-occupied single-family house

(*Jones v. United States*). To explain how that house was involved in interstate commerce, federal prosecutors pointed out that it had a mortgage held by a national bank. Oh—and the owners had received shipments of out-of-state natural gas. Not even the court's liberals could accept that. The conviction was overturned unanimously.

What looked like a trend, however, was more or less a last hurrah. Although the Supreme Court's decisions in *Lopez*, *Morrison*, and *Jones* triggered hundreds of commerce clause challenges to federal criminal laws, the lower courts simply pretended as though nothing had changed since 1937. As of 2003, only one federal statute had been struck down as beyond the commerce power, and that decision was later reversed.[40] The following year, the Supreme Court—in particular, Justices Anthony Kennedy and Antonin Scalia—lost its nerve, upholding a federal drug bust against two seriously ill women in California who had been prescribed marijuana for medicinal purposes (*Gonzalez v. Raich*). All of this was allowed under California's medical marijuana law, which had been approved in a popular referendum. The court's majority acknowledged this, as well as the fact that, without the marijuana, the two women and thousands like them would be left to suffer excruciating pain.

The court held that the federal Controlled Substances Act trumped California law because of the supremacy of the commerce clause. But wait: there was no "commerce" here. The case involved people who grew pot in their own home, and for their own consumption. Alas, *Wickard v. Filburn* was still good law—and *Wickard* involved a farmer who grew wheat on his own farm for his own consumption. In both cases, the idea was that your own personal consumption is a matter of federal law because, in the aggregate, consumption affects interstate commerce. Still, the analogy with *Wickard* was not perfect. The statute at issue in *Wickard*, the Agricultural Adjustment Act, at least had the (perverse) New Deal logic of restricting agricultural production to drive up prices in national markets, thus assisting farmers. But as far as I know, no one in the *Raich* case argued that the Controlled Substances Act was necessary to boost the income of marijuana growers.

It's worth remembering that the *Raich* case was prosecuted by the Bush administration against highly sympathetic defendants who had acted properly under California law. One would have expected liberals and progressives to rise up in protest against the court's decision. David Morris, a liberal activist with the Institute for Local Self-Reliance, urged, "This is the moment where we need to demand that our states defend us against this encroaching tyranny." Quite right—but progressives were basically silent, "paralyzed," wrote Morris, by "their near worship of the magic of the Constitution's Commerce Clause."[41] The official voice of the liberal establishment, the *New York Times*, admitted to "mixed emotions" about the *Raich* decision, but ultimately, the *Times* argued, "protecting the Commerce Clause" was the most important principle involved in the case.[42]

It would be another eight years before the court could discover any limitations in the commerce clause. In *NFIB v. Sibelius*—the ObamaCare case—the court held that the commerce clause did not give Congress power to regulate inactivity—namely, the failure of citizens to purchase federally approved health insurance policies. But Congress could hardly complain about that decision, since the court graciously rewrote the statute to characterize it as an exercise of Congress's taxing power—despite the president's repeated insistence that the individual mandate was not a tax.

The Rise and Fall of the Tenth Amendment

Although the postwar Supreme Court has happily enforced the first eight amendments of the Bill of Rights—particularly against the states through the doctrine of "incorporation"—it continues to pretend that the Ninth Amendment does not exist, and it has yet to make up its mind about the Tenth.

In 1974 Congress made federal wage and hour regulation (the Fair Labor Standards Act, or FLSA) applicable to state and local governments. In other words, Congress decreed that the states could not be trusted to regulate the working conditions of their own employees. The FLSA was a New Deal law that displaced 150 years of state law over employment practices—as we saw in the previous chapter, that particular usurpation was upheld in the egregious *Darby* decision of 1941. Back then, Congress at least had the decency to exempt state and local governments from the provisions of the FLSA.

In placing the states under federal employment law, Congress did not even bother to invoke any particular constitutional justification. Nobody claimed that the law was "necessary and proper" to regulate interstate commerce. Nor did Congress attach the FLSA to a conditional spending bill so as to make compliance "voluntary." As William Van Alstyne, a law professor at Duke University, wrote, "The Act of Congress was all stick and no carrot. The Act was entirely coercive federalism."[43]

A lawsuit challenging the FLSA reached the Supreme Court in 1976. Miraculously, the court held that Congress had exceeded its constitutional powers—specifically, it had violated the Tenth Amendment (*National League of Cities v. Usery*). Assuming that the FLSA was within Congress's power in the first place, the statute impaired an important "attribute of state sovereignty"—namely, the power to set wages for state employees. The court held that the Tenth Amendment forbids any legislation that would take away the states' freedom "to structure integral operations of traditional government functions."

Given the court's track record, the *Usery* decision was a huge victory for states' rights—and for original meaning. Even Archibald Cox, a liberal scholar and former Watergate special prosecutor, conceded that the *Usery* decision was "almost surely consistent with the original conception of the federal union and might not have surprised any constitutional scholar prior to the 1930s."[44]

It took less than a decade for pronationalist forces on the court to convince Justice Harry Blackmun—the swing vote in *Usery*—to reverse himself. Writing for a new majority, Blackmun overruled *Usery*, declaring that Congress was perfectly entitled to impose the FLSA on municipal transit authorities (*Garcia v. San Antonio Metropolitan Transit Authority*, 1985). Indeed, the *Garcia* decision declared that the judiciary would no longer enforce *any* limits on federal power vis-à-vis the states. If states felt threatened by federal power, they would have to seek protection in the "procedural safeguards" of the political system. However, the primary "procedural safeguard" to protect states at the federal level—the election of senators by state legislatures—had been abolished by the Seventeenth Amendment in 1913.

The Battle for the Bureaucracy

Garcia was a boon to nationalists not only in Congress but also in the Washington bureaucracy, who had been delegated more and more power to determine the extent to which federal rules should trump state laws. In the wake of *Garcia*, the Reagan administration looked for ways to restrain the bureaucracy from doing any further damage to federalism. In 1987, after lengthy consultations with state and local officials, Reagan issued Executive Order 12,612, entitled "Federalism." The order begins with nine fundamental principles that ought to be tattooed on the forehead of every civil servant and congressman, including:

- Our political liberties are best assured by limiting the size and scope of the national government.
- The people of the states created the national government when they delegated to it [certain] enumerated powers.
- In most areas of government concern, the states uniquely possess the constitutional authority, the resources, and the competence to discern the sentiments of the people and to govern accordingly.

And most important: "In the absence of clear constitutional or statutory authority, the presumption of sovereignty should rest with the individual states." In other words, states should not have to prove that they are sovereign entities—under the Constitution, they are presumed to be sovereign, except in those limited areas delegated to the national government. Any federal agency looking to infringe on that sovereignty should bear the burden of proving that the infringement is necessary—and constitutional.

The executive order had a number of mechanisms designed to keep bureaucrats in tow. First, whenever a proposed federal rule would limit the "policymaking discretion" of states, the agency was required to consult with a designated state official. Also, each agency would have to prepare a "Federalism Assessment" to accompany any proposed rule that had significant federalism implications. The assessment had to address whether or not the rule interfered with "traditional government functions" of the states (the *Usery* test), as well as an estimate of any additional financial burden on the states.

President Clinton repealed Reagan's federalism order and replaced it with his own directive on the proper manner of consulting with state and local officials. Characteristically, neither Clinton nor anyone in his administration actually bothered to consult with state or local officials before issuing the order. Had they done so, they might not have issued an order that "permitted federal agency regulation under almost any imaginable scenario," as the law professor Brian Bailey puts it.[45] Gone were Reagan's nine principles of federalism; instead there were nine broad and overlapping conditions under which federal agencies could preempt state law, even in the absence of clear authority from the Constitution or Congress.

Following an outcry by state and local government organizations as well as members of Congress, Clinton hastily revoked the order and replaced it with a new one based on the Reagan federalism order. The new Clinton order (Executive Order 13,132) preserves some of the federalism principles of the Reagan order, but it removes the "presumption of sovereignty"—that was too much, even for a political shape-shifter like Clinton. Also, critically, the Clinton order empowers bureaucrats to enact rules that preempt state law without congressional authorization whenever they believe that state powers would conflict with "the exercise of Federal authority under the statute." That's a blank check, since virtually any state regulatory power might conflict with "the exercise of Federal authority."

In place of the Federalism Assessment of the Reagan era, the Clinton order—which remained in effect under both George W. Bush and Barack Obama—requires a Federalism Impact Statement, but without an explicit requirement to calculate the costs to states. In any event, federal agencies pretty much ignored this direct order from the president. A 1999 study by the Government Accountability Office found that federal agencies had prepared Federalism Impact Statements for exactly five rules—out of more than eleven thousand final regulations issued in the last years of the Clinton administration. Things were no better under Bush.[46]

Indeed, under Bush, preemption became one of those issues—like medical marijuana—that made liberals rally around the cause of states' rights. The left's main grievance arose from a series of health and safety regulations issued by Bush officials that claimed to preempt state tort laws—that is, laws that concern things like negligence and malpractice. The federal rules thus threatened to wipe out some of the state laws that feed the multibillion-dollar personal injury business of America's trial lawyers, who, along with organized labor, provide the Democratic Party with the bulk of its cash. The trial lawyers' main political action committee, the American Association for Justice, has given over $30 million in campaign contributions over the past two decades, 90 percent of which went to Democrats.[47]

Liberal scholars lashed out at the administration's attempt to gut state "regulatory autonomy," as the law professor Nina Mendelson put it in a 2008 article.[48] In November 2008, the Center for Progressive Reform published a paper calling on the incoming Obama administration to amend Clinton's executive order on federalism to include "a statement supporting a vibrant tort system."[49]

No matter what one thinks about tort reform as a matter of policy, liberals were right on the constitutional issue: tort reform should be a matter of state law, not federal regulation. And the Bush administration *had* used questionable tactics—in one case, slipping preemptive language into a regulatory preamble after publicly declaring that the rule would not preempt state law. Within four months of taking office, President Obama ordered the entire federal bureaucracy to review each preemptive federal regulation issued within the past ten years (with the implicit aim of increasing the opportunities of trial lawyers to sue under state law). Whenever federal regulations bumped up against state tort laws, Obama officials spoke the language of John C. Calhoun. At a 2010 congressional hearing, David Strickland—an African American lawyer appointed by Obama to run the National Highway Traffic Safety Administration—assured the House that he would refrain from preempting state law because "states' rights are incredibly important."[50] Imagine the uproar if a conservative president had sent an African American official to sing the praises of "states' rights" on Capitol Hill.

The administration's concern for states' rights, however, turned out to be selective at best. In other areas, Obama proved to be a hypernationalist. On immigration, for example, the Obama administration sued Arizona to block that state's efforts to add state enforcement measures to reinforce federal law. In 2012 the Supreme Court largely adopted the administration's aggressive view that states have no right to pass any laws whatsoever on immigration, even laws that are consistent with federal standards[51]—an example of the "field preemption doctrine" pioneered by the Progressives.

In financial services, the administration championed the Dodd-Frank law, which created a new financial regulator—the Consumer Financial Protection Bureau—that would be an "independent agency" and therefore exempt from Executive Order 13,132 (the federalism order). In fact, the law gives the bureau total authority to determine whether its rules preempt state laws.[52] The same law exempted the Office of the Comptroller of the Currency from the federalism executive order.

On the environment, it was Obama's EPA that glorified in the FIP-as-crucifixion strategy mentioned earlier. In Obama's first term, the EPA unleashed nineteen FIPs; in the preceding twelve years, there had been exactly two FIPs.[53] During the same period, the EPA vetoed ninety-five state environmental programs, a 300 percent increase over the previous three presidential terms. In 2011, state officials across the country (even in Democratic states like New York and Massachusetts) balked at a proposed EPA regulation that would have given the agency jurisdiction over roadside ditches—on the theory that those ditches become "navigable waters" once they fill with rain water. This was all part of trend described in 2014 by Mario Loyola, a policy analyst, as "a vast federal takeover of the states."[54]

Moreover, EPA functionaries have often failed to consult with state officials, even though they are supposed to do so in order to set national priorities. Instead, EPA officials prefer to deal with environmental groups, using a strategy known as "sue and settle." Under this strategy, the EPA waits for an environmental lobbying group to file a lawsuit accusing the agency of neglecting this or that mandate, and then immediately enters into friendly settlement discussions with the group.[55] The states are not invited to these negotiations; in fact, the EPA has "made a practice of opposing participation by states— the regulated entities—in settlement discussions with environmentalist organizations," according to William Yeatman, a policy analyst.[56] All the litigants need is a single federal judge to bless the settlement and—voilà—there you have it: a new batch of environmental regulations without any input from the state officials who are legally required to implement them.

Tenth Amendment Reborn?

Since the early 1990s, a shaky pro-federalism bloc on the court has managed to chip away at the *Garcia* decision—mainly through the "anticommandeering rule."

The anticommandeering rule holds that Congress may not hijack the legislative or administrative machinery of a state by forcing the state to adopt or administer regulatory programs designed in Washington. The doctrine emerged in a 1992 case (*New York v. United States*) in which the court struck down a federal law that gave states two options for dealing with radioactive waste: either (1) take ownership of all the waste generated within the state's borders, or (2) regulate the waste according to Congress's instructions. How could this be commandeering? protested the government. We gave states a choice! But it was a choice between two options that Congress had no power to foist upon the states. It was as though Congress gave states a "choice" between banning smoking and withdrawing from the Electoral College.

The government made the same argument in *New York* that FDR's men had made in *Schechter*—that a national "crisis" (this time, radioactive waste rather than the Depression) demanded federal intervention in state affairs. But the majority rejected the argument, wisely pointing out that "the Constitution protects us from our own best intentions. It divides power . . . precisely so that we may resist the temptation to concentrate power in one location as an expedient solution to the crisis of the day."

In a later decision, the court also struck down parts of the Brady Handgun Violence Prevention Act that required local law enforcement officials to conduct background checks on prospective gun purchasers (*Printz v. United States*, 1997). Just as Congress cannot force states to adopt particular internal policies, it also cannot "commandeer" state employees to administer federal laws. Again the majority cited founding-era evidence that the Constitution does not authorize the federal government to act through the states. In the *Federalist* no. 36, for example, Hamilton suggested that the federal government could try to attract the services of state officials by paying them higher wages ("an accumulation of their emoluments," as he delicately put it). But there is no evidence that the Founders thought the central government could force state officials to do its bidding.

More recently, the Supreme Court conceded in *Bond v. United States* (2011) that the Tenth Amendment is not a meaningless "truism"—as the New Deal court described it—but a fundamental right that individuals can actually enforce through the courts. *Bond* involved the federal government's attempt to prosecute a run-of-the-mill assault as a violation of an international treaty banning chemical weapons. Finally, there was the 2012 decision in which the court held that ObamaCare's Medicaid expansion was unconstitutionally coercive for the states.

All in all, there has been a modest but encouraging ascent in states' rights at the Supreme Court. Although this so-called federalism revival only nibbles around the edges of the post–New Deal order, it has been decried by the media as a judicial apocalypse. The *New York Times*' Linda Greenhouse, for example, denounced the court's pro-federalism decisions as "stunning" and "unnerving,"[57] while the *Times*' editorial board found it "chilling" that the court was "inching closer to states' rights."[58]

I'd describe it a different way: a good start. Read on.

The Present:

THE CASE FOR
STATES' RIGHTS
TODAY

The Blessings of Liberty

Has the federal government become a threat to individual liberty? Depends on whom you ask. Put that question to a K Street lobbyist, or a defense contractor, or a member of the Harvard faculty, and the answer will be no. But if you ask the average American, the answer, more likely than not, will be yes.

A 2014 survey found that 54 percent of likely voters "consider the federal government today a threat to individual liberty rather than a protector." By contrast, just 22 percent would describe the federal government as a protector of individual rights. The year before, a Fox News poll found that more than two-thirds of likely voters "feel like the federal government has gotten out of control and is threatening the basic civil liberties of Americans." More Democrats agreed with the proposition that DC is out of control than disagreed.[1] While hostility toward the federal government has been steadily rising among members of both parties, respect for state and local government is high—and has been so for decades.[2] The growing gap between Americans' trust in Washington and their trust of the states reinforces one of the Founders' key insights: in a federal system, the states serve as a permanent bulwark against the abuse of power by the central government.

This is where enlightened folks start to roll their eyes. Harvard's Cass Sunstein, for example, insists that the New Deal forever demolished the "ludicrous" idea that the growth of government poses a risk to freedom. William Greider, writing in the *Nation*, argues that conservative hostility to federal power represents a desire "to roll back the twentieth century."[3] Sunstein, Greider, and their allies may concede that the federal government went a bit too far with the Sedition Act or the Fugitive Slave Act, but such things simply do not happen today. And if the federal government no longer represents a threat to individual liberty, who needs states to protect them?

Lots of people. Just ask Catherine Engelbrecht.

Tough Times for Patriots

Catherine Engelbrecht and her husband run a small business in Houston. For nearly two decades, the Engelbrechts and their little business had chugged along with virtually no interaction with government agencies save routine tax filings. But that began to change in 2010.

After the 2008 election of Barack Obama, the previously apolitical Catherine became excited and energized about politics. Good, right? Unfortunately, she had the appalling taste to become energized in *opposition* to President Obama. She got involved in Tea Party politics and, in 2010, submitted applications to the Internal Revenue Service seeking nonprofit status for two organizations: the King Street Patriots and True the Vote (a group that combats voter fraud).

Suddenly, the federal government became intensely interested in the Engelbrechts and their business. The Occupational Health and Safety Administration made its first-ever inspection of Engelbrecht Manufacturing—an inspection that ended with a $25,000 fine for such grave violations as having the wrong type of seat belt on a forklift. Not that there wasn't any seat belt, mind you—but it was the *wrong type*.[4]

The FBI came calling six times, including a visit by the Domestic Terrorism Unit looking for information about a person who had attended a King Street Patriots meeting. The IRS demanded mountains of information about the King Street Patriots, including every Facebook post and tweet issued by the organization—supposedly necessary information to determine whether the group qualified for nonprofit status. There were five rounds of IRS questioning regarding True the Vote. And just for good measure, the IRS conducted multiple audits of the Engelbrechts' personal and business tax returns.

All told, Catherine and her husband endured more than fifteen audits or inquiries by federal agencies in the years following the 2010 applications. Even the Bureau of Alcohol, Tobacco, Firearms and Explosives got into the act. The ATF had jurisdiction because Engelbrecht Manufacturing had obtained a license to make firearms over a decade earlier—but in fact the company does not use its license. No matter, the ATF conducted comprehensive audits of the family business in 2012 and then again in 2013. In an April 2014 congressional hearing, the ATF's director, B. Todd Jones, said he could not think of any reason why the Engelbrechts were singled out for consecutive audits.[5] Can you?

As we now know, in 2010, the Obama administration began a coordinated effort to stem the rising tide of conservative political organizations. The administration used various tactics, but the most brazen was the IRS's harassment of conservative groups. In March 2010, the IRS decided to put organizations with names containing phrases like "Tea Party" or "Patriot" on a special "be on the lookout" (BOLO) list, meaning that nonprofit applications from such organizations would get extra scrutiny. And when I say "extra scrutiny," what I mean is that the hapless applicants were made to feel like characters in a Kafka novel. The San Fernando Valley Patriots, for example, were treated to a questionnaire with thirty-five parts and eighty subparts including requests for details of how the organization "conducts or promotes" illegal activities—the IRS's version of "Have you stopped beating your wife?" The Richmond Tea Party—in the swing state of Virginia—spent nearly three years and seventeen thousand dollars in legal fees on its nonprofit application, which was finally approved in December 2012—conveniently one month after Obama's reelection.[6]

By 2012, the IRS had expanded the BOLO list to include organizations "involved in educating on the Constitution and the Bill of Rights."[7] There was no similar scrutiny of groups devoted to *denigrating* the Constitution; rather, only those groups seeking to *elucidate* the Constitution were deemed uniquely suspicious.

Yesterday's Tyranny—Today!

When the central government can use all the levers of power to stifle dissent, you have a textbook case of tyranny—different from the Sedition Act only by degree. The most effective check against such abuses is the right of each state to protect itself and its citizens against federal overreach. Don't take my word for it. The Supreme Court has said so again and again. In 2011, a unanimous court—including the most liberal justices—held that federalism "secures the freedom of the individual. . . . By denying any one government complete jurisdiction over all the concerns of public life, federalism protects the liberty of the individual from arbitrary power."[8] In 1990, a seven-member majority of the court, including such liberals as John Paul Stevens, stated that "a healthy balance of power between the states and the federal government will reduce the risk of tyranny and abuse from either front."[9]

In fact, liberals are often in the vanguard of warning about federal tyranny—whenever the federal government is run by conservatives. Progressives may think that conservatives are paranoid about the war on "patriot" organizations, but they would never admit to being paranoid about the PATRIOT Act—that George W. Bush–approved legislation passed by Congress in the wake of the September 11 attacks. Entire libraries could be stocked with books detailing the excesses of the federal government's war on terror. There were reports, for example, that the Bush administration spied on religious and political organizations. There was the fear that federal agents could target you by race or ideology, or detain you without cause, or, at the very least, subpoena your library history.[10]

Like the Sedition Act of yesteryear, the PATRIOT Act was a heavy-handed, take-it-or-leave-it federal law justified on national security grounds. And—just like in 1789—the only effective resistance to the act came from state and local governments, dozens of which passed resolutions against various aspects of the war on terror. At least fifteen states, for example, refused to implement the 2005 REAL ID Act, a Homeland Security measure that prescribes certain standards for state-issued driver's licenses and other identification cards. As a result of this—dare I say it?—nullification, the act has yet (as this book goes to press) to be fully implemented.

When the Bush administration called for state and local participation in antiterrorism measures, ultraliberal towns like Madison, Wisconsin, asserted the right of *interposition*: that dreaded and putatively racist doctrine we invariably see associated with John C. Calhoun. Madison's Common Council enacted a resolution refusing to participate in any type of surveillance activity "in the absence of probable cause of criminal activity," thus defying the Bush administration's desire to dismantle the wall between intelligence and law enforcement.[11]

Contrary to popular belief, it wasn't the Tea Party that resurrected the Virginia and Kentucky Resolutions; it was the anti-Bush left. The striking thing about anti–PATRIOT Act measures like the one in Madison is that the local jurisdictions reserved for themselves the right to determine when rights had been violated, regardless of what federal officials or judges said. "These assertions of interpretive autonomy," writes the law professor Ernest A. Young, "recall a similar challenge to federal supremacy two centuries ago in the Virginia and Kentucky Resolutions."[12]

With Barack Obama's election, however, the progressive magical thinking machine kicked into high gear. Liberals who had dreaded Washington's gestapo tactics under Bush suddenly welcomed federal power as the source of everything good. But had things really improved? Consider the outrage over the Bush administration's Operation TIPS, a short-lived program that allowed ordinary citizens to report to the Justice Department "suspicious" terror-related behavior or even conversations. A dubious program, to be sure, but was it any worse than Obama's 2009 launch of flag@whitehouse.gov? In case you've forgotten, the White House created that email address so that ordinary citizens could report "fishy" information about healthcare reform—including information received "via chain emails or through casual conversation."[13] In short, it was a place where people could snitch on their neighbors who oppose ObamaCare. As bad as it is to invite people to report "suspicious" behavior to the Department of Justice, the TIPS initiative at least had a veneer of respectability since it was restricted to terrorism-related information. The "flag" email address, on the other hand, had no purpose whatsoever except to assist the White House in compiling a list of political enemies who would presumably be short-listed for the full Engelbrecht treatment. Even though the White House shut down the email address fairly quickly, there were reports of citizens getting IRS audits shortly after being named in the "flag" email inbox.[14]

It's a sure bet that future presidents and future Congresses will think up new ways to try to suppress political dissent. Having a Bill of Rights is a necessary, but not sufficient, antidote to that. A nice piece of parchment does you no good if politicians are too corrupt to respect it and courts too cowardly to enforce it. Remember that the Constitution's framers believed that the best defense of liberty lay in diffusing political power through federalism and separation of powers. "Ambition must be made to counteract ambition," as Madison wrote in the *Federalist* no. 51. Today, federalism is more important than ever. Given the vast resources of the federal government, only the states have the necessary heft to resist Washington's abuses. Or, as professor

Ernest Young puts it, "Sometimes it takes a government to check a government."[15]

Challenge the Surveillance State

Do you lose sleep worrying that your state government is reading your emails, intercepting your phone calls, or stalking you with drones? Of course not, that's the federal government's job! Say what you like about Edward Snowden—the former National Security Agency contractor who in 2013 leaked details of the NSA's spying operations—his revelations provided a rare glimpse into the federal government's incredibly intrusive surveillance operations. Among other things, the NSA gathers nearly five billion records a day, including cell phone location data on millions of Americans, all without warrants. Legions of NSA analysts pore over this data.[16]

The information gathered by the NSA does not remain locked in a vault until a major terror threat is detected. Rather, the NSA feeds warrantless data directly to state and local law enforcement officials. Typically, this information relates to routine criminal matters—nothing to do with national security—and the local officials use the information to make arrests. As much as one likes to catch bad guys, the simple fact is that the federal government is giving local police information that they could not obtain themselves if they were forced to play by the boring old rules and get a warrant.

That's a problem—but it's also an opportunity for states to deflate the NSA by prohibiting the use of warrantless data. The anticommandeering rule means that the federal government cannot force state or local governments to use NSA data.

There is an encouraging trend of state legislatures considering bills to block state police and prosecutors from using evidence obtained in violation of the Fourth Amendment's protections against unreasonable searches and seizures. That is classic interposition, and it's a step in the right direction.

Unfortunately, citizens don't always know when NSA data is being used against them. The NSA actually *requires* law enforcement officers to lie about the source of their information. According to a 2013 Reuters report, "Federal agents are trained to 'recreate' the investigative trail to effectively cover up where the information originated."[17] In other words, federal agents create a fictional narrative to explain how they got information that, in reality, came from warrantless surveillance. As one blogger marveled about NSA surveillance, "You just can't make this stuff up."[18] Actually, you can. That seems to be the point.

The states do have leverage over the NSA for a rather simple reason: the agency has to put its computers *somewhere*, and that somewhere is always within the borders of some state. NSA supercomputers need to be placed close to a very robust electrical grid and a large body of water—the cooling systems require millions of gallons of water. Knowing all that, the whiz-bang experts in the federal government decided to locate a major NSA data center in America's second *driest* state: Utah. When the *Salt Lake Tribune* asked local officials exactly how much of the state's most precious natural resource was being diverted to the data center, the NSA ordered local officials not to answer. Why? According to David Sherman, the NSA's associate director for policy and records, water usage statistics could be used to reverse engineer the computing power of the data center. If the NSA's computing power were known, then ordinary citizens might find out "how much intelligence NSA is collecting and maintaining."[19] And where would we be then?

Officials in Bluffdale, Utah—where the data center is located—did the NSA's bidding and refused to divulge the center's water usage information. Ultimately, however, the Utah State Records Committee unanimously ordered that the information be released.[20] Summing up: the *federal* government—the supertransparent Obama administration, no less—sought to block the media from getting information about a vital natural resource, while the *state* government vindicated the public's right to know. Sometimes it takes a government to check a government.

The larger point is this: neither Utah nor any other state is obliged to make its water supply available to the NSA. Various state lawmakers are pushing to withhold material support for federal programs they consider objectionable or downright unconstitutional.

End the Prosecutors' Reign of Terror

Surveillance may be dirty business, but too many Americans are willing to accept it in the belief that the federal government goes after only really bad guys. It's not like the feds are going to prosecute *me*, for heaven's sake!

That's probably what Nancy Black used to think—until that morning in November 2006 when more than a dozen armed agents in bulletproof vests raided her home and seized a chunk of her life's work. Black is a well-regarded marine biologist who finances her research by conducting whale-watching cruises in Monterey Bay, California. Her saga actually began more than a year before the raid, when officials at the National Oceanic and Atmospheric Administration (NOAA) alleged that some of Black's whale-watching crewmates had violated federal "natural resource protocol" by—brace yourself—*whistling* at a humpback whale.

Let's pause there for a moment. NOAA is actually a subdivision of the US Department of Commerce, an agency whose sole constitutional basis lies in the federal government's ability to "regulate Commerce with foreign Nations, and among the several States, and with the Indian Tribes" (Article I, Section 8). How did that narrow grant of power turn into a mandate to control a citizen's ability to whistle in the vicinity of a whale? It's not as though Ms. Black had been attempting to sell the humpback whale across state lines. NOAA itself is not shy about its jurisdiction: "Our reach goes from the surface of the sun to the depths of the ocean floor," according to the agency's website.

But Black did not concern herself with such technical questions; she assumed at first that the federal government was genuinely concerned about the whales' well-being. At NOAA's request, Black provided a video of the incident, but she edited it to *highlight* the whistling. The tape made it clear that there was no illegal harassment of whales, but NOAA then indicted Black for editing the tape, with intent to "impede, obstruct, and influence a [NOAA] investigation." She also faced a misdemeanor charge arising from an earlier incident in which Black had fed blubber to an orca. Well, actually, it was blubber from a whale that the orca itself had just killed and, one suspects, would have been eaten with or without Black's assistance.[21]

And now the nightmare really began—with Black suddenly facing a possible twenty-year prison sentence. In the November 2006 raid on her house, agents seized over thirty hours of Black's research videos, making it impossible for her to continue

with her work, which, incidentally, is entirely devoted to helping killer whales. Prosecutors threatened not only jail time but
also the forfeiture of Black's research boat. It would take seven
more years for Black to reach a plea bargain in which she agreed
to pay $12,500 to NOAA and perform three hundred hours of
community service.[22]

So in the end, you might think that Nancy Black got off
pretty lightly. But the salient point is that *she did nothing wrong.*
Nor did Angel Raich and Diane Monson, the two seriously ill
California women arrested by the federal Drug Enforcement
Agency for possessing marijuana that had been legally prescribed for them under state law. Their prosecution was upheld
by the Supreme Court in *Gonzales v. Raich.*

Nor did John Rapanos, a Michigan property developer who
was threatened with more than five years of jail time because he
moved sand on his property without getting a federal permit. The
judge presiding over his case observed that federal prosecutors had
recently sought a ten-month sentence for an illegal immigrant
caught selling dope, but in the case of Mr. Rapanos, "We have an
American citizen who buys land, pays for it with his own money,
and he moves some sand from one end to the other and the government wants me to give him 63 months in prison. Now, if that isn't
our system gone crazy, I don't know what is. And I'm not going to
do it." Because his case was heard by a sane judge, Rapanos avoided
jail time. But thousands of others are not so lucky.

Everyone's a Criminal

Unfortunately, the Rapanos prosecution does not represent the
system "gone crazy"—it's just the system, period. Each and ev-

ery citizen should be worried about federal prosecutors, for once you do something that attracts their attention, they will find a way to get you.

There are over 4,500 federal statutory crimes and over 300,000 regulatory crimes—that is, criminal penalties for violating bureaucratic rules. Mind you, those numbers are approximate and outdated, based as they are on a 2008 analysis of federal law. But no better numbers are available for the simple reason that nobody in our highly efficient, scientifically driven national government is responsible for compiling, counting, or rationalizing the hundreds (thousands?) of new federal crimes created every year. As Julie Rose O'Sullivan, a professor at Georgetown Law, put it in 2014, "No definitive count of federal crimes is extant, and such a count is probably not possible without too much trouble to make the task worthwhile."[23]

Whatever the number is, it is higher than the number of federal crimes provided for in the Constitution: four. In the framers' original plan, Congress was delegated the power to punish (1) treason, (2) counterfeiting, (3) piracies and felonies committed on the high seas, and (4) offenses against the law of nations. As Thomas Jefferson observed in the Kentucky Resolutions, Congress may punish those four sets of crimes "and no other crimes whatsoever."

In the *Federalist* no. 17, Alexander Hamilton argued that the states would enjoy a "transcendent advantage" over the central government, because the states would control "the ordinary administration of criminal and civil justice." That was why the Sedition Act was a states' rights issue—it was not only oppressive, it usurped power from the states.

Granted, the amendments to the Constitution have expanded federal criminal jurisdiction slightly: under the Thirteenth Amendment, for example, Congress surely has the power to make it a crime for one person to enslave another. Under the Twenty-First Amendment (repealing Prohibition), it is a federal offense to import liquor into a state in violation of the laws of that state. So maybe there are six, seven, or even eight legitimate areas of federal criminal jurisdiction. Instead we have an uncountable heap of federal crimes enforced by 120,000 full-time officers working for 73 different federal agencies, all with full authority to carry guns and make arrests.[24] There—you feel safer?

Federal criminal laws do not fill some gaping hole in state law. To the contrary, serious federal crimes almost always target conduct that is already forbidden by state law. As previously noted, the federal Gun-Free School Zones Act (GFSZA), for example, was hailed by gun control advocates, but it essentially duplicated laws that already existed in virtually every state.[25] The case that brought the GFSZA to the Supreme Court, *US v. Lopez*, involved a student who had initially been charged with violating a *state* prohibition against guns in schools—but state prosecutors dropped their case once the feds got involved.

Why does Congress create so many redundant laws? Because it's Congress: a body of political entrepreneurs forever on the lookout for cheap ways to take credit for tackling some tough problem or another. When, for example, the media focused on the rise of deadbeat dads, Congress made it a federal crime to fail to pay child support, even though that was already illegal under state law. After a spate of church fires, Congress passed the Church Arson Prevention Act of 1996—as though the states had never bothered to outlaw arson against churches. Forget any pretense of coherence; federal criminal law is not driven by expert opinion on how to reduce crime, it is driven by the calculations of politicians seeking reelection.[26]

The sheer number of federal crimes, however, tells only half the story. The breadth of federal crime is the other half. It's certainly true that some criminal laws are of the narrow don't-whistle-at-whales variety. But when those laws don't do the trick, there is always a broader law that prosecutors can fall back on. In Black's case, when it became clear that she did not actually harass the orcas, prosecutors charged her with making a "false statement." Under Section 1001—a favorite with federal prosecutors—it is a crime to lie about any matter within federal jurisdiction. Think about that: there is now no matter that is entirely *outside* of federal jurisdiction, so virtually any untruth becomes a federal crime. And, according to Harvey Silverglate, a criminal defense lawyer, when the FBI accuses you of making a "false statement," what they mean is that you have said something that contradicts the handwritten notes of an FBI agent—which is impossible to verify, because the FBI forbids the tape-recording of interviews.[27] For that, you can forfeit your liberty and property.

You don't even have to lie *to* federal employees, provided your lie concerns a "matter of federal jurisdiction." In one case, federal officials prosecuted an Idaho farmer, Cory King, for lying to state officials about his violation of a state irrigation policy. Years after King settled the matter with Idaho authorities, federal prosecutors continued to pursue him, ultimately leading to a conviction that was upheld by the Ninth Circuit Court of Appeals. As Vikrant Reddy, a legal analyst, puts it, the court's logic amounted to this: "You violated a state law and you lied about it to a state official. That's a federal offense."[28] Stephen Salzburg, a law professor at George Washington University, argues that "there's no statute out there that's more pernicious" than Section 1001.[29]

Actually, here's one that gives Section 1001 a run for its money: honest services fraud. Under this law, to deprive anyone of "the intangible right of honest services" is a crime. The statute grew out of earlier efforts to target corruption in state and local governments, but the current incarnation of the law includes private citizens who defraud their private employers. As Justice Scalia noted in a 2009 dissent, the statute, taken literally, "would seemingly cover a salaried employee's phoning in sick to go to a ball game" (*Sorich v. United States*). Or, as Professor Julie Rose O'Sullivan puts it, if you violate your employer's policy by, say, using your work computer to buy a pair of shoes online, "you may have committed a 20-year federal fraud felony."

Congress has devised a novel way to commandeer state law enforcement officials to enforce federal law. Under a program known as "equitable sharing," state and local police who participate in federal criminal investigations are allowed to keep 80 percent of any resulting forfeitures. In case you're not familiar with the concept, forfeiture is a legal doctrine that allows the state to seize not only the proceeds of crime (say, money stolen from the bank) but also any property involved in the crime (the getaway car).

Forfeiture is an illogical and outdated practice that assumes that the getaway car is itself somehow "guilty" of a crime. And the federal government thrives on it. Since 1985, when federal agencies were first allowed to keep any property they gained through forfeiture, the federal government's forfeiture receipts have soared; the Department of Justice's main fund had $4.2 billion in deposits in fiscal 2012.[30] And with equitable sharing, state-level forfeitures are booming, too. Granted, most states have forfeiture laws themselves, but many of them have built in significant protections for property owners, and have tried to remove perverse incentives by requiring forfeited assets to go to the general treasury of the state rather than to the local police department. The federal government, however, actively pushes state and local police forces to evade the state protections and participate in the lowest-common-denominator rules that prevail in federal cases.[31]

Left to themselves, the states are less likely to seize your property than the federal government is. They are also less likely to take away your liberty. While federal courts continue to throw citizens in prison for trifling "crimes" that nobody has heard of, there has been an "avalanche of state-based initiatives to reform the criminal justice system," according to a 2014 report by the Texas Public Policy Foundation.[32] Since 2007, various states have decriminalized certain low-level offenses and have eliminated custodial sentences for others; they have eliminated mandatory sentencing laws and developed smart nonprison alternatives for technical parole and probation violations.[33] The states have achieved results that have so far eluded the federal government: simultaneous reductions in crime and prison populations.

Shut Up and Trust the Prosecutors

Apologists for the federal police state insist that there's nothing to worry about. According to a 2012 *Emory Law Journal* article by Professors Susan Klein and Ingrid Grobey, the growth of federal criminal law is "largely irrelevant," because many of the offenses are "virtually ignored or overlooked by prosecutors."[34] Sorry, professors, but that is exactly the problem with the overfederalization of criminal law. The depth and breadth of federal criminal law empowers prosecutors to pick and choose which citizens to pursue "for having broken laws by committing acts that they did not, and could not reasonably, know were illegal," according to Silverglate.[35] In short, when everyone's a criminal, then no one is—except for those singled out by federal prosecutors.

In case you're tempted to rely on federal prosecutors to use their discretion wisely, consider the case of Carol Anne Bond, a Pennsylvania woman who spread abrasive chemicals on the doorknobs and the mailbox of another woman who had been carrying on an affair with her husband. She had hoped to give her romantic rival an uncomfortable rash, but succeeded only in inflicting a minor thumb burn that was easily treated by rinsing with water. Still, what Ms. Bond did was wrong—and it was almost certainly an ordinary assault under Pennsylvania law. But Bond was not prosecuted under state law; instead, federal prosecutors swooped in and charged her with violating a federal law implementing the Chemical Weapons Convention, an international treaty seeking to outlaw the "stockpiling" of chemical weapons. Whereas Bond might have received a few months' jail time in a state-level assault case, the federal district court sentenced her to six years' imprisonment plus five years of supervised release for being a purveyor of weapons of mass destruction, including chemicals she had ordered on Amazon.

Had the Bond prosecution been the work of a rogue prosecutor, one would expect his or her supervisor, or the attorney general, or the president, to correct the mistake. It would have been easy to do: Bond appealed her conviction, giving the administration ample opportunity to drop the case. Instead the Obama Justice Department spent years and untold prosecutorial resources litigating the case—including two trips to the Supreme Court—all to preserve the ability of federal prosecutors to exploit a federal law that was plainly never meant to reach purely local crimes. Ultimately, the Supreme Court held unanimously that the federal chemical weapons statute could not be applied to Bond's crime. The majority of justices applied the "clear statement" doctrine—that is, a rule that federal statutes should not be interpreted so as to usurp traditional areas of state sovereignty unless Congress clearly says so. While the clear statement rule is better than nothing, it still allows Congress to violate the Tenth Amendment so long as it does so explicitly—not exactly an ironclad protection. Three of the justices (Scalia, Thomas, and Alito) had a much stronger rationale—namely, that because the federal statute was written so broadly as to potentially cover run-of-the-mill assaults, it should be struck down for violating the Tenth Amendment (*Bond v. United States*).

Resist Civil Laws That Invade Liberty

Criminal laws may pose the gravest threat to liberty, but even when the federal government exercises its civil—that is, noncriminal—jurisdiction, the results can be pretty scary. In fact, in some ways it's worse, because citizens in civil suits lack the protections afforded to criminal defendants.

Consider the Food and Drug Administration's relentless pursuit of honest farmers who do nothing worse than sell unpasteurized milk to willing consumers who happen to believe that "raw milk" is healthier than the supermarket variety. It's worth noting that unpasteurized milk—although largely obliterated by large dairy concerns in the United States—is a common drink in much of Europe. But the central government has taken up the challenge of ensuring that we all eat and drink exactly the same thing, right down to school bake sales, regardless of local preferences.

In 2011, the FDA brought a lawsuit against an Amish farmer named Dan Allgyer, based on evidence obtained by agents in a predawn raid on Allgyer's Pennsylvania farm. The FDA sought not only to stop Allgyer from selling raw milk but also to give federal officials a permanent right, without prior notice, to conduct further raids on his farm. The judge alleviated some of the FDA's most intrusive requests, but in the end, Allgyer ditched the farm altogether rather than try to fight the federal government.[36]

In a 2012 argument before the Supreme Court, the Obama administration argued that the federal government has an unfettered right to induce flooding of private property without ever having to compensate the property owners under the "takings clause" of the Fifth Amendment. Again, this was a civil matter—it's not as though the government was flooding land as a punishment for the owners' crimes. Rather, the administration asserted matter-of-factly that part of the federal government's job is to "adjust the benefits and burdens" of living near a river. Not much fun for those who end up with uncompensated "burdens" courtesy of Uncle Sam (*Arkansas Game and Fish Commission v. United States*).

And then there's ObamaCare, a federal law that invades personal liberty by subjecting every person's health choices to government scrutiny and control. Even though the courts have held that Americans have the right to refuse medical treatment altogether, ObamaCare forces every resident not only to buy a health plan but also to divulge on an ongoing basis his or her most sensitive medical details to an insurance carrier.

But ObamaCare requires cooperation from the states, which makes it vulnerable to state interposition: thirty-four states refused to create the healthcare exchanges that federal experts blithely assumed they would, while twenty-two states decided not to relax Medicaid eligibility rules, notwithstanding federal bribes that the experts assumed would be irresistible. Such efforts did not wipe the Affordable Care Act off the map, but by withholding their support, the states have exposed the technical incompetence of the federal government, seen most spectacularly in the botched rollout of the national marketplace website, healthcare.gov. In the longer term, state resistance means that—as ObamaCare teeters from disaster to disaster—Congress will have to either scrap the law entirely or radically revamp it in a way that suits the states.

The state resistance to ObamaCare exemplifies a much larger national trend: since 2010, more and more state legislatures have enacted laws refusing to recognize federal jurisdiction over purely intrastate affairs. In the final chapter, I review this legislation as well as other proposals that citizens and state legislators should endorse.

The point is not that assertions of states' rights will magically increase individual freedom overnight. Federalism is a long-term proposition, not a silver bullet. It is a system that "best protects liberty over time, through the day-to-day operations of a government in which nothing much can get done without the cooperation of multiple actors at multiple levels."[37] Continued resistance to overreaching federal laws will ultimately force the central government to negotiate with the states.

Let Dissent Bloom

The temptation to suppress dissenting views is an equal opportunity employer; Richard Nixon and George W. Bush, for
example, may have succumbed to the temptation, but their
efforts now seem halfhearted compared with the Obama administration's war on dissent. The war began in earnest following the Supreme Court's 2010 decision in *Citizens United
v. FEC*, which threatened to exacerbate the then-growing dissent against Obama. The decision upheld the right of private
corporations and unions to make independent expenditures in
political races, rather than having to set up separately regulated
political action committees, or PACs.

The president's first reaction to *Citizens United* was to denounce the Supreme Court on live television while the members of the court were sitting in front of him. All that was
missing from the performance were the golden epaulettes and
ceremonial sash of the traditional Latin American despot. Then
the president's allies in Congress pushed legislation intended
to force corporations (but not unions) to give up their First
Amendment rights to be eligible for federal contracts. When
that legislation failed, the president attempted to enact the exact same law by executive order—who needs Congress?—but
was eventually shamed into withdrawing the order. The baton
then passed to the IRS, which began to target conservative
501(c)(4) organizations—but not liberal ones—for extra scrutiny. This was no coincidence. Since at least September 2010,
Obama and Senate Democrats had been denouncing conservative nonprofits for engaging in political activity (which, in
fact, had been permitted for decades under IRS rules).[38] In
any event, if 501(c)(4) organizations were supposed to avoid

politics, why not scrutinize the liberal ones as well as the conservative ones?

After the harassment of conservative groups became a public scandal, the IRS proposed new rules regarding the permissible political activities of 501(c)(4) organizations—a topic normally covered by the Federal Election Commission; but unfortunately for the president, the FEC is a bipartisan group, and less amenable to White House pressure. Although the new rules cover all 501(c)(4) organizations, the IRS exempted unions—which are organized under 501(c)(5)—from any restrictions on political activity. Summing up: if the administration and its allies had succeeded in their full program, there would be nationwide restrictions on the free speech rights of corporations and conservative nonprofits, but not unions or liberal nonprofits.

In May 2013, the Federal Communications Commission launched an initiative to root out "perceived station bias" in broadcast news media. The commission planned to send federal bureaucrats into newsrooms to interrogate reporters and editors about how they decide which stories to run and whether they are responsive to "underserved populations." Translation: Obama's FCC wanted to put pressure on Fox News and conservative talk radio. The entire effort was so ham-fisted that the FCC suspended the study before it started.[39]

In a democracy, what could be more important than the ability of citizens to make their views heard, particularly when those views are unpalatable to those in power? The lesson of *Citizens United* is that Americans don't give up their First Amendment rights when they join a corporation or a union; but unfortunately, the federal government wields enormous leverage over both corporations and unions. States, however, are a little more difficult to push around. Even in the era of federal grants and crossover sanctions, states remain the most reliable channel for dissent.

States' rights matter because those very rights can be used to vindicate citizens' views on national questions. If we return to the Founders' design—in which the central government depends upon the states rather than the other way around—states will provide an even more powerful check against federal overreach. As it is, states must continue to find creative ways to block federal tyranny. If Congress tries to curtail the political activity of federal contractors, states could, for example, shut off water and electricity to NSA data centers. If the IRS denies, or indefinitely postpones, the tax-exempt status of conservative nonprofits, how about a state tax credit to make up the difference? The details are less important than the principle—the principle that we started with: sometimes it takes a government to check a government.

8

Democracy, for a Change

For the people of Tombstone, Arizona, democracy means the right to choose whether to die of thirst or burn to death as the town's reservoir runs dry. Well, actually, if Tombstone's residents had a say in the matter, they wouldn't have to do either. They would vote to take advantage of the twenty-five freshwater springs in the nearby Huachuca Mountains that the city owns outright. But the federal government has assumed the power to decide when, if ever, Tombstone will get its water, and the residents have no control over that decision.

Tombstone's problems began in June 2011, when a fire in the mountains, followed by monsoons, damaged the town's water pipeline, shutting off the flow from the mountain springs. The city was forced to rely on its 1.2-million-gallon reservoir, which, by August, was running dry. Governor Jan Brewer declared an emergency and freed up some state money to repair the pipeline. Tombstone officials got permits from all the necessary government agencies—except the United States Forest Service, which had to sign off because much of the work would have to take place in a federally protected wilderness.[1]

Eventually, city officials got tired of waiting for the Forest Service to act, so they sent workers with an excavator up to Miller Canyon and started to clear out a reservoir. That's when they found out that the Forest Service wasn't merely being slow to approve the repairs; to the contrary, the service actively opposed the repairs. Federal rangers threatened to have them arrested if they did not immediately remove the excavator. According to the rangers, the Wilderness Act of 1964 prohibits the use of "mechanized" equipment in the protected area—and they were not about to make an exception to save one measly town. One of the rangers told Tombstone's mayor, Jack Henderson, that if he didn't agree with the Forest Service, "I suggest you call Barack Obama." As Henderson later told CNN, "That's when I began to get a sense of the smugness we were dealing with."

So city workers put away the excavator and came back with a wheelbarrow. Again the rangers turned them back, arguing that even a wheelbarrow constitutes forbidden "mechanized" equipment—because it has a wheel.

Then the town sent people up the mountain with picks and shovels—no wheels. They managed to get a makeshift pipeline working with water from two of the town's twenty-five springs. A few more months and Tombstone might have secured its water supply with a durable pipeline. But then the Forest Service blocked the work again, saying that even manual labor might disturb the nests of Mexican spotted owls, some of which had been sighted in the mountains above the pipeline.

In the meantime, Tombstone had sued the federal government for the right—which shouldn't be controversial—to fix its own springs, pipeline, and reservoirs in the name of self-preservation. Tombstone's legal argument was based on the Tenth Amendment—namely, that its ability to preserve the lives and property of its residents by repairing its municipal water supply is a traditional government function reserved to the states, even when it involves federal land. After all, the Supreme Court has previously held that states retain the power to regulate behavior on federal lands to further environmental goals (*California Coastal Commission v. Granite Rock Co.*, 1987). If the states can intervene on federal land to protect owls, why not to protect people?

Unfortunately, Tombstone lost at the trial court, and on appeal—the federal appeals court issued a mere three-paragraph decision saying that Tombstone had failed to raise any "serious questions" under the Tenth Amendment. The town's survival, therefore, remains at the tender mercy of the Forest Service. Lest there be any doubt about the Forest Service's priorities, consider an exchange that took place at the trial. Tombstone's lawyer asked a Forest Service supervisor: "Sir, just tell me: What is more important? Owls or people?" The supervisor refused to choose favorites between the species, simply saying that "we have to balance" both. But as this book goes to press, the owls still have the advantage: the US government continues to block Tombstone's efforts to access its own water.[2] "While federal administrators fiddle," says the Cato Institute, "Tombstone literally burns or at least dries up."

What About Local Self-Government?

Tombstone's plight is not unusual in places like Arizona, where the national government owns 42 percent of the land. The situation is worse in other states. In Idaho, for example, 62 percent of the land is owned by the federal government; in Utah, it's 67 percent. The prize goes to Nevada, where 81 percent of the state's landmass is federal property.[3] Admittedly, these areas were once federal territories, but with statehood the federal government was supposed to relinquish the land.

In what universe can anybody claim that a state like Nevada enjoys democracy when its citizens and legislature have no direct say over the management of 80 percent of its territory? Democracy means that the citizens of a community have a meaningful voice in shaping their own destinies. That's not exactly a radical idea: it's the principle of self-determination, endlessly parroted by the United Nations in documents such as Resolution 1514, which declares that self-determination means the right of "all peoples" to "freely pursue their economic, social and cultural development." In *American Society: How It Really Works*, the notably left-wing professors Erik Olin Wright and Joel Rogers equate freedom—"the capacity to make choices over one's life"—with democracy—"the capacity to participate in the *effective* control over collective choices that affect one's life as a member of a wider society" (emphasis mine).[4] Thus, say the professors, "in a democracy, decisions which affect our common fate and common interests should reflect the collective will and choices of equal citizens rather than powerful elites." The reference to "powerful elites" may have been intended to capture corporate titans, bankers, and other liberal bogeymen, but why shouldn't it apply just as forcefully to national groups like the Sierra Club and their unelected enablers in the federal bureaucracy?

The Constitution itself guarantees to each state a "Republican form of government" (Article IV, Section 4). The text does not define what a "republic" is, but James Madison considered the distinguishing feature of a republic to be a government operated by persons "appointed, either directly or indirectly by the people" (*Federalist* no. 39). In other words, a "republican" government is one in which the leaders are directly accountable to the people they serve.

Compare that ideal with the situation in Nevada, where 80 percent of the territory is controlled by 535 politicians in Washington (only six of whom directly represent the citizens of the state), and by unelected federal bureaucrats and judges, and where 80 percent of its natural resources—and tax base—are off-limits to the citizens who need them.

Nevada's status as a de facto colony of Washington is typified by the case of Wayne Hage, a cattle rancher whose family farm had been in operation since the days when Nevada was still a territory. In 1991, the federal Bureau of Land Management (BLM) arbitrarily shut off Hage's access to grazing lands and water rights (some of which had vested as long ago as 1866)—evidently all part of some personal grudge harbored by two federal employees. There was nothing that state or local officials could do except to wait for the matter to work its way through the courts. When a federal court finally ruled, in 2013, that the two BLM employees had engaged in an illegal "conspiracy" to deprive the Hages of their vested rights, Wayne Hage was completely vindicated. Unfortunately, he was also dead, having waited more than two decades for his day in court.[5]

Local self-government has yet to arrive in the American West. Not that Eastern opinion leaders are overly concerned; the idea of Westerners (other than Californians) governing themselves is inherently distasteful to them. If only Tombstone, or the Hage ranch, had been located in Tibet—then they would have had the elites' sympathy. According to a statement issued by the Dalai Lama's supporters, and published on a variety of websites, the Tibetan region of China lacks "genuine autonomy" because its own local government cannot make decisions on such issues as "environmental protection" and "utilization of natural resources."[6] Shouldn't the same considerations weigh in favor of "genuine autonomy" for Nevada?

In fact, the argument for Nevada is even stronger. The US federal government has no constitutional authority to create an inland empire under its exclusive control; to the contrary, the Founding Fathers went to a lot of trouble to prevent that from happening. Under the Constitution, Congress's exclusive control extends to only (1) the District of Columbia, and (2) other places "purchased by the consent of the legislature of the state . . . for the erection of forts, magazines, arsenals, dockyards, and other needful buildings" (Article I, Section 8). In other words, the federal government was not meant to be a big landlord outside the federal district. How did it end up owning 28 percent of the land in the United States? The short answer is: by flouting the law.

After the ratification of the Constitution, each new state was admitted to the Union under an "enabling act"—that is, a congressional guarantee that the new state would be placed on an "equal footing" with the original thirteen states. A critical part of that equal footing was an express promise that all of the federal lands in the state "shall be sold" expeditiously, with 5 percent of the proceeds going to the state, and the land thereafter becoming part of the state's permanent tax base. That's how it worked in the Eastern states, where today only about 4 percent of the land remains under federal control.

By the time the Western states were coming into the Union, however, our old friends the Progressives were in charge. They decreed that federal agencies must be created to manage the lands in the new states. "The widely-held belief of the day," according to Holly Fretwell, a policy analyst, "was that an elite group of experts could dispassionately use science to determine best resource use, and . . . align management to provide for those uses."[7] Yet again we see the imposition of central government control in the name of "science." And you know that science has finally triumphed when the federal government declares the *wheel* to be a dangerously mechanized innovation.

Predictably, once Congress created federal bureaus whose very existence depended upon federal land ownership, the government lost all interest in selling its land—never mind the legal requirement that the land "shall be sold." Not only did the government hold on to the land, but it forbade economic development on huge swaths of it. In 1976, Congress gave up the pretense that it was ever going to sell its Western possessions by passing the Federal Land Policy and Management Act (FLPMA), which declares "it is the policy of the United States that the public lands be retained in Federal ownership, unless . . . it is determined that disposal of a particular parcel will serve the national interest." Note how the presumption of sovereignty has been turned on its head. The framers had assumed that public lands would be held by the states, and the burden was on Congress to establish a national need to acquire federal land. Now the burden falls on those trying to persuade Congress to dispose of federal lands. In the late 1970s, following passage of the FLPMA, politicians throughout the West staged protests that became known as the "Sagebrush Rebellion." Nevada and Utah passed laws asserting state title to public lands, but those laws were ultimately struck down by federal courts. With at least five states actively seeking title to their public lands, there is still hope of bringing democracy to the American West.

One-Man Rule, Not Cool

Another undemocratic aspect of federal land management is the immense power it places in the hands of a single person: the president. This has been the case since the Progressive Era's Forest Reserve Act, which gave the president the unilateral power to set aside federal lands as public reservations. Teddy Roosevelt used his powers under that law so enthusiastically that Congress passed another law forbidding him to make further reservations in six Western states without congressional approval. Having just been told by the people's representatives to stop reserving Western land, TR set aside an additional 30 million acres during the ten days before the bill became law.[8] How's that for government by the people?

Rule by executive order is a problem that extends far beyond the question of land management and into the most sensitive areas of domestic policy. That's not to say that all executive orders are illegitimate. As the chief executive and commander in chief, the president has every right to issue written instructions to the employees of the executive branch and the armed forces. The problem is that American presidents find it increasingly handy to use executive orders as a means of achieving domestic policy goals that cannot be achieved by democratic means. In the summer of 1998, for example, when President Clinton failed to push his domestic legislation through Congress, he launched a series of executive orders to get around Congress.

His aide Paul Begala—whom we last saw cheering the federal government as the greatest force for good in human history—had a similarly stirring defense of executive orders: "Stroke of the pen. Law of the land. Kind of cool."[9]

Clinton certainly wielded the presidential pen with flair. In 1996, he unilaterally established the Grand Staircase-Escalante National Monument in Utah, setting aside 1.7 million acres of land—an area more than twice the size of Yosemite—with no advance consultation with local residents. In 2013 congressional testimony, John Jones, a *Democratic* commissioner from Carbon County, Utah, was still fuming over Clinton's Grand Escalante order as a "cowardly, infamous act" that devastated the local economy, shut off development of the nation's cleanest low-sulfur coal supply, and had triggered such an exodus of residents that the school system was about to shut down. Jones concluded: "One man's signature changed our lives completely."[10] Kind of cool, huh, Paul?

President Obama has used an expansive definition of executive powers to run an alternative Congress out of the White House. When he could not win on immigration reform, Obama stretched the concept of prosecutorial discretion to exempt millions of illegal immigrants from the reach of federal law. When Obama failed to get gun control or campaign finance laws through Congress, he tried to achieve the same results by executive order. Unable to pass education reform, Obama effectively created his own educational policy by granting more than half the states "conditional" waivers from the provisions of the No Child Left Behind Act—but at the cost of states' agreeing to the administration's education policy, including the "Common Core" curriculum. When Republicans try these tactics, it's known as the "imperial presidency."

Rein In the Rogue Bureaucrats

The doctrine of "preemption"—when federal rules displace state laws on the same subject—poses a serious threat to states' rights, as we've seen in the Supreme Court's efforts to strike down state regulations of railroads during the Progressive Era, as well as more recent controversies, such as the federal government's alleged monopoly over marijuana regulation. But preemption also threatens democracy since it involves a small group of Washington decision-makers overriding the will of democratically elected state legislatures. It was bad enough in the old days, when preemption came from Congress, but now federal agencies play the dominant role in asserting federal preemption.[11] The validity of state laws lies in the hands of executive branch mandarins who will never have to justify their actions to ordinary voters.

The US Supreme Court, instead of standing up for democracy, has endorsed the trend toward rule by executive agency. In 2011, the court held that in disputes over the preemptive effect of federal rules the key factor is not the Constitution, not the *Congressional Record*, but the statements of the federal agency itself (*Williamson v. Mazda Motor of America, Inc.*). Justice Stephen Breyer, the principal author of the majority opinion in *Williamson*, argued that it was only "practical" to defer to federal bureaucrats because they are "most likely to know what 40,000 pages of agency record actually mean." In effect, the court encouraged federal agencies to bury their decisions beneath mountains of turbid prose so as to maintain their interpretive monopoly.

Perhaps the most elegant solution to federal overreaching is the Repeal Amendment, a proposal championed by the law professor Randy Barnett. The Repeal Amendment would allow two-thirds of state legislatures to repeal any federal statute or regulation. In May 2011, Utah representative Rob Bishop attracted twenty-two cosponsors for the proposal, but like all amendments, it's a long shot. Therefore, in chapter 12, I'll review some of the more readily achievable ideas for arresting the regulatory rampage coming from Washington, including legislation that would codify Ronald Reagan's federalism executive order.

Make Politics Less Expensive

The one tactic that will not solve Washington's democracy deficit is simply transferring power from the civil service back to Congress. First of all, it would never last. Congress creates and funds federal agencies, so it will always have the ability to stick bureaucrats with the politically difficult decisions. But more fundamentally—and I think my liberal friends will be with me on this one—Congress does not faithfully represent the wishes of the people. "The average congressional district now contains 647,000 persons," observes the writer (and former staffer to Senator Daniel Patrick Moynihan) Bill Kauffman. "How is anything like representative government possible on such an enormous and impersonal scale?"[12]

Good question. Given the expense of campaigning for federal office, most senators and representatives "effectively represent national special interests" according to a recent analysis.[13] That charge is often hurled at Republicans, but it is equally true of Democratic politicians, who rely on labor unions, trial lawyers, environmental groups, and left-wing political action committees to fund their campaigns. And it feeds a vicious cycle: expanding federal power means expanding your national constituency. As the law professor Steven Calabresi puts it: "Pass a national speed limit, collect a donation from the insurance companies. Pass a national drinking age, collect a donation from Mothers Against Drunk Driving. Every breach of the constitutional fabric becomes a new fundraising opportunity and new television spot."[14]

The influence of money in national politics is a common liberal refrain. But while liberals have correctly diagnosed the problem, the proposed remedy is a little odd. Mainstream liberals would let Congress keep all of its existing powers—and add new ones, to boot—but would restrict the ability of certain groups to engage in political speech, as we saw in the Obama administration's response to the Supreme Court's *Citizens United* decision. By penalizing people who choose to speak through corporations and conservative groups, the thinking goes, we can remove all vestiges of corruption in politics and let the people's voice be heard.

Actually, there's a better way to go about this. Instead of trampling on the First Amendment, how about enforcing the Tenth Amendment? Put power in the hands of state legislators, city councilors, and county commissioners—none of whom needs the National Rifle Association or the AFL-CIO to bankroll their election campaigns. And citizens don't need a high-priced lobbyist to gain access to their local officials. As the late New York mayor Ed Koch once said, "If you don't like the president, it costs you 90 bucks to fly to Washington to picket. If you don't like the governor, it costs you 60 bucks to fly to Albany to picket. If you don't like me—90 cents [the price of a subway token at the time]."[15]

Let Communities Set Their Own Priorities

The rise of conditional federal grants and crossover sanctions is yet another assault on democracy because the point of such measures is to coerce states into doing things that their voters do not want, or at least would not be willing to pay for themselves. The pressure is usually irresistible. In the aggregate, states depend on federal funding for 35.5 percent of their revenue. In Mississippi, the most dependent state, federal aid comprises 49 percent of all state revenues. Even in the least dependent state, Alaska, the federal government provides nearly a quarter of all revenues. Federal aid, as Neal McCluskey, a scholar at the Cato Institute, puts it, is "the mighty tool that Washington uses to make states do its unconstitutional bidding—taking tax dollars from state citizens whether they like it or not, and forcing states to follow federal rules to 'voluntarily' get some of the money back."[16] Most Americans are probably unaware of the basic dynamic of federal coercion.[17]

Worse yet, most federal aid programs (and all of the really big ones) require states to match all or part of the federal grant—and thus, to get the federal dollars, the state has to spend its own money. And once a state is locked into a program, it generally has to go along when Congress decides to expand it. In practical terms, this means that federal aid programs crowd out other spending priorities at the state and local level, be they "education or pothole repair," says John Kincaid, a federalism expert at Lafayette College—a conclusion he says is firmly based on "empirical data."[18]

Already state spending on healthcare (Medicaid and Medicare) has surpassed spending on education, the next-biggest recipient of federal funding ("Hurrah," says Michael Greve, a professor at George Mason University, "the entitlement state has begun to eat its own.").[19] With entitlement programs on a path to consume 75 percent of all federal grant programs by 2020, education funding will be further squeezed. Sit back and watch: whereas the teachers unions used to blame the Pentagon for hogging all the federal dollars, they now have to blame the healthcare unions and AARP.

What Congress ought to do is easy enough to describe: phase out all conditional grant programs, cut federal taxes proportionately, and let state and local governments decide what to do and how to pay for it. Surely each state would continue to maintain welfare programs, public schools, and good roads— but why not let the states divvy up the money as they see fit? Such a policy is sometimes referred to as "turn-back," as in "turning back" responsibility to the states.

This won't be easy, given Washington's resistance to decentralization, particularly among the Democratic Party establishment. Proposals like Medicaid block grants—which preserve today's federal funding stream but liberate states from micromanagement—are considered "untested" and "hazardous" by the Obama administration.[20] Apparently, it is better to stick with Medicaid's rigid national fee structure, which has turned away so many potential providers that low-income people chronically fail to get the care that the law promises.[21]

Even in state capitals there is fear of change: in 2011, seventeen Democratic governors wrote to congressional leaders to oppose Medicaid block grants—with Washington's governor, Christine Gregoire, writing separately to the *Wall Street Journal* vowing to fight "any congressional effort to impose Medicaid as a block grant." It's an odd spectacle to behold: elected governors fighting against the "imposition" of flexibility.

Why are governors like Christine Gregoire afraid of being forced to *govern*? It's because state flexibility means state competition—and competition means hard work and long hours for state politicians. Rough sledding for them, perhaps, but that's why they get paid the big bucks. The virtue of states' rights is not that it makes life easy for politicians; rather, it is that interstate competition will make life better for citizens—as we'll see in the next chapter.

9

Real Diversity

Celebrate diversity. Go ahead—liberals do it, conservatives do it, businesses and universities, too. But nobody, it seems, devotes as much energy to diversity as the federal government. On August 18, 2011, President Obama issued Executive Order 13,583, which mandated a "government-wide initiative designed to promote diversity and inclusion in the federal workforce." That order built on various federal statutes and at least half a dozen earlier executive orders over three presidential administrations—all aimed at a "diverse" government. By law, the federal government is required to seek "a workforce from all segments of society."

But why? The only sensible answer is that a diverse government is a better government—that is, a government that produces better results. Certainly that is the thrust of President Obama's diversity push. When the government workforce "reflects the population we serve," argues Obama, "we are better able to understand and meet the needs of our customers—the American people."[1] Geographic diversity is an important part of the Obama approach, because "differences among people concerning where they are from and where they have lived" will also help government to serve the "customer."

Speaking as one of the president's customers, I'd like to make a suggestion: If you really want diversity to bloom, stop trying to run people's lives from Washington. America is naturally diverse: we have 314 million inhabitants spread out over a landmass of more than 9.6 million square miles. Different states and regions have sharply different political cultures, and if diversity is your goal, then why not let states govern themselves? What works for Hawaii may not be right for Maine; why should they be forced to have the same policies? Or, as the political commentator Bill Kauffman argues, "if Marin County wants to serve joints with school lunches and Tupelo, Mississippi, wants the Ten Commandments in the classroom, well, that's up to the people of Marin and Tupelo."[2]

When Washington politicians promote "diversity," they usually mean nothing more than having a demographically varied federal workforce, all of whose members are busy cramming the same one-size-fits-all policies down our throats. The federal diversity agenda is bound to fail on its own terms: a bureaucracy that must implement *national* laws laid down by the 535 members of the *national* legislature will never be able to tailor its programs to serve the "customers." Speaking of customers, according to the American Customer Satisfaction Index, the federal government ranks lower than just about every private-sector industry, including airlines and cable television companies.[3]

When the federal government is in charge, "uniformity wins but diversity loses," according to a 2014 essay in the *Atlantic*.[4] But when state and local governments are empowered, the result is both political and demographic diversity. As Heather Gerken, a Yale law professor, observes, progressives should embrace federalism because state and local governments have become more effective "sites of empowerment for racial minorities and dissenters" than the federal government.[5] Under a system of states' rights, an ambitious Hispanic lawyer in, say, Santa Fe can actually make a difference in his community by participating in state or local government. Instead, far too many talented individuals are drawn to Washington, where they end up as anonymous cogs in the federal machine.

Let States Be States

States continue to outpace the federal government in many policy areas, including those high on the progressive agenda. While Congress has perennially failed to reform rigid federal criminal sentencing laws, for example, the majority of states have fixed theirs.[6] While the federal EPA has not even evaluated 98 percent of chemicals in use today, twenty states have passed more than seventy-seven laws aimed at protecting consumers from specific chemicals.[7] Local and state governments enacted measures to protect the public from asbestos and lead poisoning long before Congress took action.[8] In addition, local authorities often provide stronger civil rights guarantees— more in line with progressive thinking—than does the federal government.

When the federal government imposes top-down policies on the states, however, the results are rarely satisfying for liberals or conservatives. Consider the sorry history of Washington's role in K–12 education. Since 1965, the federal government has spent roughly $2 trillion on education, adjusting for inflation.[9] Federal spending per pupil nearly tripled from $446 in 1970–71 to $1,185 in 2008–09, and it has continued to climb. Congress and the federal education bureaucracy dole out this money according to ever more complicated formulas and programs. When it was first adopted, the 1965 Elementary and Secondary Education Act—the main vehicle for federal K–12 policy—was a mere thirty-two pages. The most recent reauthorization of the act—the No Child Left Behind (NCLB) law—takes up six hundred pages with ten separate titles and more than fifty programs.[10]

This forty-year surge of federal dollars and supposed expertise has had little discernible effect. From 1970 to 2010, math and reading scores for American high school students were stagnant, while science scores showed a slight decline. In essence, American taxpayers are paying three times as much to get the same quality of education they enjoyed in 1970.[11] Could this be a problem of state or local incompetence? Not likely. Consider the school system of Washington, DC, which is unambiguously subject to Congress's ultimate control and which was historically "regarded as one of the worst urban school districts in the country," according to USA Today.[12] The DC schools began to improve in the early years of the century, but only because they adopted a reform that had been pioneered by states: vouchers.

Voucher systems, in which parents get a fixed amount of money that can be used to pay tuition at the school of their choice—public, private, or parochial—are revolutionizing education policy. They foster competition, encourage educators to innovate, and allow parents to match their kids with the most suitable schools. On top of all that, they save taxpayers money, since the vouchers are invariably less expensive than the per-pupil cost of public school. The most rigorous academic studies of such programs have concluded that school choice raises educational standards.[13]

Vouchers began in Wisconsin in 1989 and gradually spread to other states. By 2003, Congress and the Bush administration decided to try vouchers to help DC's failing school system and enacted the DC School Choice Incentive Act. Although the program was successful and popular, the Obama administration killed it in 2009, and then, after it was briefly revived by Congress in 2011, killed it again. Obama justified his opposition to the program by saying that it didn't make "that much of a difference"—as though there is something wrong about a program that helps poor students only *a little bit*.

The president did endorse charter schools—that is, public schools that are organized by local parents and operated by private companies. Just like vouchers, charters are a creature of state innovation: originally proposed by a Michigan educator and first adopted by Minnesota in 1991. Charter schools now operate in forty-two states. They cost less than traditional public schools and do a better job at serving disadvantaged children.[14]

Not one person in Washington's education bureaucracy has been able to produce an idea as powerful as charter schools or vouchers, notwithstanding the billions of dollars funneled through the federal Department of Education every year. These innovations—and countless other small, everyday miracles in K–12 education—come from the states. "The federal government should pretty much get out of the business of education," says Professor John Kincaid of Lafayette College, who points to Canada and Switzerland, where schools are locally controlled and which achieve better education outcomes than those in the

United States.[15] Utah Republican congressman Rob Bishop—a former high school teacher and founder of the Tenth Amendment Task Force—argues that "we've tried everything except giving schools the freedom to be different."[16]

State and local educators now dread each new education initiative coming out of Washington. During the Bush administration, some thirty states of varying political hues passed resolutions denouncing the rigid mandates of No Child Left Behind. Lawsuits challenging aspects of NCLB were filed by the state of Connecticut as well as school districts in Michigan, Texas, and Vermont.[17] Under President Obama, states and school districts have learned to resent the straitjacket of "the Common Core," a set of uniform math and English curriculum standards designed behind closed doors by two private organizations. States were coerced into adopting the Common Core in the depths of the Great Recession as the price for applying for a piece of Obama's $4.35 billion Race to the Top grants, and/or as a precondition for getting a presidential waiver from the NCLB's expensive mandates.

The Common Core has generated its own set of critics, from the left-leaning Brookings Institution to the right-leaning Heritage Foundation, many of whom point out that the curriculum falls far short of its goal of making American schools internationally competitive.[18] Besides, if the Common Core truly represents a world-class curriculum that will make students thrive and parents proud, then presumably states will adopt it without having a gun held to their head. What are the rabid advocates of centralization so afraid of? Afraid that states will arbitrarily reject a fabulous education policy? Or is there some existential threat in the idea that one or two states might want to try something different?

When a policy makes sense, state politicians have every in-centive to adopt it, with or without federal nudging. In im-migration, even though Congress failed to enact a national DREAM Act (providing educational benefits to undocu-mented students), at least sixteen states went ahead and passed their own mini–DREAM laws.[19] For decades, states have pushed ahead in areas where Congress faces perennial gridlock: campaign finance, school vouchers, predatory lending, welfare reform—the list goes on. This is how it should be: when states are free to pick their own packages of reforms, they can actu-ally respond to the needs of their "customers."

Break the Federal Cookie Cutter

Despite the long tradition of state innovation, the entire fed-eral apparatus—Congress, president, bureaucracy, courts, you name it—appears determined to squelch all state and local ef-forts to build policies around their own citizens' preferences. A kid can't ride his bike around the block without implicating federal law. Literally. In order to get their full allotment of fed-eral highway dollars, states have to sign on to the Department of Transportation's "Livability" standards, right down to the requirement that each community connect its bike paths to the US Bicycle Route System, whatever that is.[20] It would, of course, be sheer chaos—anarchy—if cities and towns got to decide for themselves where to put bike paths.

As for ObamaCare, not only did that law prevent red states from pursuing market-based health reforms, but it also deprived deep-blue states of the option of going to the left of Congress. Vermont, for example, might well have adopted a Canadian-style single-payer system by now, but is barred from doing so, unless it can persuade the federal government to grant the state a waiver to get out of the ObamaCare box.

Another thing Vermont would like to do is get rid of the Vermont Yankee nuclear power plant, which the federal Nuclear Regulatory Commission has authorized to operate for twenty years beyond its original forty-year design. The legislature voted to revoke the plant's license, only to be rebuffed by the Obama administration on the grounds that state laws regarding nuclear energy are entirely preempted by federal law. A federal court agreed that the Vermont legislature was illegally attempting to "thwart" the federal regulatory scheme that puts the "radiological safety" of nuclear power exclusively in the hands of the federal government. In other words, once the federal government decides to put a nuclear reactor in your state, you and your representatives have no say in the matter.[21]

The Obama administration has fought to overturn democratically enacted state voter-identification laws, even though opinion polls show that upward of 70 percent of Americans support the simple requirement of voters showing a photo ID at their polling places. Medical marijuana laws—adopted by twenty states and supported by 55 percent of voters[22]—are all preempted by the federal Controlled Substances Act. To the extent states have been able to operate "compassionate use" programs, they have been purely at the sufferance of the federal government. In 2012, federal authorities moved to shut down pot dispensaries in California, prompting Governor Jerry Brown to warn against intrusion by "federal *gendarmes*"— perhaps the first assertion of American states' rights in French.[23] More recently, Obama has pursued a stealth strategy of using the Bureau of Reclamation to block marijuana growers from accessing water for irrigation, even in states where pot is legal.[24]

Competition Works

In recent decades, Congress has also moved to take over the rules governing corporations, which are (or were) pure creatures of state law. After the 2001 revelations of accounting shenanigans at Enron and other corporations, Congress passed the Sarbanes-Oxley Act, which, for the first time, dictated how corporate boards are to be elected, who may serve on the audit committee of the board, how many directors must be independent—and what it means to be "independent." The law represents an "unprecedented intrusion into corporate governance" by the Congress, according to the law professor Jill E. Fisch.[25]

The standard progressive response to anyone who questions the wisdom of a law like Sarbanes-Oxley is that, without such federal laws, states will descend into a ruthless "race to the bottom." Ever since the Progressives warned about a "race" for corporate charters, reformers have argued that unscrupulous corporate managers naturally gravitate to states that allow them to exploit investors. But as Frank Easterbrook, a federal appellate judge, asks, "Why should investors be stupid? They can choose where to put their money."[26]

That's the key: as long as capital is free to migrate elsewhere, states will compete to attract corporations that maximize shareholder value. A similar dynamic holds in banking law, in which states compete to create the most customer-friendly banking regime, because that is how state-chartered banks

A Less Perfect Union

attract deposits. The race to the bottom occurs when a single all-encompassing regulatory regime blocks states from competing for consumers and investors. Which brings us back to Sarbanes-Oxley, which, in fact, did not lead to an enlightened model of corporate governance. Instead, as Judge Easterbrook observes, "the statute requires every corporation that engages in interstate commerce to be governed just like Enron—which had a majority independent board, an 'independent' compensation committee, and met the Act's other requirements."[27] Thus, after reviewing the wreckage of Enron's poor corporate governance, Congress perversely decided to impose the Enron model of governance on the entire nation.

Oddly enough, the nationalists who insist that competition among states is bad are often the very same people who extol the virtues of competition in the private sector. After all, competition is the central tenet of antitrust law: a progressive invention if ever there was. On the website of the Obama Justice Department—the agency responsible for enforcing antitrust law—one learns that "free and open competition benefits consumers by ensuring lower prices and new and better products." If competition among widget makers is good for consumers, then why not competition among governments? President Obama could hardly object to the private sector analogy; after all, he's the one who refers to citizens as "customers."

One gets the distinct impression that the problem with competition is that it hurts politicians, not citizens. Consider the minimum wage. In the spring of 2014, Maryland's governor, Martin O'Malley—who successfully pushed his state to raise the minimum wage to $10.10 over a period of three years—publicly called on Congress to approve a national $10.10 minimum wage because "the truth of the matter is that when workers earn more, businesses have more customers and our economy grows."[28] If that were the truth—if Maryland were enjoying an economic edge over its lower-minimum-wage neighbors Virginia and Delaware—why would O'Malley let the cat out of the bag? Why on earth would he want Congress to wipe out Maryland's comparative advantage by raising the minimum wage everywhere?

The answer is that O'Malley knows that hiking the minimum wage is an economic loser. But it's a political winner, so O'Malley wants to enjoy the political credit for raising the minimum wage while having Congress insulate him from the economic consequences. What happened to the virtues of competition? Essentially, the O'Malley position amounts to an assertion that only Maryland and a few other Democratic states can be trusted to enact decent wage laws; the rest must be forced.

The notion that most states are untrustworthy has become liberal orthodoxy—particularly in the area of green politics. The journalist Conor Friedersdorf notes that, even as progressives embrace states' rights to advance marijuana legalization, most liberals "insist federal power is still needed to protect . . . the environment."[29] At the extreme end of the spectrum, the left-wing blog *Daily Kos* asserts that organizations like the American Legislative Exchange Council that advocate states' rights are part of a vast corporate conspiracy to "gut the laws against environmental degradation."[30] The reigning assumption appears to be that, left to their own devices, the states will drop all environmental standards and let business do whatever it wants. But that assumption runs counter to historical fact, since the states have often enacted environmental protections before the federal government has done so. As Indur Goklany, a former EPA consultant, demonstrates in his book *Clearing the Air*, for each pollutant, there has been a "period of perception" during which the public becomes increasingly concerned about the substance.[31] As the perception of danger grows more widespread, politicians respond to public demands for action—but the faster and more effective response has usually come from state and local governments. An environmental race to the bottom also runs counter to common sense: states are competing not only for industry but for people—taxpayers and workers. Those people, by and large, demand environmental protections.[32]

More broadly, why would any governor—blue or red—engage in a race to the bottom? Why would states compete for the worst infrastructure, the poorest schools, the dirtiest water? And if states get things so wrong, how could one trust Congress to get it right? The exact same voters who elect congressmen also elect governors and state legislators.

Finally, even if the "race" were true, isolated policy fixes like the minimum wage or the Clean Water Act would not solve the problem. If Congress imposes a higher minimum wage, the dodgy states would simply relax some other regulation in order to attract business. As the law professor Richard Revesz points out, "Race-to-the-bottom arguments are frontal attacks on federalism," since the logical conclusion of such arguments is that *every* regulatory and fiscal decision must be federalized—in which case, you might as well shred the Constitution.[33] So much, then, for the race to the bottom.

Small Government, Small Mistakes

The financial crisis that sent so many states into a tailspin was a direct consequence of the national government's meddling in affairs—housing—that properly belong to the states. Under its reserved Tenth Amendment powers, a state may, if it chooses, decide to expand home ownership by subsidizing people to buy houses that they could not otherwise afford. It wouldn't exactly be prudent, and would eventually lead to local housing bubbles as demand outstripped the natural supply. But when Congress decided to make this reckless policy into a national priority, we ended up with a full-scale housing meltdown and a collapse of credit.[34]

"The virtue of small government is that the mistakes are small as well," as Kirkpatrick Sale, the upstate New York liberal guru, wisely observes.[35] More important, the mistakes made in one state serve as a lesson to other states: they naturally try to avoid bad ideas. At the same time, states do try to replicate good ideas. Here again is the virtue of diversity: the failures stay local while the successes go national.

What is the best way to fix America's broken healthcare system? There's no easy answer, but in recent decades the states have experimented with a wide variety of health policies, and have learned from each other's experiences. If Massachusetts had benefited from its individual-mandate health system, other state governors and legislatures would have rushed to follow suit. But they didn't; to the contrary, many states expressly rejected the Massachusetts approach of forcing people into the insurance market. Judge James Graham of the Sixth Circuit Court of Appeals, who voted to strike down ObamaCare as unconstitutional, lamented that the law "brings an end to state experimentation and overrides the expressed legislative will of several states that had guaranteed to their citizens the freedom to choose not to purchase health insurance."[36]

For a glimpse into the future of a one-size-fits-all national health system, consider the federal takeover of mental health, which took place over fifty years ago. In 1963, President John F. Kennedy proposed creating a national system for treating the mentally ill, a responsibility that had previously belonged exclusively to the states. Kennedy outlined a policy to encourage the closing of state psychiatric hospitals and the opening of federally funded community mental health centers, or CMHCs. It was time, said the president, to replace the "cold mercy" of hospital confinement with the "open warmth of community concern and capability."

Congress obliged, ultimately throwing billions at the nascent CMHCs while the states—happy to be relieved of their burdens—promptly shuttered, or shrank, their psychiatric hospitals. But the CMHCs were neither equipped for nor interested in treating patients with the most severe illnesses—for example, schizophrenia and bipolar disorder—who were left on the streets, thanks to the national embrace of "deinstitutionalization." Twenty years into this grand experiment, Dr. Robert Felix, the chief architect of the program, declared it to be a failure. "The result is not what we intended," Felix conceded, "and perhaps we didn't ask the questions that should have been asked when developing a new concept but . . . we tried our damnedest."[37] Well then, A for effort, but what did Congress do about the breakdown of the CMHC program? It has continued to fund it for another thirty years and counting.

Meanwhile the untreated mentally ill have drifted into homelessness—and crime. According to E. Fuller Torrey, a psychiatrist and nationally recognized expert on mental health policy, these individuals "are responsible for 10% of all homicides (and a higher percentage of the mass killings), constitute 20% of jail and prison inmates and at least 30% of the homeless."[38] How's that for the "open warmth of community concern and capability"?

Dr. Torrey is unambiguous about the cause of this mess: it is the hubris of a national government that believed it could replace a century of state-based care with untested theories. "It is fatuous," he argues, "to think that a planning office in Washington can draft coherent regulations to cover both California's Los Angeles County and Montana's Garfield County, both of equal size geographically but one with a population of 9.8 million and the other with a population of 1,184." To build better mental health services, says Dr. Torrey, "the single most important change is to give the responsibility for these services back to the states."[39]

End the Culture War—Now

One reason the Anti-Federalists sought to oppose, or at least limit, government centralization was the sheer difficulty of legislating for a large, diverse population. This was conventional wisdom at the time; as the late historian Herbert Storing observed, eighteenth-century theorists believed that "free, republican governments could extend only over a relatively small territory with a homogenous population."[40] Where a republic is not homogenous, the Anti-Federalists feared, the legislature "would be composed of such heterogeneous and discordant principles as would constantly be contending with each other."[41] A fair description of the US Senate every time a judicial nomination comes up for a vote.

The Federalist response to this concern was a central government that would limit itself to a narrow set of truly national issues in which coordination was essential—trade, defense, patents, bankruptcy, and so on. As Madison observed in the *Federalist* no. 45, the powers delegated to the federal government "are few and defined," whereas the powers of the states "are numerous and indefinite." This was, indeed, a lasting solution to the problem of an extended republic. To this day, congressional gridlock does not arise in debates about weights and measures; even in debates about foreign policy, the need for unity is generally understood. Instead, gridlock is a phenomenon that accompanies federal intervention in areas that properly fall under state jurisdiction: things like environmental protection, labor relations, health and safety, and cultural issues.

In a centralized system, "forty-nine percent of the country may vehemently disagree with the national position yet be powerless to challenge it," as one law review commentator pointed out.[42] Both conservatives and liberals find themselves in the powerless 49 percent, depending on the issue. After passage of the 1996 Defense of Marriage Act (DOMA), which created a federal definition of marriage for the purposes of federal benefits, liberals complained of federal intrusion on the states' right to define marriage. But after 2013, when the Supreme Court and lower federal courts struck down DOMA and began striking down state laws banning same-sex marriage, it was the conservatives' turn to complain about the federalization of marriage law.

Granted, a state can be politically polarized. A liberal in Austin might feel disgruntled by Texas law; a conservative in Sacramento might feel powerless to change the Golden State. But here's the thing: they can vote with their feet. The California conservative can move to Texas; the Texas liberal can move to California (well, if he can find a job). But when socially divisive issues are nationalized, the disaffected citizens have nowhere to go but Canada.

A genuine commitment to states' rights would defuse many of the most hot-button social and cultural issues. Thus, the solutions I discuss elsewhere in the book to restore legislative and regulatory autonomy to the states would inevitably lead to a healthy diversity in public policy as states and cities respond to local preferences. And that means that a much higher percentage of citizens—the "consumers" of government services—would come to believe that they are getting the government they bargained for.

One complicating factor: much of the federalization of social issues has come, not from Congress, but from activist courts that have superseded state laws with judge-made "rights." At first blush, this seems an intractable problem, since nobody can force federal judges to decide cases a certain way. But actually, under the Constitution, Congress has complete control over the appellate jurisdiction of federal courts. In other words, Congress can decide what kind of cases make it to the courts of appeal and the Supreme Court. Congress could, for example, limit or even eliminate the ability of federal courts to overturn state court decisions.

Nothing would better ensure state diversity than letting each state's judiciary have the last word on the laws that touch that state—particularly in the divisive areas of social issues. The only people threatened by that kind of diversity are the control freaks who dominate our current political leadership. Liberals at the national level will have to learn to live with the fact that some states will restrict abortion but not guns—but then, conservatives will have to accept that some states will restrict guns but not abortion. That's what diversity is all about. Celebrate it.

10

A More Competent Government

On March 31, 2014—the final deadline for signing up for ObamaCare coverage—the federal government's online marketplace crashed. Twice.

Critics described this malfunction as an epic failure, but to be fair, it was really just business as usual for healthcare.gov, the jerry-rigged contraption built by the Obama administration to implement its signature policy. When the site launched on October 1, 2013, only 1 percent of those who attempted to enroll were able to do so. In other words, as an e-commerce site, the federal marketplace had a 99 percent failure rate on its opening day. And that was after the government had spent nearly $300 million in contractor payments—three times the initial estimates—to build the site.[1]

When insurers started getting reports from the federal site, it was clear that healthcare.gov could not be trusted to get even basic details, like an individual's gender, right. But then, perhaps that was just as well, since cybersecurity experts testified to Congress that the site could not be trusted to keep such information secure, either.

Two weeks after its launch, healthcare.gov had managed to sign up fewer than 27,000 people from the thirty-six states that relied on the site. Interestingly, the fourteen states that built their own online marketplaces had managed to sign up 79,000 customers. By the end of November 2013, those fourteen states accounted for 62 percent of total health insurance enrollments. In the meantime, the Obama administration threw millions more dollars at the site in a haphazard "tech surge." Finally, by the end of 2013, the federal site, with its thirty-six-state catchment area, had finally caught up with the fourteen go-it-alone states.

Uncle Sam the Incompetent

Let us remember that the main argument for entrusting Washington with extraconstitutional powers is that the federal government allegedly possesses special competence to administer the laws efficiently and fairly. According to the conventional narrative, you can't trust the states to run things. The truth is just the opposite: it is the federal government that is utterly hopeless at running things. Consider the Department of Veterans Affairs, whose secretary was forced to resign in the spring of 2014 after it turned out that officials at VA hospitals had been manipulating patient waiting lists.[2] Or take the Transportation Security Administration (please)—the federalized airport security agency that has proved to be even worse than the private cartel it replaced. And then there's the US Department of Agriculture, which from 2008 to 2012 paid $22 million to some 3,400 crop insurance policyholders, all of whom were dead.[3]

It has been thus since Franklin Roosevelt realized that the central government could not actually implement his New Deal programs, leading him to launch the Second New Deal, which was primarily administered by the states. Likewise with Lyndon Johnson's Great Society programs—they were designed in Washington but implemented via the states. The states have much more hands-on administrative experience than the federal government. Think your local DMV is bad? Just try getting answers from the Social Security Administration or the IRS.

The myth of central government competence has been handed down from generation to generation. Woodrow Wilson argued that the biggest problem facing American democracy is the fact that power is "dispersed," whereas it ought to be "concentrated." With a firm belief in "the almost unlimited potential of science and administration," as the historian Richard L. McCormick notes, Wilson and his fellow Progressives envisioned a powerful central government composed of "independent" administrative agencies staffed by technical wizards who would correct the mistakes of the free market.[4] The independent federal agency proved to be an indispensable vehicle for future presidents—from FDR and his "Brain Trust" of Mussolini-worshipping academics to Barack Obama, who vowed to make government "cool" with tech-savvy initiatives.

The actual results have been less than impressive. The majority of federal employees, according to recent surveys, do not believe that their agencies attract employees with the right skills, make promotions based on merit, or take steps to deal with poor performers. Indeed, the firing rate for poor performers in the federal government is about 0.03 percent—or 1 in 3,000—per year.[5] In the early 1990s, a survey revealed that federal employees themselves considered 25 to 50 percent of their colleagues to be utterly useless. Among the useless employees was the Federal Aviation Administration weather checker in Kansas who repeatedly told his superiors that his job was pointless.[6] Small wonder the American people gave the federal government low marks in recent customer satisfaction surveys. While nearly half of all Americans trust state and local government to deliver competent service, only a third trust the federal government to do so.[7]

It's hard enough for any government entity to produce a decent policy, but the problems are "vastly magnified by the centralization in Washington of most key decisions, despite the fact that the information needed to formulate and implement them is located a universe away," notes Peter Schuck, a Yale Law School professor. "How can central policy makers gather and aggregate all of this vastly dispersed information into effective policy?" asks Schuck. "The short answer is, they can't—however smart they are and however hard they try."[8]

It should come as no surprise, then, that so many of the federal government's grand experiments have been flops: Consider the perennial attempts to determine the "scientifically" best use of public lands, the optimal amount of competition in the private sector, the most effective treatment for mental illness, the proper composition of school lunches, the ideal level of home ownership—all of these efforts, and hundreds more, have been either ineffective or counterproductive.

Honest observers on both sides of the aisle have recognized that the federal bureaucracy is simply not up to the job that Congress has given it. For that matter, Congress is not up to the job it has given itself. By 2000, the late New York senator Daniel Patrick Moynihan—a New Deal liberal—was ready to concede that federal micromanagement had gone too far:

> After some 40 years in Washington, I attest that we get involved in far too many miniature issues. School uniforms. This need not be done from Washington. *Can't* be done effectively. It belongs to levels of government closer to the problems involved.[9]

This tendency to meddle in "miniature issues" is partly responsible for the federal government's inability to cope with big issues. The central government should be focused on its core constitutional duties, such as defense, foreign affairs, international trade, and immigration. Instead, it regularly succumbs to the temptation to expand its reach into new domestic initiatives. Each new initiative is a further distraction for Congress and federal agencies.[10] Is it pure coincidence that the president and Congress have consistently fumbled national security issues at a time when they have been obsessed with regulating health insurance, student loans, school lunches, and greenhouse gases?

In 2010, Michael Waddoups, the president of the Utah Senate, and David Clark, the Speaker of the Utah House, made the unimpeachable argument in the *Washington Post* that "535 members of Congress and the president [cannot] educate our children, provide healthcare, pave our roads and protect our environment as well as the nation's 8,000 state legislators and tens of thousands of local officials." Accordingly, the legislators made a "modest proposal" to the federal government: "select a few programs—say, education, transportation, and Medicaid. Let Utah take over these programs entirely."[11] The federal government did not take them up on the proposal. The results would have been too embarrassing.

Get Money Where It's Needed

One advantage of states' rights is that your tax dollars might actually end up doing some good instead of feeding multiple levels of bureaucracy. The current system, in which taxes from residents of the fifty states get funneled through Washington and then redistributed back to the states, is based on the "belief that policy makers can dispassionately allocate large sums of money across hundreds of activities based on a rational plan designed in Washington," according to Chris Edwards, an economist who runs the Cato Institute's Downsizing Government project.[12] In other words, it's the old Progressive faith in the all-knowing central government.

The reality is that there is no overall plan—rational or otherwise—by which the federal government doles out money to states, cities, organizations, and individuals. Federal grants arise from a jumbled collection of overlapping programs with no organizing principle whatsoever. In 1960, there were a mere 132 of these programs; today, there are over 2,200.

You can learn all about federal financial aid in the *Catalog of Federal Domestic Assistance* (*CFDA*), a publication not to be read unless strong coffee is at hand. Today's federal grants include a program to promote "nursing workforce diversity," assistance for "socially disadvantaged farmers," grants for "healthy marriages," and subsidies for solar panels at bus stops. Since 1971, the federal government has provided grants for "recreational boating safety"—in 2013 alone, the government spent $118 million reminding yachtsmen to wear their life jackets. So vital is this program that it comes under the purview of the Department of Homeland Security—and so rationally administered that landlocked Nebraska gets more money for recreational boating safety than Hawaii.

Even if one thinks that every program in the *CFDA* represents a worthy cause, it would be hard to imagine a worse mechanism for funding those causes than federal grants. Consider the life cycle of a typical grant program. First, taxpayer money is shipped to Washington, where a large slice is taken off the top to feed the bureaucracy needed to administer the program. Then state governments must spend money for personnel to make the necessary applications to get a portion of their money back. That's no small endeavor: a single antidrug grant program required a seventy-four-page application that references thirteen hundred pages of regulations. The federal government then spends more money picking winners and losers among the applicants. When the states finally get their money, they must take a further cut to pay for the overhead costs of distributing the funds to local governments. In programs like this, "bureaucracy [could] eat up a quarter of the overall funding," according to Chris Edwards.[13]

What if, for example, cities and towns that border on recreational waterways took responsibility for their own boating safety programs? These could be funded by a small tax on vessel licenses or marina slips. Safety courses could be outsourced to any number of nonprofit organizations; indeed, the Coast Guard already uses such organizations to teach boating safety. Instead of paying for bureaucrats, nearly all of the money would be put to use in the very communities where it is needed. No longer would the landlubbers of Hawaii be forced to subsidize the salty old dogs of Nebraska.

Cut the Waste

Federal grants are not merely inefficient, they're positively wasteful. For one thing, they push states into massive over-spending. State politicians create gold-plated programs that wouldn't exist at all, or that would be much smaller, if the state were not incentivized to capture its maximum share of federal dollars. There is little downside for a state politician bringing home federal funds that are widely perceived as "free money."[14]

And then there is the more prosaic form of waste—old-fashioned mismanagement. In 2011, for example, federal agencies made roughly $115.3 billion in "improper payments"—that is, they paid too much, or they paid the wrong recipient. Disaster assistance loans were off by a whopping 28 percent; school breakfast grants, 25 percent; the Child Care and Development Fund messed up over 11 percent of its payments.[15]

Overall, federal agencies had an error rate of nearly 4.7 percent—compared with the private sector, in which an error rate of less than one half of 1 percent is more typical.[16] This level of mismanagement has been going on for some years; in a 2006 hearing, Senator Tom Coburn asked (rhetorically), "Can you imagine the Accounts Payable Department at Microsoft or Wal-Mart reporting an error rate of 28 percent, or even 3 percent?"[17] Heads, as they say, would roll.

In case you were wondering, we know about these improper payments only because Congress has forced the agencies to divulge the information under the Improper Payments Elimination and Recovery Act of 2010—a law that replaced earlier efforts to root out fiscal malfeasance. The law mandates that agencies do their best to recapture improper payments, but according to the Office of Management and Budget, the

agencies managed to claw back a mere $1.25 billion in 2011—
not much out of a total of $115.3 billion.[18] Indeed, according to
the Government Accountability Office, only forty-two of the
seventy-nine federal programs reporting improper payments
even bothered to analyze the causes of their costly mistakes.[19]

Even when federal expenditures are technically "proper,"
they are often misused. In 2014, Congress appropriated $65
million for Pacific salmon conservation—$15 million more
than the administration had requested—even though environmental experts argued that the government was already over-
spending on salmon conservation.[20] Professor Paul C. Light, an
expert in public administration (and generally sympathetic to
federal power), estimated in 2011 that the federal government
could cut $1 trillion in wasteful spending over ten years—if
only it could muster the political will to do so.[21] Good luck
with that one.

On top of all that, there are less noticeable forms of waste,
such as the opportunity cost represented by millions of acres of
idle federal land, as well as "spillover costs" arising from the fact
that federal regulations often impose burdens that far exceed
any quantifiable benefit to society. According to a 1995 study
by two public policy experts, if you added up all the varieties
of waste in federal programs, "the total could easily exceed half
of the federal government's exhaustive expenditures."[22] Think
about that: half of your federal taxes up in smoke, with no net
benefits to the citizen. So remind me: Why do we insist on
centralizing more and more power in Washington?

None of this is meant to suggest that state and local governments are immune from waste; rather, the point is that transferring responsibility and money to Washington yields absolutely no advantage in terms of efficiency. The way to achieve

efficiency in government is through competition, a virtuous competition among the states. When states have control over their own fiscal houses, they engage in two forms of competition that balance each other out. On the one hand, there is "expenditure competition," in which states compete to provide better infrastructure and services than their neighboring states. The urge to spend, however, is kept in check by a countervailing "tax competition"—nobody wants to be the high-tax state in the region.[23] But when states rely on Washington for upward of half of their revenue (and when bailouts are implicitly on offer for imprudent states), there's nothing left but the expenditure competition. Trillions of dollars later, what we've accomplished is mainly the enrichment of a class of bureaucratic middlemen, lobbyists, and government contractors.

Help the Poor, for a Change

And still nationalists will defend the Washington money merry-go-round in the name of "helping the poor." We must have a *national* redistribution of wealth, the argument goes, to even out economic disparities among regions. In other words, only the federal government can force Silicon Valley to subsidize Appalachia. Even on those terms, federal grants fail miserably. In the decades since President Lyndon Johnson declared a war on poverty in 1964, Americans have spent around $16 trillion on means-tested welfare programs; and yet, poverty rates today are higher than in the 1970s.[24] As Peter Ferrara, a scholar at the Heartland Institute, puts it, "We fought the War on Poverty, and poverty won."[25]

Only a fraction of the dollars spent on federal antipoverty

programs actually make it to the poor. Study after study—going back to the 1980s at least—has shown that federal aid programs have never consistently transferred money from rich areas to poor ones.[26] A good example is Title I, a federal grant program for disadvantaged schools. In 2013, Fairfax County, Virginia—one of the top ten richest counties in the nation—got over $19 million in Title I aid. Some Title I money does reach poor school districts; however, the state and county governments simply make corresponding budget cuts, meaning that the schools are no better off than they were before they got the Title I aid.[27]

In 2007, federal Medicaid spending per person in the five poorest states averaged $3,547, while in the five richest states it averaged $5,405—almost $2,000 more per capita for rich states.[28] In other words, when it comes to Medicaid, Appalachia is subsidizing Silicon Valley. Forty percent of all direct federal transfer payments go to families with above-average incomes, according to a 1993 study[29]—a figure that is unlikely to have improved, particularly given such recent trends as the "green energy" programs that force middle-class taxpayers to subsidize rich people who want to buy solar panels and six-figure electric cars.

The reason for this misallocation is not hard to find: politics. Federal grants are divvied up according to formulas ultimately set by congressmen who are primarily interested in getting reelected, or by cabinet secretaries who are primarily interested in scoring political points for the president. When politics dictates the allocation of tax dollars—as it always will—money will flow to the well connected. In 2004, for example, Senator Conrad Burns redirected a $3 million grant for Indian tribal schools in poor reservations to the Saginaw

Tribe of Michigan—already wealthy from casino money—at the behest of a major campaign donor.[30]

The Community Development Block Grant (CDBG) program—intended for impoverished communities—is perennially misallocated. In 1995, wealthy Greenwich, Connecticut, received five times more funding per low-income resident than poorer Camden, New Jersey.[31] In the 2002 budget, CDBG money went toward traffic lights in upscale Newton, Massachusetts—which happened to be the home of Congressman Barney Frank, then the ranking member of the Committee on Financial Services, who had a history of intervening to preserve CDBG funds for his district.

Restoring control to states would not end political corruption, but it would put a big dent in pork barrel politics as currently practiced. As long as citizens see Washington as a magical ATM, there is no price to pay for delivering pork; to the contrary, it's a virtue. Congressman Frank did not suffer politically for steering money to Newton. Why should he? It wasn't Massachusetts's money, it was Washington's money. Now, imagine that a *Governor* Frank took state money that was meant for depressed areas of Boston and redirected it to his politically connected neighbors. Suddenly, there would be real outrage, because Bay Staters would correctly perceive that their own tax dollars were going to waste.

Historically, the other major argument for federal grants was Keynesian—that is, that federal spending helps the poor by stimulating the economy. There are some economists who still believe that theory, but after the disastrous stimulus efforts of the Obama administration, those economists must be counted as delusional (see, e.g., Krugman, Paul). The American Recovery and Reinvestment Act of 2009—Obama's primary stimulus package—sucked nearly a trillion dollars out of the private economy and put the money into such economic growth engines as "victim services," preserving "cultural artifacts," and restoring "native plant habitats." The stimulus also included a series of grants known as Transportation Investment Generating Economic Recovery, or TIGER, an acronym presumably meant to evoke images of East Asia's economic "tigers." The TIGER-funded projects included new and improved bike lanes and pedestrian walkways in Boston and "traffic calming and streetscaping improvements" in Olean, New York. Look out, China!

And what was the return on our trillion-dollar investment? The deepest recession followed by the most anemic recovery since . . . well, since FDR's ill-conceived stimulus programs. In a true federalist system, states would be free to try to spend their way to economic growth, if they must, but the consequences would be local, state taxpayers would hold politicians accountable, and other states would soon learn their lesson.

End Duplicative Programs

Would waste and inefficiency be even worse in a world of states' rights? There is a belief—reasonable in theory—that the federal government at least manages to consolidate and, therefore, streamline the otherwise disparate efforts of the fifty states. The mainstream view is captured by Rick Newman, a columnist for *U.S. News & World Report*, who argues that returning power to the states is a "bad idea" because we'll end up with "fifty different sets of rules."[32]

Take homelessness. It's a national problem, so under the

Newman logic, the federal government must take responsibility for it, lest the nation be saddled with fifty different programs for the homeless. Actually, the federal government *did* take responsibility for homelessness and there *are* fifty different programs—all of them federal and spread out over eight different agencies. On top of that, there are twenty-three different programs for housing aid in four agencies.[33]

The federal government's fragmented approach to homelessness is par for the course. Economic development? There are 342 federal programs for that. At-risk youths? One hundred and thirty federal programs for them.[34] Employment and training? Forty-four different programs. There are at least a hundred different federal programs for surface transportation, eighty-two for teacher quality, fifty-four for financial literacy, eighteen for food assistance. No fewer than seven federal agencies share responsibility for water quality along the US–Mexico border.[35]

If you live in rural America, you've hit the jackpot. Over 1,300 federal programs in multiple agencies are devoted to shoveling money into rural areas. Are those programs coordinated? Take a guess. Federal officials cannot even agree on the meaning of the word "rural." According to a 2013 report in the *Washington Post*, "The U.S. government has at least fifteen official definitions of the word 'rural,' two of which apply only to Puerto Rico and parts of Hawaii."[36] Under one definition, Pennsylvania's capital, Harrisburg, counts as rural.

Nothing prevents Congress from merging similar programs except politics. There are approximately 250 committees and subcommittees in Congress, and each one wants to have its own set of grant programs to oversee. Even when a program proves to be ineffective, Congress rarely kills it, for fear of offending somebody. Instead, Congress creates a new program to exist side by side with the old one.[37] In 2008, for example, Congress created a new office in the Department of Agriculture to inspect catfish, even though the Food and Drug Administration already had a long-standing program that covered catfish. By 2013, the USDA had spent $20 million to establish the office and $14 million a year to run it, but had yet to inspect a single catfish.[38]

Whenever an issue becomes "hot," federal agencies will design programs around it to attract yet more congressional funding. The September 11 attacks, for example, led to a huge outpouring of support for first responders—as one would expect—and now there are at least sixteen overlapping federal grant programs to subsidize first responders. President Obama followed in his predecessor's footsteps, pouring money willy-nilly into anything that smacked of homeland security. The administration's fiscal 2014 budget proposed $670 million of federal grants to subsidize local fire departments—an institution that had survived without federal subsidies since Ben Franklin's day.[39] In general, the Department of Homeland Security grant programs are plagued by incompetence. One county in Washington State, for example, got $63,000 for hazmat equipment even though the county had no hazmat team.[40]

Fewer and more precisely defined federal programs are anathema to empire builders in Congress and the bureaucracy. And so the federal budget is riddled with hundreds of overlapping programs with nebulous mission statements. Consider the Rural Strategic Investment Program, whose purpose is to "provide rural communities with flexible resources to develop . . . strategic planning processes; and implement development strategies." Who knows what that means?

Yes, if the problem of homelessness were left to the states—as intended by the Tenth Amendment—we would have fifty different homeless programs as in the current system. But at least those programs would be organized by a rational principle— physical geography—rather than political turf. And if there was some interstate spillover of the homeless population between, say, Illinois and Missouri, then the states could easily coordinate or even form an interstate compact to address the issue.

End It, Don't Mend It

The federal government is impervious to reform. Not that various administrations haven't tried to overhaul the executive branch. Indeed, it is safe to say that a more efficient federal government is right around the corner—and has been since 1910. In that year, President William Howard Taft convened a commission on economy and efficiency, a group of "accountants and experts" who would, for the first time, analyze the entire federal machinery with a view toward "the integration of all administrative agencies of the Government, so far as may be practicable, into a unified organization for the most effective and economical dispatch of public business." The commission's best-known proposal—the creation of a consolidated budget—is significant mainly in that it demonstrates that the federal government lasted for more than a century without having a coherent spending blueprint. The commission's other recommendations tended toward trivial administrative matters, including a hearty recommendation to introduce window envelopes in federal service.[41]

Reform of the federal government became a standard gimmick of each new presidential administration: Hoover, Carter, Reagan, Clinton, and Bush, among others, all pushed administrative reform.[42] Congress has been even more active— hyperactive, in fact. Between 1945 and 2002, Congress passed 177 "major" bureaucratic reform statutes, according to Paul C. Light.[43] Notwithstanding these efforts, the federal bureaucracy remains mired in the organizational structure laid down by Hoover in the 1930s. Meanwhile, the dream of executive efficiency is dashed by the metastasizing layers of management. The number of federal executive titles nearly doubled between 1992 and 2004 (the last time anyone counted), meaning that we now have twice as many principal associate deputy undersecretaries who are responsible for—well, they're not actually responsible for anything. That's the point.

Instead of launching Reform #178, how about changing the whole mission of the national government? Letting states exercise their right to self-government will bring a host of benefits, not least of which is fidelity to our supreme law, the Constitution. The notion that real federalism entails a loss of federal government expertise is a pure myth. This isn't France, where the top national bureaucrats are trained in special academies reserved only for them. Waddoups and Clark—of the "modest proposal" fame—point out that Utah's civil servants "attend the same public administration schools, go to many of the same conferences, [and] read the same journals as do their federal counterparts. Our administrators belong to professional organizations where they meet with their peers, learn the latest management techniques, and exchange information about best practices."[44]

Moreover, although both state and federal officials must ultimately answer to politicians, state politicians tend to be more pragmatic and disciplined than their federal overlords.[45] They have to be: every state save Vermont is legally required to balance its budget; nearly half of the states have overall tax or expenditure limits; and most governors, and many state legislatures, are subject to term limits. While Congress increasingly bundles unrelated pieces of legislation into vast omnibus bills that nobody reads, most states have rules that limit bills to a single subject.[46]

The common knock that states' rights is anachronistic—the Tenth Amendment is "quaint," says *U.S. News*'s Newman—has no basis. Look at Switzerland, where the majority of taxing and spending is done by the cantons, their version of states, and where the central government accounts for just 14 percent of total expenditures. Compared to the United States, Switzerland has healthier public finances, stronger infrastructure, and better schools. Interestingly, Swiss citizens also have a much higher degree of trust in their national government—the highest, in fact, among all industrial democracies.[47] Perhaps when the central government sticks to its core competencies, the people will trust it more.

Centralization is the real anachronism. It reflects the mindset of the early twentieth century, when rapid industrialization created new and complex interstate problems, but primitive information technology made it difficult to coordinate the response to such problems. When only a limited group of experts had the ability to access and interpret the relevant data, and when communication was difficult, it arguably made sense to centralize decision-making. Be that as it may, those conditions no longer obtain. Expertise is far more diffuse than it was in the Progressive Era; any state government can hire or consult with the experts that it needs. In fact, most of the federal government's experts are not full-time employees but independent contractors. They can just as easily be contracted out to the states.

And then there's technology, which allows people in Anchorage to access the exact same data as people in DC. The Internet also makes it easy for state officials to collaborate with their counterparts in sister states on common problems. Technology favors decentralization—federalism is just one flavor of decentralization in which state and local officials crowdsource, if you will, the best policies. We no longer need the central bureaus and blue-ribbon commissions of the "horse and buggy" set. Nowadays, the best ideas come from the bottom up—from state and local governments.

11

A Lasting Peace

Tennesseans watching the news on March 16, 2014, could hardly avoid the emotional footage of local families bidding farewell to the National Guard units that had left the state that morning on their way to Afghanistan. The deployment order had come without much advance warning. Each guardsman was allowed to spend about an hour with his or her family before going overseas for thirteen months. "This is my third deployment," said Captain Daniel Isley, "and I thought it would get easier. It's actually a little harder leaving the family."[1]

Scenes like this were not supposed to play out under President Obama. Five years earlier—in fact, on the day after Obama's January 20, 2009, inauguration—a coalition of peace groups converged on the National Press Club in Washington to announce the Bring the Guard Home campaign. Ben Manski, the executive director of the Liberty Tree Foundation, assailed the outgoing president, George W. Bush, for using the state National Guard units as a tool of "empire building."[2] But now Manski and his colleagues were going to put an end to this misuse of the National Guard.

How? They would push legislation allowing each state governor to *nullify*—there's no other word for it—federal orders to
deploy National Guard troops. The constitutional argument
for this flavor of nullification is straightforward: under the
Constitution, the National Guard (as the presumed successor
to the state militias) can be pressed into federal service for three
reasons—and invading other countries is not one of them. To
be precise, the militia may be called into federal service (1)
to defend against invasions; (2) to suppress insurrections; or
(3) to execute federal laws (Article I, Section 8). Those three
circumstances, said James Madison, represent "the only cases
wherein [Congress] can interfere with the militia." Otherwise,
the militia was intended to remain firmly under state control.
Constitutionally speaking, the federal government has no right
to compel a governor to deploy his or her Guard units in support of a foreign war—assuming, again, that the Guard is the
equivalent of the state militia.

Bring the Guard Home (BTGH) resolutions began to appear at the state and local level during the Bush years—they
had no effect, but progressives blamed that on the reactionary forces in the Bush-Cheney White House. In January 2009,
however, hope and change were in the air. Vermont BTGH activist Ben Scotch cheerfully predicted that the inauguration of
a new president with "a humane ethic and a sound view of the
Constitution" meant that the movement to bring the Guard
home would finally have a sympathetic ear in Washington.[3]

How's that "humane ethic" working out? Not so well for
the Tennessee Guard—nor for any of the thousands of guardsmen deployed to Afghanistan, Iraq, or other hot spots under
President Obama's leadership. Although Obama accelerated
the withdrawal from Iraq, and moved to wind down the war in

Afghanistan, he has never endorsed the BTGH movement—to the contrary, he has opposed efforts to give governors greater control over Guard deployments.

Since September 11, 2001, there have been over 760,000 individual mobilizations of National Guard members. At the peak of the war on terror, the Army Guard provided about 40 percent of the troops on the ground in Iraq and Afghanistan—and earned 5,703 Purple Hearts in the process. Army Guard members are serving or have served in thirty-one countries, including Kosovo, Bahrain, Qatar, Kuwait, and Djibouti. The special forces units of the Guard are even better traveled: in fiscal 2014, they deployed to sixty-five countries worldwide.[4] The National Guard, in short, is pretty much everywhere *but* home.

Defenders of the status quo argue that today's National Guard is a fantastic deal for the states because it provides an all-purpose local response force and the federal government pays 95 percent of its costs. But why is that a great deal? Why should state taxpayers have to pay even 5 percent of the cost of a federal reserve force—which is how the Pentagon views the Guard? What do the states get in return? A body of troops that the governor may occasionally borrow when the president isn't using them. Which isn't very often. In 2005, for example, Montana's governor, Brian Schweitzer, had to ask permission to deploy his own state's Guard units to combat devastating wildfires. Permission was denied—the units were needed overseas.[5]

Cut Back on Foreign Adventures

Once upon a time, state governors played a useful role in restraining Washington's war fever. Remember that in 1812 a number of New England states refused to contribute their militia units to President Madison's initial troop mobilization, the purpose of which was to mount an invasion of Canada. The states were justified in doing so since, as already noted, an offensive war is not a legitimate basis to federalize state militia units. Of course, when the British retaliated by invading the United States, it was time to defend the homeland. But the British would not have been provoked in the first place had the hawks in Washington appreciated the level of state resistance to their plan of conquest.

There's a basic principle at work here: the larger one's military force, the more tempting it is to throw one's weight around. At the Constitutional Convention of 1787, one of the delegates, Elbridge Gerry, famously compared a standing army to an erect penis: "an excellent assurance of domestic tranquility, but a dangerous temptation to foreign adventure."[6] Gerry was referring to the proposed federal standing army, not state militias. But today, the two are merged: the Army National Guard provides 52 percent of the "Total Army" infantry brigade combat teams, and 50 percent of the combat engineers.[7]

Can there be any question that the federalization of our state militias has increased the temptation to embark on "foreign adventures"? Is there any question that we'd have fewer such adventures if the president suddenly had only half as many troops at his disposal to send overseas?

The Founders made a deliberate decision to keep the militias under state control—it's not as though they were unaware of alternative possibilities. At the Philadelphia convention, the delegates decisively rejected Alexander Hamilton's proposal that the "Militia of all the States [should] be under the sole and exclusive direction" of the central government. During the first Congress, the secretary of war, Henry Knox, proposed legislation to establish a national militia organized, trained, and outfitted by the federal government. Not even the Federalist-dominated Congress would approve such a centralized plan. Instead, Congress passed the Militia Act of 1792, which perpetuated the decentralized model dating back to colonial times.[8] In 1820, the Supreme Court affirmed that the states retain concurrent authority with the president to mobilize the militia, even in times of foreign invasion.[9]

Throughout the nineteenth century, the state militias remained largely independent, and received only modest financial aid from Washington. That began to change with the Militia Act of 1903, which, in classic congressional style, dangled the possibility of more money for state militias—provided the governors accepted federal dictates on the organization and use of the militia.

The states succumbed to federal bribery. By 1908, federal aid for state militias—or National Guard units, as they had become known—had increased tenfold over the levels of the 1890s. Now that the states were hooked, Congress declared that the Guard must be available for federal service at any time and at any place—including overseas. In 1912, Attorney General George Wickersham advised President Taft not to make use of this new power, because nothing in the Constitution authorizes the president to order militiamen to serve outside the United States.[10] But the Constitution was rapidly being swept aside. Woodrow Wilson engineered further legislative gimmicks to federalize the Guard, and when the United States entered World War I in 1917, guardsmen made up over 20 percent of the American Expeditionary Force.[11]

The "Dual Status" Charade

In 1933, Congress took the next logical step by making the National Guard into a reserve component of the US Army. Technically, the state Guard units now had "dual status," state and federal. Each incoming guardsman would also become a member of the Army Reserves—whether he liked it or not— and would swear an oath to serve both masters. "Dual status" may sound like a compromise between state and federal governments, but that's the problem—there was no need or constitutional authority for such a compromise: the militia was intended to remain under exclusive state control, except in dire emergencies. It's as though Congress passed a law declaring that each state's governor now has "dual status," as the head of state government but also as a functionary of the federal government. Come to think of it, that wouldn't be too far from the truth.

In any event, "dual status" was a constitutional fig leaf to cover up the naked takeover of the state militias by the federal government. According to John Brinkerhoff, a former FEMA and Department of Defense official, "The National Guard is no longer the militia. . . . the National Guard is funded, organized, trained, and equipped by the Federal Government to wage war overseas."[12] For much of the Cold War, dual status was tolerated because Guard units saw little active duty overseas. For the most part, the units remained in their states but were hypothetically available to the Pentagon in the event of war with the Soviet bloc. Moreover, federal law prohibited the president from calling guardsmen to active duty without the consent of the affected governors. Governors would always face pressure to consent to mobilizations, whether out of patriotism or from the fear of jeopardizing federal funds, but still, they could withhold their consent. That's what happened in 1985, when Maine's governor refused to allow forty-eight members of the state's National Guard to participate in a training mission to Honduras. The point was symbolic—we're talking about fewer than fifty guardsmen—but the governor wanted to protest President Reagan's policies in Central America. So great was the furor over Maine's defiance that Congress enacted (after a ten-minute debate) the Montgomery Amendment, which prohibits governors from withholding consent to Guard deployments outside the United States because of objections to the mission.[13] Keep in mind, Congress was not saying that governors could *never* object to foreign deployments—heaven forbid!—they just could not object to the "location, purpose, type, or schedule" of such deployments. Governors would remain perfectly free to critique the color of the uniforms.

A number of governors, led by Minnesota's Rudy Perpich, challenged the Montgomery Amendment in court. But they made a glaring strategic error: they refused to challenge the "dual status" charade—apparently, because they were afraid they might win, and thus lose the money that dual status brings.[14] Lacking the courage to strike at the root cause of National Guard subservience, the governors got what they deserved: the Montgomery Amendment was upheld by a divided panel of the Eighth Circuit Court of Appeals. After all, if a state guardsman is also a federal reservist, then he is subject to the president's orders just like any other member of the national army (*Perpich v. Department of Defense*).

Two dissenting judges in the *Perpich* case blasted the Montgomery Amendment for making the state militias "available to the federal government any time the federal government wants, to do anything the federal government desires. This cannot be right."[15] The governors took their case to the Supreme Court, but lost again, in a unanimous decision handed down in June 1990. And just in time for Uncle Sam: the following February, more than two hundred thousand reservists/guardsmen were called up for service in Operation Desert Storm. The rest, as they say, is history.

Thwart Domestic Despots

The Founding Fathers thought it was a bad idea to put all of America's military forces under the control of a single centralized government—so bad that few statesmen of the founding era, other than Hamilton, even considered it. The Constitution recognizes the practical need for the federal government to have a standing army, but Federalists and Anti-Federalists alike worried about the potential use of a standing army in the hands of a despot. The way to neutralize this danger was to guarantee to each state an independent militia as a counterweight to the federal army. As Professor Akhil Amar states, the militias were viewed as a necessary defense of freedom "should tyrannous national leaders attempt a coup."[16]

In the *Federalist* no. 46, James Madison argued that if national leaders attempted to use the standing army to oppress the people, the states "would be able to repel the danger" because they could collectively deploy "a militia amounting to near half a million citizens with arms in their hands, officered by men chosen from among themselves."

These days, anyone who seriously believes that states should resist federal *military* power is pretty much written off as a nut

job. The idea that the federal government has even the potential to behave despotically is considered anachronistic, and
thus, people who quote the Founding Fathers on the topic are,
at best, nostalgic Tea Party types and, at worst, domestic ter-
rorists.

But wait: during the George W. Bush presidency, it was
liberals who insisted that the National Guard had become an
instrument of "empire building"—and they argued that states
must block federal mobilization orders. In 2005, the Democratic governor of Louisiana snubbed President Bush by refusing to cede control of her state's Guard units during Hurricane
Katrina.[17] When Congress responded by granting the president
expanded powers to federalize the National Guard, progressives (and many conservatives) howled that tyranny was just
around the corner. The president now had "king-like power,"
according to the former adjutant general of Washington State.[18]
Forty-nine governors of all political stripes protested that the
new legislation—it was part of the 2007 Defense Authorization
Act—was a dangerous attempt to "usurp" their constitutional
powers over the Guard. Patrick Leahy, the famously progressive senator from Vermont, objected that the law would "make
it easier for presidents to declare martial law."[19] Within a year,
Congress repealed the offending provision.

If federal tyranny is something that sensible people no longer worry about, why should anyone care about presidential
control over the Guard? Why fret over a president having
"king-like" powers, if we are so sure that he or she will never
use them? Why raise the specter of martial law unless it was
within the realm of possibility?

The fear of a reactionary president imposing martial law
goes way back—at least to the 1980s. In 1987, the *Miami Herald*

reported that the Reagan administration had a secret plan to declare martial law in the event of a perceived emergency, including "national opposition to a US military invasion abroad."[20] Although this secret plan was never confirmed, a 1996 book written by a progressive academic, Christian Smith, and published by the University of Chicago Press states that "evidence strongly suggests that in 1984, the [National Security Council] and FEMA collaborated in designing a top-secret contingency plan, named Rex 84, to suspend the US Constitution, declare martial law, appoint military commanders to run state and local governments, and detain masses of people considered to be national security threats."[21] People continue to write about Rex 84 amid allegations that subsequent administrations harbor the same, or similar, contingency plans.

Right, Left, Right

I have no idea whether Rex 84 or anything like it currently exists or ever existed. If such a plan does exist, the federal government probably lacks the basic competence to carry it out properly. Be that as it may, we do know that both the Bush and Obama administrations have asserted the right to detain US citizens indefinitely as part of the war on terror—just as FDR detained thousands of Americans in World War II. Moreover, the fact that progressive academics, journalists, and politicians consider it plausible that a president might someday use military power for illiberal purposes suggests that the Founding Fathers were onto something when they sought to preserve the state militias. If a centralized military apparatus evokes fear of martial law—even remote fears—why not try a decentralized one?

Conservatives and liberals both espouse a decentralized military structure. The problem is that they don't espouse it at the same time. In the fiscal 2015 defense budget, the Republican House of Representatives included a provision clarifying that governors and state adjutants general would have "principal" authority over Guard units performing domestic operations such as firefighting. Based on their Bush-era rhetoric, progressives should have welcomed this assurance of local control of the Guard, but the Obama White House immediately blasted the measure as an "unwarranted intrusion on the authorities of the president and secretary of defense."[22] Sounds awfully like somebody wants "king-like" powers over the Guard.

During Obama's presidency, peace groups that once sought gubernatorial control over the Guard quietly dropped the issue. The Bring the Guard Home movement cannot be found on the web; the site of the Liberty Tree Foundation no longer mentions BTGH. Indeed, the most prominent organization promoting BTGH legislation during the Obama years has been the Tea Party–aligned Tenth Amendment Center.

For many progressive groups, the only problem with the National Guard under Obama is that states have *too much* control. This "problem" came to light in 2013 when the secretary of defense, Chuck Hagel, ordered equal spousal benefits for same-sex partners throughout the military, including the National Guard. Governors in four states resisted the order because it conflicted with their state constitutions, which define marriage in the traditional way. There is, after all, a certain logic to a governor wanting to abide by his own state's constitution. The progressive solution? Federalize the Guard! Liberal journals like *Slate* and the *Washington Blade* enthusiastically reported on the possibility that Obama might federalize the Guard to enforce the federal definition of marriage in those four states. A spokesman for the American Military Partner Association, Lieutenant Colonel Chris Rowzee, said that federalization would be a viable option for Obama, "and in that case, the state governor would have zero say over what a Guard unit then does."[23]

We've landed in a strange place when progressives believe that it is tyrannical for the president to unilaterally control the Guard's deployments internationally or domestically—but that it's perfectly okay for him to dictate the Guard's personnel policy. "This is a true Rubicon moment for the National Guard," wrote the law professor Jonathan Turley in 2013. "If the federal government can now dictate the benefits and treatment of guardsmen, there remains very little of the original state control."[24] By the end of 2013, the four holdout states had reached a compromise whereby same-sex partners of guard members could obtain spousal benefits, provided the benefits were processed by federal officials.

Forward, March!

Presidential control over the armed forces is an important topic. The government's power to project military force feeds both the dream of national security and the nightmare of martial law. Who controls the 463,000 US Army and Air National Guard troops, along with their tanks, planes, and firearms? Are they simply appendages of the Pentagon? Should they be available to the president at any time, for any purpose? These are the central questions. Same-sex marriage—no matter how you feel about it—is peripheral. Conservatives and liberals should forget these side issues and work to give governors more control over the use of their troops.

There's no need to amend the Constitution; rather, we just need to enforce it. First, Congress should repeal the Montgomery Amendment, restoring to each governor the power to block a federal mobilization order. At the same time, state legislatures should continue to enact BTGH laws declaring that the governor should approve federalization of the state troops only for constitutional purposes: to deal with invasions, insurrections, or defiance of federal laws. As Ben Scotch, a Vermont activist, said, such legislation authorizes a governor to do "no more than due diligence would require in determining if a document on the governor's desk is or is not a valid federal order."[25] But BTGH is more than "due diligence"—when a governor asserts the right to determine the constitutionality of a federal order, that's nullification.

Unfortunately, as long as the Guard retains its dual status—and remains dependent on federal funds—gubernatorial autonomy will be largely symbolic. The long-term key to restoring states' rights in military matters is to forget the Guard altogether and to focus on building genuine state militia forces. Doing so is perfectly legal. In 1956, Congress authorized states to create traditional state-run militias, known as State Defense Forces, or SDFs—effectively conceding that the Guard had been federalized. The SDFs are funded exclusively by the state, and can be deployed only within their home state.

The SDFs serve the same function as the original state militias; indeed, the Heritage Foundation refers to them as "today's modern state militias."[26] Why has nobody heard of them? For starters, only twenty-three states have established SDFs, and nationwide they command only 14,000 troops.[27] Money is the problem: when the federal government pays for 95 percent of the Guard, and zero percent of the SDF, governors have little incentive to cultivate SDFs. Besides, state residents pay federal taxes, so they expect to get the maximum value in return. Not surprisingly, SDFs are poorly funded and equipped.

The best way forward, then, is to give states their fiscal freedom over military affairs. Congress should return to the states the revenues that it takes for the National Guard—this could be either in the form of tax rebates or State Defense block grants. The states would use this revenue to develop their SDFs into effective forces for homeland security as well as disaster relief. The federal government could—with the states' consent—continue to house reserve units in the states, but we would do away with the fiction that those reserve forces are state militias.

When federal reserve units and SDFs compete on a level playing field, it seems highly likely that a large number of today's guardsmen would switch their loyalty to the SDFs, where they would have the same opportunities to serve and defend their communities without the risk of being forced to participate in foreign wars—although nothing would stop an SDF member from *volunteering* for an overseas mission. In this new world, the president would have a much smaller force available for overseas missions, making it much harder to commit to an engagement like the Iraq war, or to enter into poll-driven interventions like those in the former Yugoslavia (Clinton) or Libya (Obama). And yet, there would be just as many—possibly more—troops available for defensive and humanitarian missions.

Fears of domestic oppression would melt away. Such fears always seem far-fetched when the "good guys" are in charge in Washington, but pretty much every president has been accused of veering toward tyranny, and occasionally those criticisms have validity. Besides, the perception that the country is vulnerable to a military coup is bad enough for its effect on patriotic spirit. In a country where partisan divisions are increasingly bitter, it might be reassuring to know that the party holding the White House does not actually command all the troops. When the president has to get fifty state governors to agree to impose martial law—well, when that day comes, people on both sides of the aisle will stop worrying about martial law.

The Future:

REVIVING STATES' RIGHTS

12

An Action Plan

On October 24, 1992, President George H. W. Bush signed the Energy Policy Act, which, among other things, imposed a national efficiency standard—for toilets.[1] Since that day, it has been illegal in the United States to sell or install a toilet that fails to meet the federal benchmark of 1.6 gallons per flush.

Before toilet flushing became a federal priority, it was subject to the vagaries of state and local regulation. To be candid, the states were wildly inconsistent in their flush policies. At least fifteen states had low-flush requirements that met or exceeded the 1.6-gallon standard, but some states allowed higher flush rates, and some states did not mandate a particular flush rate at all. But you know what? Nobody died.

In fact, state autonomy rarely leads to fatalities. Federal power, on the other hand, has cost America a fortune in blood and treasure. The glacial pace of the FDA's drug approval process,[2] the corrupt management of veterans hospitals,[3] Congress's bungled takeover of mental healthcare, and our nonstop foreign military interventions have cost thousands of lives in recent decades. On top of that, there are the economic costs of federal regulation—estimated at 2 percent of GDP per year since 1949, or nearly $40 trillion.[4] Finally, there is the steady erosion of our liberties under the weight of the Code of Federal Regulations that, as of 2012, already contained more than 170,000 pages, with more than one million restrictions.

We Can Do Better

Must we sit back and watch while our lives, liberties, and property are flushed down the federal crapper at a stately pace of 1.6 gallons per flush?

Hell no. It is possible to revive states' rights. Contrary to the critics, states' rights is not anachronistic, reactionary, or nostalgic. In fact, it is the critics of states' rights who are wedded to the past. In 2014, for example, Abbe Gluck, a Yale law professor, asserted that the doctrine of states' rights is out of sync with "modern federalism" because "the New Deal is here to stay." Got that? States' rights is old-fashioned because we're permanently stuck in a regulatory regime from the 1930s.

Centralization is the great anachronism, based on the perceived benefit of gathering experts together in one location so they can design policies for the entire nation—an idea that never worked in the best of times, and which has been rendered obsolete by information technology. In twenty-first-century America, the progressive faith in the national government's power to solve problems is as dated as a box of Gerald Ford's WIN buttons ("Whip Inflation Now!"). "Liberal antipathy to federalism seems so *Sixties*," as the law professor Ernest Young observed.[5]

Advocates of states' rights are promoting a thoroughly modern agenda that speaks to modern sensibilities. What would states' rights look like today? Under a revived system of states' rights, Americans would see that:

- States compete openly for citizens and businesses by offering the best mix of infrastructure, tax rates, and social services.
- The decisions that most affect our lives are made closer to home, in local elections that cannot be bought by special-interest groups.
- Regulation is smarter—tailored to local conditions by experts with local knowledge.
- Students are better prepared, thanks to a decentralized education system that promotes innovation and competition.
- Crime rates and incarceration rates are lower.
- The federal government is freed from gridlock, as the most divisive social issues are devolved to the states.

With all due respect to Professor Gluck, the New Deal is not etched in stone. Consider the 1996 welfare reform law, which took a centerpiece of the New Deal—Aid to Families with Dependent Children—and fundamentally transformed it into a block grant program in which each state could design its own welfare-to-work policy. A decade earlier, Ronald Reagan managed to consolidate eighty federal programs into just nine block grants. Reagan also managed to work with a Democratic House of Representatives to adopt a package of reforms of Social Security—that famously untouchable "third rail" of American politics. When the American people want something done, politicians don't stop to ask permission from Ivy League professors.

History is chock full of examples of leaders achieving the impossible. President Andrew Jackson paid off the entire national debt, for heaven's sake. Compared to that, states' rights is a cakewalk. It doesn't cost the taxpayers a dime. To the contrary, it saves money by ending the merry-go-round in which tax dollars must go through Washington before returning to the states, encrusted with wasteful mandates. States' rights means pushing policy decisions to the states, which, unlike the federal government, must balance their budgets rather than passing on ever-greater bills to future generations.

To revive states' rights, we don't need constitutional amendments, national plebiscites, or supermajority votes. The reforms I outline require simple majority votes in Congress or state legislatures, or executive action by the president or state governors. What is needed is a *coalition*: an alliance of political groups that share some common goals even if they don't agree on everything. The states' rights coalition would include conservatives and Tea Party Republicans, of course, but it should also include Democrats from states like Texas that thrive on procompetitive policies, but which are constantly being undermined by federal mandates. The coalition should include the progressive groups that embraced federalism under George W. Bush but grew strangely silent during the Obama years. It should include civil libertarians concerned about the reach of federal surveillance and law enforcement, medical marijuana advocates, environmentalists, and peaceniks. And that's just for starters.

In the pages that follow, I outline steps that lawmakers can take to limit federal power and restore states' rights. But the movement begins with you, because none of the measures I discuss will succeed without active support from citizens. The first step is to stop being afraid of the term "states' rights"— it's not toxic. If you believe that states have a right to local self-government and should exercise that right, then speak up. You'll find you're in good company. In poll after poll, a majority of Americans are expressing an increasing distrust of a federal government gone out of control. At the same time, trust in state and local government remains high.

As a citizen, you can press your local candidates for state and federal office to support legislation that protects states' rights. If your representatives need a little prodding, you can always draft legislation yourself—seriously. The Firearms Freedom Act, which I discuss below, was drafted by a private citizen who had never held elective office. And yet, that single piece of legislation inspired a national movement. You can also encourage your state representatives to join the American Legislative Exchange Council (ALEC), a private organization of state legislators throughout the country that works to promote constitutional federalism. If all else fails, you can run for office. Politics can be an honorable profession for those who manage to stick to their principles.

You can also do your part to expose and correct the false history of states' rights. If you're a student, challenge the teachers and professors who lazily perpetuate the myth that "states' rights" is a coded reference to racial segregation. As a citizen, you can influence the state and local boards that make curriculum and textbook decisions for public schools: Are they presenting the issues fairly, or are they setting up yet another generation to learn the fairy tale of the Good Federal Government versus the Wicked States?

There are a variety of organizations that promote states' rights or related concepts such as self-governance, limited federal government, and fidelity to the Tenth Amendment. Joining these groups and signing their petitions is another way to advance the goals outlined below.

Put an End to Fiscal Coercion

The federal government controls our lives because it controls our pocketbooks. Federal taxes crowd out the ability of states to raise their own revenue, and so states have to beg Washington to get their taxpayers' money back. State governors typically will do everything in their power to maximize federal grants—even if it means creating programs that their constituents don't particularly want—lest they suffer at the ballot box for failing to bring home the bacon.

Breaking Washington's coercive hold on the states is the holy grail of states' rights. There are three basic approaches that could eliminate or greatly reduce federal fiscal coercion: turnback, opting out, and block grants.

Turn-back is the most straightforward approach: you eliminate federal grant programs, cut federal taxes proportionately, and let state and local governments set their own spending priorities and tax their residents accordingly. In other words, you "turn back" responsibility to the states. Not long ago, this basic idea was championed by the liberal icon Daniel Patrick Moynihan. Toward the end of his career, the late New York senator, having seen New York consistently run a negative balance of payments with the federal government, suggested letting states keep more of their own money. "It is time to trade," wrote

Moynihan in a 1999 report for the Kennedy School of Government. "Less activism in Washington in return for more revenue at home, for whatever measures recommend themselves to the state or municipality in question."[6] The case for this brand of fiscal federalism is far stronger now than when Moynihan proposed it, when the federal budget was in the black. Today, the seemingly intractable problems of the Obama era—nonexistent budgets, debt limit showdowns, fiscal cliffs, and sequestration scare tactics—would largely disappear if Washington returned the bulk of taxing and spending decisions to the states.

Granted, Congress isn't likely to turn back all, or even most, federal grant programs to the states—but with the right coalition and a receptive president, it might turn back *some*, especially our egregiously inefficient federal transportation funding. The money for the federal highway program comes largely from gas taxes that are collected at the pump, and those revenues are spent by state agencies to build and maintain roads. In a sensible world, taxes collected at Ohio gas stations would go straight to the Ohio Department of Transportation to be spent on the upkeep of Ohio's highways. Instead, the gas taxes are shipped to Washington to be reallocated by federal bureaucrats. About half the states (or "donor states," to use the polite term) end up as losers—that is, they contribute more to the federal highway trust fund than they get back.[7] To make matters worse, when the states finally get their diminished highway funds back, they're not actually allowed to spend it all on *highways*. Instead the money has to be spread out among politically motivated programs, including nature trails, museums, flower plantings, bicycles, parking lots, and historic renovation. Up to 35 percent of the gas taxes we pay at the pump ends up going to projects that have nothing to do with roads.[8]

Politicians from donor states should favor legislation that allows states to keep 100 percent of the gas taxes collected within their borders—and many do. Turn-back legislation was first introduced in Congress in 1997, and it has been coming back in recent years. Typically, the proposals require the federal government to incrementally reduce the federal gas tax and allow states to increase their own gas taxes proportionately. From the motorist's perspective, there's no difference—you pay the same tax (currently about 18 cents per gallon), but more and more of that revenue stays within the state.[9] To make this more palatable to Congress, some proposals retain a small federal gas tax—say, 2 cents per gallon—to allow the federal government to ensure the integrity of the interstate highway system. Strictly unnecessary, since every inch of the interstate highway system falls within the border of some state, but a small price to pay.

If turn-back is too radical, then there is "opt-out" legislation, which gives states the flexibility to withdraw from federal grant programs. Such a move is politically feasible: a 2011 Rasmussen poll found that 54 percent of Americans believe that states should be able to opt out of federal programs.[10] The trick is to let a state turn down federal programs without forcing the state's taxpayers to subsidize the other states. Take the highway program. In 2013, New Jersey Republican congressman Scott Garrett introduced a bill (the STATE Act) that allows each state to choose the mix of state and federal gas taxes within its own borders. Whenever a state increases its own gas tax, it would get a proportionate cut in the federal tax. The state would receive less in federal aid, but it would now have its own gas tax revenue that it could spend without federal strings. And if a state actually prefers the federal system, it can stick with federal grants and the accompanying micromanagement. Who can object to choice?

Opting out could also work for education spending. Here again, Garrett has created a model for future legislation. His bill—known as the LEARN Act—would give each state the power to opt out of federal education programs entirely and receive a tax credit equivalent to its share of federal education funding. The credits would flow through to individual tax-payers, leaving states and school districts the breathing room to impose additional taxes to fund their own education priorities. The LEARN Act template would work equally well for Med-icaid, which is already administered by the state governments but subject to a mountain of federal regulations.

One attraction of Garrett's model is that taxpayers would see the tangible benefits of states' rights in the form of tax cred-its. Imagine a revised Form 1040 with a "State Flexibility Tax Credit" that reflects the number of federal programs your state has opted out of. You go to the accompanying table and—bang!—you see that it pays to be an opt-out state. If you're a Maryland taxpayer, for example, you might wonder why your friends in Virginia get a tax credit while you get none. Politi-cians who now brag about snagging pork barrel projects could start bragging about getting tax credits. Yes, yes, I realize that states would have to increase their own taxes somewhat, but without the perverse incentives of federal matching programs, and given the need to keep tax rates competitive with nearby states, the state tax increases would be modest.

While we're on the subject of taxes, Congress should also eliminate withholding—that insidious mechanism for conceal-ing the true cost of government. If every taxpayer had to write checks to the IRS four times a year, the movement for a smaller federal government would gain momentum fast.[11]

Finally, where turn-back and opting out don't work, Congress should turn federal aid programs into block grants with flexible conditions. The success of the 1996 welfare reform law—which replaced the Aid to Families with Dependent Children program with a block grant—has been hailed by Democrats and Republicans alike. The only problem is that it reformed only one program while leaving untouched the nearly two hundred other means–tested welfare programs operated by the federal government. These programs, which run the gamut from nutrition assistance to housing programs to job training, cost American taxpayers over $1 trillion every year, and are expected to do so through 2018 at least. Peter Ferrara, a scholar at the Heartland Institute, proposes combining all these programs into a single block grant that states could use to help poor and low-income families, so long as that assistance is provided in return for work (as with the 1996 welfare reform), with exceptions for the disabled and seniors. By eliminating Washington red tape and empowering states to design their own "workfare" programs, the block grants "would save trillions of dollars over the next 10 years alone," according to Ferrara.[12]

Education is another area ripe for block grants, since federal intervention has done little good, and has often been counterproductive. In 2011, Utah Republican congressman Rob Bishop introduced the A–PLUS Act, which would give each state the choice to turn its federal K–12 funding into a block grant, subject to minimal federal conditions. In other words, the state would be allowed to spend its own taxpayers' money according to local preferences. According to the Heritage Foundation, "A–PLUS would . . . place the responsibility for educational improvement with states and schools, which have the strongest incentive to get policymaking right."[13]

As I write this, block grants are a high priority among

congressional Republicans. The House Budget Committee—
chaired by Congressman Paul Ryan—has proposed a fiscal
2015 budget that turns Medicaid into a fixed block grant in-
dexed to inflation and population growth.[14] Ryan has also proposed consolidating most federal education programs into a
single block grant, and combining eleven of the biggest federal
welfare programs into "Opportunity Grants" for each state.[15]
Like Ferrara's proposed block grants, the Opportunity Grants
would mandate that states require able-bodied welfare recipients to work or do things like training that could lead to work.
To be clear, although I personally consider the work requirement to be good policy, I would prefer a cleaner turn-back or
opt-out solution to welfare spending. As long as the federal
government is dictating any conditions, the states are denied
their sovereignty and, more important, the people are denied
the benefits of interstate competition. If, say, New Hampshire
likes workfare and Vermont likes traditional welfare, why not
let them each go their own way?

Congress should also take the funding that it currently devotes to the National Guard and turn it into a "State Defense
Block Grant." The states would use this revenue to create or
strengthen their own State Defense Forces, thus building effective forces for homeland security as well as disaster relief.
As the constitutional state militia, the SDFs could be called
into federal service to (1) defend against invasions, (2) suppress
insurrections, or (3) execute federal laws (Article I, Section 8),
but not to fight overseas.

Although Democratic leaders have recently tried to de-
monize them, block grants are historically a bipartisan idea.
Democrats, in fact, pioneered block grants in the 1960s. The
Reagan block grants were passed by a Democratic House of

Representatives, while the 1996 welfare block grants were signed into law by a Democratic president. In the spring of 2012, Linda Bilmes, a former Clinton administration official and an outspoken Iraq war critic, suggested that Obama scrap his ill-fated American Jobs Act in favor of simple block grants to each state "with no strings attached."[16] The blue state of Rhode Island began experimenting with a Medicaid block grant program in 2009.

The five programs I have highlighted—Medicaid, transportation, education, welfare, and defense—account for more than 90 percent of federal grants to state and local governments. If those five areas could be reformed through a combination of turn-back, opting out, and block grants, the relationship between the states and the central government would be revolutionized. Again, this doesn't take a constitutional amendment, just ordinary legislation backed by a broad coalition.

In the meantime, states can make themselves less vulnerable to coercion by learning to say no to federal aid programs. That may not be possible for a program like Medicaid, but there are a host of federal grant programs that end up being more trouble than they're worth. The challenge, however, is convincing state voters that it is sometimes wise to turn down the money offered by Uncle Sam. In 2013, Indiana's governor, Mike Pence, created the Office of State-Based Initiatives (OSBI) to conduct cost-benefit analyses on federal grant programs. Indiana's state agencies now have to get approval from OSBI before participating in federal grant programs—and if OSBI determines that Indiana would be a net loser, it can withhold approval. The governor can override the OSBI, but then the burden would be on the governor to justify imposing the increased costs on state taxpayers. So far OSBI's results have been modest—in its first year, it turned down less than a million dollars of federal money—but then, any amount is impressive.

Another part of OSBI's mandate is the creation of block grant contingency plans—that is, specific plans to demonstrate how Indiana would allocate federal funds if liberated from federal micromanagement. Such a plan can help build support within the state for greater autonomy, and can also help persuade Congress that giving states flexibility will not lead to chaos. Every state should have an OSBI—or like-minded states could pool their resources to form a multistate OSBI to stiffen the spines of governors trying to resist the siren song of "free" federal money.

Interposition Now!

When it comes to resisting federal mandates that are *not* tied to grant money, states have an extremely powerful weapon: the anticommandeering rule. As we saw earlier, the Supreme Court has held that Congress cannot force states to adopt policies that the federal government could not impose directly (*New York v. United States*, 1992), nor can it "commandeer" a state's administrative machinery to implement federal law (*Printz v. United States*, 1997).

The anticommandeering rule is the modern analog of James Madison's principle of interposition. In the Virginia Resolutions, Madison explained that, when faced with an unconstitutional law, a state had a duty to use its own power not to repeal the law but to "arrest the progress of the evil." A state can, for example, prohibit its officials from assisting in enforcing federal laws that the people of the state do not support. That was the principle behind the personal liberty laws that Northern states adopted in the nineteenth century to shelter fugitive slaves. The anticommandeering rule protects the right of interposition by declaring that Congress cannot force a state to implement federal policies.

Interposition and its more aggressive cousin, nullification, have been on the rise in recent years from both left and right.[17] The 2010 ObamaCare train wreck, for example, was just begging for interposition, and it got it. Thirty-four states refused to create the health insurance exchanges called for in the law, while twenty-two states declined the desired Medicaid expansion. The health law's individual mandate inspired a wave of "healthcare freedom" laws—adopted by statute or constitutional amendment in seventeen states—declaring the right of individuals not to be forced into any particular healthcare scheme. The Supreme Court's 2012 decision upholding ObamaCare has lent greater urgency to these state efforts—if neither the court nor Congress will slay the beast, it's up to the states. In the 2014 legislative session, at least 173 bills and resolutions in thirty-seven state legislatures included opposition to, or proposed legislative alternatives to, parts of the Affordable Care Act. A growing number of these states expressly prohibit any state official from taking any action to implement the act. Notwithstanding the Supreme Court's decision, these measures of state interposition remain perfectly valid, thanks to the anticommandeering rule.

The healthcare freedom laws were themselves inspired by a separate batch of state laws designed to protect intrastate transactions from federal regulation. The movement began in 2009 with the Montana Firearms Freedom Act (FFA), which declared that any gun that is made in, and stays in, Montana "is not subject to federal law or federal regulation." The FFA is pretty much a restatement of what ought to be Con Law 101: the Constitution grants Congress power to regulate only *inter*state commerce; thus, it leaves to the states the power to regulate *intra*state commerce. Naturally, a federal district court struck down the law—offering the highly sophisticated rationale that "when Congress makes an interstate omelet, it is entitled to break a few intrastate eggs."[18]

Despite its defeat in court, the Montana FFA triggered, as it were, a movement: similar legislation has been debated during seventy-eight legislative sessions in thirty-seven states over the last decade.[19] So far, eleven states have enacted FFAs, although in three states the bills were vetoed.[20] Moreover, the FFA has inspired a wave of other "freedom acts," including food freedom, tobacco freedom, and even lightbulb freedom—asserting the right of state residents to use locally produced incandescent bulbs notwithstanding the federal mandate to switch to alternatives like compact fluorescents and LED lights. The freedom acts will continue to invite litigation, which at least has the potential to push the Supreme Court into tightening the limits on federal power, as it has several times since the mid-1990s in cases like *Lopez*, *Printz*, and even the court's 2012 ObamaCare decision, which held that Congress could not use the commerce clause to force citizens to buy products or services. Freedom acts are also valuable as tools to channel the dissenting views of millions of citizens alienated by federal policies.

Liberals—although they hate to admit it—rely on interposition and nullification as much as, or more than, conservatives. How else to explain the seventy-odd "sanctuary" cities and states where police are forbidden from helping to enforce federal immigration law? That's interposition. How else to explain the twenty states that have legalized marijuana use in open defiance of the federal Controlled Substances Act?[21] Or the fifteen states that vowed not to implement the Bush-backed REAL ID law? Nullification!

Unfortunately, the anticommandeering rule does not apply to fiscal coercion—the courts still merrily repeat the fiction that states accept federal grant conditions "voluntarily" because they're free to turn down the money (which is why turn-back, opting out, and block grants are all needed). But when Uncle Sam is not picking up the tab, why should states play along?

States should adopt the State Regulatory Responsibility Act, a model law that flatly prohibits state agencies from taking any action to implement a federal mandate unless Congress provides the funds to do so *and* the action is consistent with state law. Alternatively, or in addition to such a strategy, states can explicitly withhold support for specific federal programs. For example, following Edward Snowden's leaks regarding National Security Agency surveillance, at least sixteen state legislatures considered the "Fourth Amendment Protection Act," a model law that forbids state police and prosecutors from using warrantless NSA data, and makes such data inadmissible in state courts.[22]

Another option is to block the use of state resources to support domestic surveillance, since, for example, the NSA data centers consume enormous amounts of electricity and water (which is used to cool their supercomputers). In February 2014, Utah representative Marc Roberts introduced a bill to shut off water to the NSA data center near the Great Salt Lake.[23] Legislation in other states would prohibit the use of water or electrical resources for any domestic surveillance operation. Some proposals would go even further: for example, barring state universities from accepting grants from federal intelligence agencies, and barring corporations from doing business with a state if those corporations also participate in warrantless surveillance. If it seems harsh to cut off water or electricity, just remember whom we're dealing with. The federal government has been using its power to order irrigation districts not to distribute water to farmers who are growing marijuana legally under state law. It's time to fight water with water. By withholding logistical support for NSA spying, and by refusing to use warrantless data for law enforcement, the states could effectively force the federal government to moderate its domestic spying.

Here's something else that states should withhold from Uncle Sam: troops. Congress should repeal the Montgomery Amendment, which would restore to each governor the power to block a federal mobilization order. But while we're waiting for that to happen, state legislatures should continue to enact Bring the Guard Home laws—embraced by conservatives and liberals alike—declaring that a governor should approve the federalization of the state troops only for constitutional purposes: to deal with invasions, insurrections, or defiance of federal laws.

Where to Begin?

Given the breadth of federal mandates, states have to be strategic about employing interposition—it's just not realistic to try to block all federal programs at once. How can states decide which mandates to oppose? One mechanism is a constitutional defense council, a state body that could include the attorney general, other state officials, and outside experts, and that has authority to retain outside lawyers. The council could identify the federal mandates that pose the greatest threat to the state and recommend measures to "arrest the progress of the evil" (as Madison put it), including litigation to challenge unconstitutional federal laws. In the 1990s, three states created constitutional defense councils (Arizona, Idaho, and Utah), but for the most part they have not been very active. It's time for states to dust off this idea and make constitutional defense councils part of a coordinated strategy of states' rights.

States should also explore the potential of interstate compacts as a means to cast off unwanted federal mandates. The Constitution envisions interstate compacts—regulatory agreements among states—and there are over two hundred currently in force, dealing with issues ranging from driver's license standards to emergency management coordination. The Port Authority of New York and New Jersey is an interstate compact that operates various transportation hubs in and around New York City.

Since 2011, states have been quietly signing up to join an interstate "Health Care Compact" in which the member states would opt out of ObamaCare and assume the responsibility of regulating healthcare within their own borders (except on military bases). No particular healthcare regime is required—each state is free to choose—but the compact includes an interstate advisory commission that would recommend best practices. Eleven state legislatures have approved the healthcare compact, although two governors vetoed the legislation. In order to trump federal law, an interstate compact must be approved by Congress; this is seemingly a tall order, but as more states join the compact, Congress will find it increasingly risky to withhold approval. The George Mason University School of Law professor Michael Greve estimates that a block of sixteen or seventeen noncooperating states could effectively defeat a federal mandate.[24] Interstate compacts are one mechanism that could be used to coordinate the efforts of procompetitive states in casting off anticompetitive federal regulations.

Preemption and Presumptions

Approving the Health Care Compact is just one step that Congress should take. It also needs to strip bureaucrats of the power to create rules that preempt state law. With a brief amendment to the Administrative Procedures Act, Congress could establish that federal agency regulations are not covered by the supremacy clause of the Constitution—a reasonable thing to do since the clause deems only statutes, treaties, and the Constitution itself to be "supreme." The result would be that when a federal regulation conflicts with state law, the state law would win.[25] At the very least, federal law should require that courts adopt a "presumption against agency preemption," a proposal put forward by the law professor Nina Mendelson.[26] The general idea would be that any federal agency proposing a preemptive rule without specific congressional authorization should bear the burden of establishing why preemption is required.

Speaking of presumptions, remember Ronald Reagan's federalism executive order, which included the all-important "presumption of sovereignty"? One congressional proposal—the Federalism Accountability Act—would codify the Reagan order in federal statute law, meaning that a future president cannot simply wipe it away, as Bill Clinton attempted to do. In fact, the act would go beyond the Reagan order by empowering federal courts to stop new regulations from coming into force if the agency failed to provide a Federalism Impact Statement.[27]

A complementary proposal is the Tenth Amendment Regulatory Reform Act, first introduced by Oklahoma congressman Tom Cole in 2011, which gives state governors, lieutenant governors, attorneys general, or state legislative leaders special standing to challenge federal regulations while they are still in the proposal stage, and provides for expedited court hearings to resolve those challenges. Failing that, federal agencies should at least be required to give early notice of proposed rules to each state's attorney general, as well as the leading nongovernmental organizations representing state and local government, like the National Governors Association, the National Conference of State Legislatures, and the United States Conference of Mayors.[28]

Get Out of Jail Free

Since 1980, the number of federal prisoners has grown by over 700 percent. The new breed of federal inmates includes such hardened criminals as Abner Schoenwetter, a commercial fisherman sentenced to eight years for importing undersize lobster tails in plastic bags—rather than boxes—in violation of *Honduran law*.

The best response to the overfederalization of crime is for Congress to pass a sweeping law that would gradually phase out all federal crimes that are neither defined in the Constitution nor incidental to one of Congress's enumerated powers.

Likely? No. But a states' rights coalition could certainly scale back the current reach of federal criminal law. Indeed, reducing federal crimes "could be one area where ACLU-style liberals concerned with individual rights find common ground with conservatives seeking in rein in federal overreach," according to the policy analyst Vikrant Reddy.[29] Congress could start by forbidding executive agencies from creating new crimes via regulation (unless specifically directed to do so by statute). With an estimated three-hundred-thousand-plus regulatory crimes already on the books, it is time to put the brakes on overzealous bureaucrats.

Congress should also stop duplicating state crime-fighting efforts. It could, for example, create a commission that would identify federal crimes that are entirely redundant of existing state laws, like federal laws against arson (a topic amply covered by state criminal laws). The commission could be modeled on the highly successful commission for dealing with obsolete military bases, the Defense Base Realignment and Closure Commission, or BRAC. Like the BRAC, the criminal law commission's recommendations would become law unless Congress votes to disapprove them. While they're at it, Congress should also eliminate the judge-made exception to the double jeopardy rule that has allowed federal prosecutors to pursue defendants who have already been tried at the state level.

Restoring states' rights over ordinary intrastate crimes would be good for individual liberty and good for the rule of law. The states have proved themselves far more adept at controlling crime than the central government has. Since 2007, the majority of states have managed to reduce both incarceration rates *and* crime rates during a time when the federal prison population has been surging.[30]

No matter what Congress does, the states must also act to blunt the tyranny of federal prosecutors. First, states should allow citizens to sue federal officials in state court when those officials violate individual rights. Such lawsuits already exist on the federal level: any citizen can sue a state government official in federal court for violating constitutional rights—these are called "Section 1983" lawsuits, after the relevant US Code section. Astonishingly, there is no equivalent remedy at the state level. The Yale law professor Akhil Amar has proposed that states create "converse 1983" laws providing for state court remedies that would come in awfully handy for people like Catherine Engelbrecht and Nancy Black.[31]

State courts used to play an important role in checking the abuses of federal officials. State court suits against overzealous federal customs collectors, for example, were "commonplace" in the late eighteenth and nineteenth centuries, according to a *Columbia Law Review* article.[32] Such lawsuits were a critical part of New England's efforts to resist Jefferson's ill-considered Embargo Law of 1807. State court habeas corpus proceedings were used by those imprisoned by federal officials to challenge the constitutionality of their confinement. The constitutional provision forbidding suspension of habeas corpus was designed to prevent the federal government from interfering with such state proceedings.[33] It was not until the eve of the Civil War that the Supreme Court held that a "writ of habeas corpus" issued by a state judge cannot be used to compel the federal government to release a prisoner—this was the case of Sherman Booth, the Wisconsin abolitionist charged with aiding and abetting the escape of a fugitive slave. In proposing converse 1983 lawsuits, Professor Amar explicitly seeks to revive this "rich antebellum tradition emphasizing state protection of constitutional norms against the federal government."[34]

Second, states can forbid their officials, including local police, from participating in the investigation and prosecution of
federal crimes, except in areas of clear federal authority, such as
treason or counterfeiting. Federal agencies rely heavily on state
and local assets to enforce federal criminal laws; thus, a consistent and principled position of noncooperation by the states
would force Washington to rethink its criminal jurisdiction.
A number of states have already passed "Second Amendment
Preservation" legislation—promoted by the Tenth Amendment Center—which prohibits state and local officials from
enforcing gun control laws that violate Second Amendment
rights.[35] Some of the laws impose criminal penalties on state
officials who attempt to assist federal agents to enforce unconstitutional gun laws. What gives states the right to determine
the constitutionality of federal laws? It is the same principle of
interposition that animates Bring the Guard Home legislation:
when the federal government seeks state assistance, each state
has its own sovereign right to assess the constitutionality of the
federal request.

To make this strategy of noncooperation work in areas beyond the Second Amendment, states should designate a central
authority—perhaps the state attorney general or a Constitutional
Defense Council—to review requests for assistance from federal authorities. If the state official determines that the alleged crime is not
properly within federal jurisdiction, then he or she should be able
to block local officials from participating. Such a system would be
perfectly legal under the anticommandeering rule—and necessary
in order to stop local police from succumbing to the temptation of
"equitable sharing."

Third, states can decriminalize conduct where public opinion
runs against the federal law. The clearest example of this tactic has

been the trend among states to legalize the use of marijuana for medical purposes and, in some states, for recreational use.

Fourth, the states can take an active role in challenging criminal laws that violate the Tenth Amendment. In *Bond v. United States* (2013), the Supreme Court affirmed that the Tenth Amendment protects individuals—not just states—and thus criminal defendants can assert Tenth Amendment rights as a defense against federal prosecution. But few criminal defendants have the resources to hire counsel to mount constitutional challenges—so why not have the states subsidize such arguments? Each state should create a "Tenth Amendment Defense Fund"—a discretionary fund that criminal defendants could apply to if they think they are being charged with overreaching federal laws. If the state agrees, then the defense fund could pay all or part of the legal fees. State assistance of this sort has a distinguished pedigree: in 1800, James Monroe, then governor of Virginia, authorized the use of state money to fund the defense of a Virginia resident charged under the Sedition Act. Indeed, in the *Bond* case itself, Virginia and ten other states submitted a "friend of the court" brief supporting Ms. Bond's Tenth Amendment argument. With a Tenth Amendment Defense Fund—which could be administered by a Constitutional Defense Council—a state could use its resources to defend its own citizens and to vindicate its sovereign police powers at the same time.

Defang the Activist Judges

The federal judiciary presents a distinct threat to states' rights, especially when it comes to social issues. National rules on abortion, marriage, prisoners' rights, school prayer, and other social issues have come, not from Congress, but from activist courts that have superseded state laws with judge-made "rights." Congress, however, has the power to put the brakes on activist judges.

The jurisdiction of federal appellate courts and of the Supreme Court itself is almost entirely a matter of congressional discretion. Under the Constitution, the Supreme Court is obliged to hear "all Cases affecting Ambassadors, other public Ministers and Consuls, and those in which a State shall be a Party" (Article III, Section 2). Everything else is gravy—and is subject to "such Exceptions . . . as Congress shall make."

By a simple majority vote, Congress should revoke, or at least restrict, the federal judiciary's ability to overturn decisions of state supreme courts. This is not some hypothetical strategy; on multiple occasions, Congress has expanded or contracted the scope of federal appellate jurisdiction. As recently as 1996, for example, Congress stripped federal courts of jurisdiction over Immigration and Naturalization Service (now Immigration and Customs Enforcement) decisions on whether and to whom to grant asylum. Historically, Supreme Court jurisdiction was far more limited than it is today. Until 1889, the Supreme Court could not hear appeals in federal criminal cases. Until 1914, the court had no right to review state court decisions striking down state laws—even if the decision was based on federal law—or state court decisions upholding federal law. Essentially, state courts had the last word unless they struck down a federal law or denied the applicability of a federal right.

In 1949, Supreme Court Justice Owen Roberts commented that "I do not see any reason why Congress cannot, if it elects to do so, take away entirely the appellate jurisdiction of the Supreme Court of the United States over state supreme court decisions."[36] The same goes for the appellate jurisdiction of lower federal courts—they have no constitutional mandate to hear appeals from state courts. A simple piece of congressional legislation—former congressman Ron Paul's We the People Act is a great example—could strip the federal courts of jurisdiction over cases that challenge state or local laws on the basis of religion, privacy, and marriage equality. Thus, state courts would have the last word on the validity of laws concerning things like school prayer, Nativity scenes on public property, abortion on demand, and the definition of marriage.

The result: instant diversity! No longer would one or two swing justices on the Supreme Court have the power, or the responsibility, to dictate social policy to a captive nation. No longer would every Supreme Court nomination end up in a three-ring filibuster circus of posturing senators claiming to represent the views of "mainstream" Americans. Instead, social issues would arise and be resolved within each state, according to the political and legal culture prevailing therein.

Does this mean that even purported federal rights would get different interpretations in different states? Yes, but as a practical matter, that is already the case. There are twelve different federal appellate courts—the "circuit courts"—and they are free to disagree with each other. It is not at all unusual for federal law to mean one thing in, say, the Second Circuit (which covers New York, Connecticut, and Vermont) and something quite different in the Ninth Circuit (California and the West). Take the Fourth Amendment, which governs the ability of the police to conduct searches without warrants and to use the evidence obtained against criminal defendants. There are over three dozen disagreements among the federal circuits regarding the meaning of the amendment—for example, whether police can search passengers in cars.[37] Only occasionally does the Supreme Court step in to resolve such disagreements. The existence of competing interpretations of federal law has not brought the Republic down; there is no evidence that a little additional state variation would be a problem.

Back to the Land

The federal government has broken its promise to dispose of federal lands in the western United States. Congress made it official federal policy in 1976 to retain federal lands, notwithstanding the previous federal commitments to restore such lands to the states or to sell them to private owners. The result is that, while the federal government owns just 4 percent of the land in the eastern United States, it owns more than 50 percent of the land in the West, including Alaska. It controls the water supply for more than 31 million people and for one of every five farmers in the West.

Starved for property taxes and other land-based revenue, the Western states have lagged behind the East in education spending. Over the past two decades, the Eastern and Midwestern states have increased per-pupil spending at nearly twice the rate of those in the West: 68 percent versus 35 percent.[38] The Western states are basically colonies of the federal government—a situation that might have been tolerable for a brief transitional period after gaining statehood, but one that has turned Western Americans into second-class citizens.

The key to bringing true democracy to the West is to give the states control over their own territory. In this struggle, Utah has been leading the way with a 2012 law (HB 148) giving the federal government an ultimatum to transfer the title to public lands to the state by December 31, 2014; the state would then be free to sell portions of the land, and the rest would be maintained as state public lands. For any land that the state sells, 5 percent of the proceeds would be used for state schools—consistent with the Utah's enabling act—with the rest going to the US Treasury to help pay down the debt. As this book goes to press, the federal government has ignored the state's deadline, and Utah lawmakers are preparing for litigation against Uncle Sam, having already set aside $2 million for that purpose.[39]

Despite the horrified reaction of the professional left—a "thinly veiled attempt" to promote "fossil fuel extraction," gasps the Sierra Club[40]—HB 148 is simply an effort to put Utah on an equal footing with, say, New York, where less than 1 percent of the land is held by the federal government. Far from being a vehicle for environmental degradation, HB 148 contains broad exemptions for existing national parks (as well as Indian reservations and military installations), all of which would remain under federal control. And for those lands that are transferred to state control, their fate will be determined— miracle of miracles—by politicians elected by the people who actually live on or near those lands. If anybody has an incentive to preserve Utah's lands, it is the Utahns themselves. Indeed, the legislature has already created a state-level wilderness act empowering the state to carve out more protected areas in the lands it hopes to wrest from Uncle Sam.[41] At the federal level, Utah representative Rob Bishop has a complementary initiative to bring competing stakeholders together to reach consensus on how to divvy up public lands in the state.

If that's extreme, then extremity is catching on. At least four other Western states—Idaho, Montana, Nevada, and

Wyoming—have passed laws similar to HB 148, and other states are considering transfer legislation. In April 2014, over fifty elected officials from nine Western states met at the Utah State Capitol to compare notes on legislative strategies to get the federal government to honor its promise to dispose of public lands.[42] If the federal government behaved rationally, it would jump at the opportunity to dispose of Western lands: land management is a huge money loser for federal taxpayers. Congress spends over $8.6 billion annually to maintain its Western possessions, but the federal government receives less than $1 billion in net revenue from those lands.[43]

To be sure, the state land-transfer laws might be struck down by the courts. However, medical marijuana laws have also lost in numerous court battles, but the states are still winning the war. That's because the state marijuana laws are supported by strong local opinion, and even by the majority of voters nationwide. So it is crucial for the Western states to win over public opinion—which means combating the hysteria whipped up by environmental groups. The fact is that most environmental issues are local, not national. As the law professor Jonathan Adler observes, "Drinking water systems serve the local communities in which they are based. Hazardous waste sites only threaten local communities. Phoenix's failure to meet the National Ambient Air Quality Standard for ozone does not affect Baton Rouge."[44] Paul Portney of Resources for the Future suggests that "states, or perhaps even individual communities" should be allowed to regulate their own drinking water.[45]

Given the local nature of environmental issues, and the federal government's poor track record on land stewardship, many experts agree that the states can do a better job. David Schoenbrod, a former attorney with the Natural Resources Defense

Council, has written that "the popular desire for a clean environment can be realized with far more common sense by returning control to local government." In 1997, the National Academy of Public Administration concluded that "[the] EPA and Congress need to hand more responsibility and decision making authority over to the states."[46] The imposition of one-size-fits-all environmental mandates is one of the factors driving public disenchantment with federal power, according to Pietro S. Nivola, a scholar at the Brookings Institute. "Is it surprising," he asks, "that taxpayers in Phoenix, Arizona, which averages seven inches of rainfall a year, question federal mandates that force the city to devote large sums every year to monitoring runoff from practically nonexistent rainstorms?"[47]

Measures like the Utah Wilderness Act help reassure the public that the states will be good stewards of natural resources. States should also consider establishing trusts to receive public lands—trusts requiring, for example, that the public lands be used to benefit schools, or agriculture. Or why not really play hardball? States could lay out plans to build politically correct projects on unused federal land: schools for the disabled, shelters for battered women, soup kitchens, and wind farms—and just dare the federal government to send in the bulldozers.

The Future Belongs to the States

History is on our side. Around the world, the political trends of the last three decades virtually all point in one direction: self-rule, local autonomy, devolution, and the breakup of empires. Spain has been steadily granting more and more autonomy to its regions since 1978; Canadian provinces have gained more powers since 1982. Britain's devolution movement of the 1990s—led by a left-leaning Labour government—created highly popular regional assemblies for Wales and Northern Ireland and a national parliament for Scotland. In a September 2014 referendum, 45 percent of Scots voted for full independence—many of them complaining about being ruled by a "distant" parliament in London (for reference, Edinburgh is about four hundred miles from London). The 1991 dissolution of the Soviet Union was hailed by international leaders— and Vladimir Putin's attempts to bring bits of the old union back into Moscow's orbit have been denounced as a threat to "self-determination," as Barack Obama put it.

Speaking of President Obama, consider his view of the Middle East conflict: "The Palestinian people's right to self-determination and justice must also be recognized," said Obama. "Put yourself in their shoes—look at the world through their eyes."[48] Whether or not you agree with him on Palestine—and I leave that question to the experts—one can't help but wonder why the president is so keen on local self-government in every country except the United States. It's all very well to "look at the world through their eyes," but why can't Mr. Obama and his Washington cohorts look at the world through *our* eyes— the eyes of Vermonters, Texans, New Yorkers, Utahns—that is, the vast majority of Americans who live outside the Beltway.

If they look through our eyes, they will see a world dominated by government programs designed by distant officials over whom we have no control. They will see a world of parents concerned about the vast and growing national debt that our children will inherit. They will see Washington stuck in gridlock over issues that never belonged at the federal level, and they will see state and local leaders stymied by one-size-fits-all mandates on education, nutrition, healthcare, the environment, and transportation totally unsuited to local conditions. In short, they will see a world in which the promise of American federalism is perilously close to extinction.

States' rights is not a matter of ideology. It's not about whether government should be big or small, interventionist or laissez-faire, conservative or liberal, peaceful or bellicose. It's about who decides these issues—state and local communities, or a tiny cadre of Washington elites and their special-interest patrons. On *that* question, left and right agree. Conservatives say they believe in Tenth Amendment rights and competitive federalism. Liberals say they want diversity and small-scale democracy. When both sides come together to support states' rights, we'll be on the way to restoring that perfectly imperfect union that our Founding Fathers bequeathed us.

Acknowledgments

My sincere thanks go to Adam Bellow, my editor at Broadside Books, whose vision and intellectual engagement made this book possible, as well as associate editor Eric Meyers, who challenged me to sharpen my arguments throughout the book. Thanks also to my agent, Geri Thoma, a font of sage advice.

Many of the ideas in this book were developed at Ricochet.com, which remains the most civilized place for political discourse on the web. A big thanks to the whole editorial team, especially Rob Long, Peter Robinson, and Troy Senik, as well as the Ricochet members who keep me honest. I also owe a debt to my allies at the Manhattan Institute, who have encouraged me in this journey, including *City Journal* editor Brian Anderson, managing editor Paul Beston, and associate editor Matthew Hennessy. Also at the Manhattan Institute, Jim Copeland, director of the Center for Legal Policy; deputy director Isaac Gorodetski; and senior fellow Steve Eide have graciously provided intellectual support, sympathetic ears, and, at times, a desk to write on.

I'm grateful to the experts who generously allowed themselves to be interviewed for this book, sometimes more than once. Thanks in particular to Congressmen Rob Bishop and

Scott Garrett, both leaders in the battle to restore the Tenth Amendment. Thanks also to Vikram Reddy of Right on Crime, Chris Williams of the Cato Institute, and Professor John Kincaid of Lafayette College, three of the most perceptive thinkers in this area.

I was lucky to have three whip-smart research assistants: Eugene Cheval, Michael Giles, and Evan Gage. They are hard-working, diligent, and creative young scholars. Any errors in the book are mine.

As ever, I'm thankful for the support of parents, siblings, co-workers, friends, and especially my two beautiful daughters, Cecilia and Fiona. But most of all, I owe this book to Kathleen, my wife, whose support never wavers. Short of writing the thing herself, she couldn't have done more.

Notes

Introduction: The War Against the States

1. Robert Enlow, "Louisiana School Choice Program Already Helping Students," *Daily Caller*, September 14, 2012, http://dailycaller .com/2012/09/14/louisiana-school-choice-program-already-helping-students/.

2. Anna J. Egalite and Jonathan N. Mills, "The Louisiana Scholarship Program," *Education Next* 14, no. 1 (Winter 2014): 66.

3. Andrea Billups and Jennifer Hickey, "Louisiana Gov. Jindal Fights Washington War on School Vouchers," *Newsmax*, January 25, 2014, www.newsmax.com/US/louisiana-education-bobby-jindal-vouchers/2014/01/24/id/548960/.

4. Ibid.

5. Michael C. Dawson, "Washington Must Redress State Injustice," *Room for Debate* (blog), *New York Times*, October 22, 2014, http://www.ny times.com/roomfordebate/2013/07/16/state-politics-vs-the-federal-government/washington-must-redress-state-injustice.

6. Jesse Jackson, "Stand Up to the Bigotry of 'States' Rights,'" *Chicago Sun-Times*, November 4, 2013.

7. Matthew Balan, "CNN's Rick Sanchez Again Hints Rick Perry is a Racist," *NewsBusters*, March 2, 2010, http://newsbusters.org/blogs/matthew-balan/2010/03/02/cnns-rick-sanchez-again-hints-rick-perry-racist.

8. "CT-04 (R) Tom Hermann Steps Up for States Rights in Confederate History Month!," *Daily Kos*, April 19, 2010, www.dailykos.com/story/2010/04/19/858906/-CT-04-R-Tom-Hermann-Steps-Up-for-States-Rights-in-Confederate-History-Month.

9. Jeffrey Meyer, "Chris Matthews: Does Tea Party Want America Where 'There Are No Gays, Blacks Were Slaves, Mexicans Were in Mexico,'" *NewsBusters*, March 21, 2013, http://newsbusters.org/blogs/jeffrey-meyer/2013/03/21/chris-matthews-asks-if-tea-party-wants-america-where-there-are-no-gay.

10. David Azerrad, "Morning Bell: New Year's Resolutions for Conservatives," *Daily Signal*, January 2, 2012, http://dailysignal.com/2012/01/02/morning-bell-new-years-resolutions-for-conservatives/.

11. Kevin R. C. Gutzman, *The Politically Incorrect Guide to the Constitution* (Washington, DC: Regnery, 2007), 23–24.

12. Brutus XII (February 7, 1788), in *The Complete Anti-Federalist*, ed. Herbert Storing (Chicago: University of Chicago Press 1981, 2008 reprint), 425.

13. Herbert Storing, *What the Anti-Federalists Were For* (Chicago: University of Chicago Press, 1981), 50.

14. Eric Posner, "John Roberts' Opinion on the Voting Rights Act Is Really Lame," *Slate*, June 25, 2013, www.slate.com/articles/news_and_politics /the_breakfast_table/features/2013/supreme_court_2013/supreme_ court_on_the_voting_rights_act_chief_justice_john_roberts_struck. html.

15. Edward L. Rubin and Malcolm Feeley, "Federalism: Some Notes on a National Neurosis," *UCLA Law Review* 41, no. 4 (April 1994): 903.

16. Michael Tanner, "DC Forgets About the Debt," *National Review Online*, July 23, 2014, www.nationalreview.com/article/383425/dc-forgets-about-debt-michael-tanner.

17. Ibid.

18. Michael S. Greve, *The Upside-Down Constitution* (Cambridge, MA: Harvard University Press, 2012), Kindle edition, chapter 17.

19. John Samples and Emily Ekins, *Public Attitudes toward Federalism*, Cato Policy Analysis no. 759, September 23, 2014.

20. Ibid., 23.

21. Ibid.

22. Glenn Hubbard and Tim Kane, *Balance: The Economics of Great Powers from Ancient Rome to Modern America* (New York: Simon & Schuster, 2013), Kindle edition, chapter 1.

23. Heather Gerken, "Federalism as the New Nationalism: An Overview," *Yale Law Journal* 123, no. 6 (April 2014): 1893.

24. Jessica Bulman-Pozen, "From Sovereignty and Process to Administration and Politics: The Afterlife of American Federalism," *Yale Law Journal* 123, no. 6 (April 2014): 1922.

25. Erwin Chemerinsky, *Enhancing Government* (Stanford, CA: Stanford Law Books, 2008).

26. David Narrett, "A Zeal for Liberty: The Antifederalist Case Against the Constitution in New York," *New York History* 69, no. 3 (July 1988): 284–317.

27. John Taylor, *New Views of the Constitution of the United States* (Washington, DC: Way and Gideon, 1823), 96.

28. Howard Dean, " 'No Child Left Behind' Should Be More Than a Slogan," *Seattle Times*, January 8, 2004.

29. Paul Begala, "I [Heart] Government," *Newsweek*, September 12, 2011.

30. William Dougan, "The Dollars and Sense of Rightsizing the Federal Workforce," *FCW*, June 15, 2011, http://fcw.com/articles/2011/06/20/ comment-william-dougan-federal-workforce.aspx.

31. Congressional Research Service, *Federal Land Ownership: Overview and Data*, February 8, 2012.
32. James Buckley, *Freedom at Risk* (New York: Encounter 2010), Sony edition, chapter 4.
33. Edward Corwin, The Constitution of the United States of America: Analysis and Interpretation (Washington, DC: US Government Printing Office, 1953), Project Gutenberg E-book, chapter I.
34. "National School Lunch Program and School Breakfast Program: Nutrition Standards for All Foods Sold in School as Required by the Healthy, Hunger-Free Kids Act of 2010," *Federal Register* 78, no. 125 (June 28, 2013), http://www.fns.usda.gov/sites/default/files/2013-15249_0.pdf.
35. Samples and Ekins, *Public Attitudes toward Federalism*, 23.
36. James H. Hershman Jr., "Massive Resistance," *Encyclopedia Virginia*, June 29, 2011, http://www.EncyclopediaVirginia.org/Massive_Resistance.
37. Ibid.
38. James R. Sweeney, "Postscript to Massive Resistance: The Decline and Fall of the Virginia Commission on Constitutional Government," *Virginia Magazine of History and Biography* 121, no. 1 (January 2013), 45–86.
39. Barry Goldwater, *The Conscience of a Conservative* (New York: Hillman Books, 1961), 32.
40. Kevin D. Williamson, "The Party of Civil Rights," *National Review*, May 28, 2012.
41. George Lewis, "Virginia's Northern Strategy: Southern Segregationists and the Route to National Conservatism," *Journal of Southern History* 72, no. 1 (February 2006): 111.
42. Ibid.
43. David Kopel, "Reagan's Infamous Speech in Philadelphia, Mississippi," *Volokh Conspiracy* (blog), August 16, 2011, http://volokh.com/2011/08/16/reagans-infamous-speech-in-philadelphia-mississippi/.
44. "Transcript of Ronald Reagan's 1980 Neshoba County Fair speech," *Nashoba Democrat*, November 15, 2007, http://neshobademocrat.com/main.asp?SectionID=2&SubSectionID=297&ArticleID=15599&TM=60417.67.
45. David Brooks, "History and Calumny," *New York Times*, November 9, 2007.
46. Joseph Crespino, *In Search of Another Country: Mississippi and the Conservative Counterrevolution* (Princeton, NJ: Princeton University Press, 2007), 1.
47. Brooks, "Calumny."
48. Thomas Byrne Edsall and Mary D. Edsall, *Chain Reaction: The Impact of Race, Rights, and Taxes on American Politics* (New York: Norton, 1991), 137–53.
49. David Greenberg, "Dog-Whistling Dixie: When Reagan Said 'States' Rights,' He Was Talking about Race," *Slate*, November 20, 2007, www.slate.com/articles/news_and_politics/history_lesson/2007/11/dogwhistling_dixie.html.

50. See chapter 6; *Hearing Before the Subcommittee on Commerce, Trade, and Consumer Protection of the Committee on Energy and Commerce, US House of Representatives*, 111th Cong. (May 6, 2010), http://www.gpo.gov/fdsys/pkg/CHRG-111hhrg76575/html/CHRG-111hhrg76575.htm.

51. Emily Bazelon, "States' Rights Are for Liberals," *Atlantic*, June 2013.

52. Paul Krugman, "Republicans and Race," *New York Times*, November 19, 2007.

53. Niall Ferguson, "How America Lost Its Way," *Wall Street Journal*, June 8, 2013.

54. Woodrow Wilson, "The Study of Administration," *Political Science Quarterly* 2, no. 2 (June 1887): 208.

55. Ibid., 214.

56. Ann E. Marimow and Lenny Bernstein, "Ex-EPA Official Pleads Guilty to Theft," *Washington Post*, September 27, 2013.

57. John Dinan, *How States Talk Back to Washington and Strengthen American Federalism*, Cato Policy Analysis no. 744, December 3, 2013, 5.

58. Hubbard and Kane, *Balance*, chapter 12.

59. Samples and Ekins, *Public Attitudes toward Federalism*, 22.

60. *United States v. Bond*, 131 S.Ct. 2355 (2011).

Chapter 1: The Bill of (States') Rights

1. Constitution of Massachusetts, Part I, Declaration of Rights, Art. IV.

2. James T. Young, *The New American Government and Its Work* (New York: Macmillan, 1920), 93.

3. Patrick Jonsson, "States Rebel against Washington," *Christian Science Monitor*, March 27, 2009, http://www.csmonitor.com/USA/2009/0327/p02s01-usgn.html.

4. George Orwell, *As I Please, 1943–1946* (New York: Harcourt, Brace, and World, 1968), 87.

5. Herbert Storing, *What the Anti-Federalists Were For* (Chicago: University of Chicago Press, 1981), 64.

6. "March 4: A Forgotten Huge Day in American History," *Constitution Daily* (blog), National Constitution Center, March 4, 2013, http://blog.constitutioncenter.org/2013/03/march-4-a-forgotten-huge-day-in-american-politics/.

7. Adam Wolkoff, ed., *The Political and Legal Structures of the Thirteen Colonies Prior to the American Revolution* (West Hartford, CT: The Graduate Group, 2008).

8. David Hackett Fischer, *Albion's Seed: Four British Folkways in America* (New York: Oxford University Press, 1989).

9. Akhil Reed Amar, *The Bill of Rights: Creation and Reconstruction* (New Haven, CT: Yale University Press, 1998), 5.

10. Wolkoff, *Political and Legal Structures*.

11. Paris Peace Treaty of September 30, 1783, available at http://avalon.law.yale.edu/18th_century/paris.asp.
12. Henry Adams, *John Randolph* (Boston: Houghton, Mifflin, 1882).
13. Alison L. LaCroix, *The Ideological Origins of American Federalism* (Cambridge, MA: Harvard University Press 2010), 154.
14. Ibid., 156
15. Glenn Hubbard and Tim Kane, *Balance: The Economics of Great Powers from Ancient Rome to Modern America* (New York: Simon & Schuster, 2013), Kindle edition, chapter 12.
16. Todd Zywicki, "Repeal the 17th Amendment and Restore the Founders' Design," *Engage,* September 2011.
17. Frederick Drake and Lynne Nelson, eds., *States' Rights and American Federalism: A Documentary History* (Westport, CT: Greenwood Press, 1999), 7–8.
18. Storing, *What the Anti-Federalists Were For,* 31–32.
19. Cass R. Sunstein, *The Second Bill of Rights: FDR's Unfinished Revolution and Why We Need It More Than Ever* (New York: Basic Books, 2006), 19.
20. Douglas J. Amy, "Government as the Primary Protector of Our Rights and Liberties," *Government Is Good,* 2007, www.governmentisgood.com/articles.php?aid=19.
21. James Madison, Speech in Congress, June 8, 1789, quoted in Kurt T. Lash, "The Lost Original Meaning of the Ninth Amendment," *Texas Law Review* 83, no. 2 (December 2004): 361.
22. Amar, *The Bill of Rights,* xi–xvi.
23. Richard E. Ellis, *The Union at Risk: Jacksonian Democracy, States' Rights and the Nullification Crisis* (New York: Oxford University Press, 1989), 3–4.
24. Forrest McDonald, "The Anti-Federalists, 1781–1789," *Wisconsin Magazine of History* 46, no. 3 (Spring 1963): 206–14.
25. Storing, *What the Anti-Federalists Were For,* 15.
26. Ibid., 53.
27. Ibid., 68.
28. Ibid., 50.
29. Lash, "The Lost Original Meaning," 350–60.
30. Brutus XI (January 31, 1788) and XII (February 7, 1788), quoted in Lash, "The Lost Original Meaning," 350, et seq.
31. Lash, "The Lost Original Meaning," 350–60.
32. Ibid., 347.
33. Ibid., 394.
34. Peter Zavoknyik, *The Age of Strict Construction: A History of the Growth of Federal Power* (Washington, DC: Catholic University of America Press, 2007).
35. Thomas Jefferson, letter to James Madison, December 24, 1825, in *Writings of Jefferson,* vol. 16, eds. Andrew Lipscomb and Albert Bergh, (Washington, DC: Thomas Jefferson Memorial Association, 1907), 140–42.

Chapter 2: Free Speech, Free Trade, and Nullification

1. John Ferling, *John Adams: A Life* (Newtown, CT: American Political Biography Press, 1992), 366–67.
2. Ibid., 367.
3. Thomas Woods, *Nullification: How to Resist Federal Tyranny in the 21st Century* (Washington, DC: Regnery, 2010), 45–48.
4. *Resolutions Adopted by the Kentucky General Assembly*, The Papers of Thomas Jefferson, https://jeffersonpapers.princeton.edu/selected-documents/resolutions-adopted-kentucky-general-assembly.
5. Ibid., 52.
6. Christian Fritz, "Interposition and the Heresy of Nullification: James Madison and the Exercise of Sovereign Constitutional Powers," Heritage Foundation, *First Principles*, no. 41, February 21, 2012, http://report.heritage.org/fp41.
7. James Morton Smith, "Sedition in the Old Dominion: James T. Callender and The Prospect Before Us," *Journal of Southern History* 20, no. 2 (May 1954): 167–68.
8. James Morton Smith, *Freedom's Fetters* (Ithaca, NY: Cornell University Press, 1956), 344–45.
9. Kentucky Resolution, December 3, 1799, reprinted by the Bill of Rights Institute.
10. Henry Adams, *John Randolph* (Boston: Houghton, Mifflin, 1883), 35.
11. William Watkins Jr., *Reclaiming the American Revolution: The Kentucky and Virginia Resolutions and Their Legacy* (New York: Palgrave, 2004), 116.
12. St. George Tucker, *Blackstone's Commentaries: with Notes of Reference to the Constitution and Laws of the Federal Government of the United States and of the Commonwealth of Virginia* (Philadelphia: William Young Birch and Abraham Small, 1803), Book I, 141.
13. Edward Hamilton, *A Federal Union, Not a Nation* (Boston: Lee and Shepard, 1880), 16.
14. David O. Stewart, *The Summer of 1787: The Men Who Invented the Constitution* (New York: Simon & Schuster, 2007), 169.
15. Hamilton, *A Federal Union,* 12.
16. James Madison, *Report of 1800*, quoted in Woods, *Nullification,* 173–74.
17. "The Matter with Kansas," *Democracy in America* (blog), *Economist*, May 7, 2013, www.economist.com/blogs/democracyinamerica/2013/05/gun-control-and-nullification-0.
18. Sean Wilentz, "States of Anarchy," *New Republic*, March 30, 2010.
19. Ibid.
20. Woods, *Nullification,* 53.
21. Ethelbert D. Warfield, *The Kentucky Resolutions of 1798: An Historical Study* (New York: G. P. Putnam's Sons, 1887), 195; Raoul Berger, *Federalism: The Founders' Design* (Norman: University of Oklahoma Press, 1987), 200.

22. Ryan Setliff, "States' Rights Apogee, 1760–1840" (master's thesis, Liberty University, 2012), 74, n. 57.

23. Ibid.

24. Woods, *Nullification*, 60–63.

25. Ibid.

26. John J. Gibbons, "The Eleventh Amendment and State Sovereign Immunity: A Reinterpretation," *Columbia Law Review* 83, no. 8 (December 1983): 1948, n. 320.

27. David Forte, "Commander of the Militia," *Heritage Guide to the Constitution*, 2012, www.heritage.org/constitution#!/articles/2/essays/87/commander-of-militia.

28. Setliff, "Apogee," 75–78.

29. Ibid., 79.

30. The Federal Reserve Bank of Philadelphia, "The Second Bank of the United States: A Chapter in the History of Central Banking," December 2010, http://philadelphiafed.org/publications/economic-education/second-bank.pdf, 1–2.

31. David P. Currie, *The Constitution in Congress: The Federalist Period, 1789–1801* (Chicago: University of Chicago Press, 1997), 80.

32. Thomas DiLorenzo, *Hamilton's Curse* (New York: Crown Forum, 2008), 67–68.

33. Kurt T. Lash, "The Lost Original Meaning of the Ninth Amendment," *Texas Law Review* 83, no. 2 (December 2004): 417–19.

34. Kurt T. Lash, "The Lost Jurisprudence of the Ninth Amendment," *Texas Law Review* 83, no. 3 (February 2005): 625.

35. Gary Gerstle, "Federalism in America: Beyond the Tea Partiers," *Dissent*, Fall 2010.

36. Setliff, "Apogee," 84.

37. Herman V. Ames, ed., *State Documents on Federal Relations* (Philadelphia: University of Pennsylvania, 1906), 152.

38. James L. Roark et al., *The American Promise: A History of the United States*, 4th ed. (New York: Bedford/St. Martin's, 2009), 322–23.

39. James Monroe, letter to John C. Calhoun, August 14, 1828, in *The Papers of John C. Calhoun*, vol. 10, eds. Clyde N. Wilson and W. Edwin Hemphill (Columbia: University of South Carolina Press, 1977), 408–10.

40. Richard E. Ellis, *Union at Risk: Jacksonian Democracy, States' Rights and the Nullification Crisis* (New York: Oxford University Press, 1989), ix.

41. Albert Gallatin, *Memorial of the Committee Appointed by the "Free Trade Convention"* (New York: W. A. Mercer, 1832), 80.

42. Condy Raguet, "An Address upon the Sovereignty of the States," *Chronicle* (Augusta, GA), April 9, 1834.

43. Alexis de Tocqueville, *Democracy in America*, trans. Henry Reeve (New York: Modern Library, 1981), 66.

44. Ibid., 70

45.	Herman Belz, ed., *The Webster-Hayne Debate on the Nature of the Union* (Indianapolis: Liberty Fund, 200), 145.

Chapter 3: States' Rights and the Abolitionists

1.	Carl Schurz, "State Rights—Reply to Criticism" (LEEAF.com Books), Kindle edition.
2.	Paul Finkelman, *An Imperfect Union: Slavery, Federalism, and Comity* (Chapel Hill: University of North Carolina Press, 1981), 239
3.	Jeanne Boydston et al., *Making a Nation: The United States and Its People* (New York: Pearson Education, 2004), 345.
4.	Interview with Terry Gross, *Fresh Air*, National Public Radio, April 12, 2011, www.npr.org/2011/04/12/135246259/looking-at-civil-war-150-years-later.
5.	Frank James, "Slavery, Not States' Rights, Caused Civil War Whose Political Effects Linger," *It's All Politics* (blog), National Public Radio, April 12, 2011, www.npr.org.blogs/itsallpolitics.
6.	Victoria Ford, "How to End the Rebirth of the 'Old Confederacy' in the 'New South': An Interview With the Reverend Jesse Jackson," *Nation*, 2014 (Web only), http://www.thenation.com/article/180555/how-end-rebirth-old-confederacy-new-south-interview-reverend-jesse-jackson.
7.	John R. Vile, ed. *Proposed Amendments to the U.S. Constitution*, vol. 1 (Clark, NJ: Lawbook Exchange, 2003), 22, 193.
8.	W. E. B. DuBois, *The Suppression of the African Slave Trade to the USA, 1638–1870* (New York: Longmans, Green and Company, 1904).
9.	Henry Adams, *John Randolph* (Boston: Houghton, Mifflin, 1883), 282.
10.	Edward Payson Powell, *Nullification and Secession in the United States* (New York: G. P. Putnam's Sons, 1897), 353; H. Von Holst, *John C. Calhoun* (Boston: Houghton, Mifflin, 1899), 133–38.
11.	Finkelman, *An Imperfect Union*, 7n10, 137.
12.	Ibid., 132–33; Thomas D. Morris, *Free Men All: The Personal Liberty Laws of the North, 1780–1861* (Baltimore: Johns Hopkins University Press, 1974), 94–106.
13.	Morris, *Free Men All*, 127.
14.	Herman V. Ames, ed., *State Documents on Federal Relations* (Philadelphia: University of Pennsylvania, 1906), 249.
15.	Jeff Forret, *Slavery in the United States* (New York: Facts on File, 2012), 287.
16.	Morris, *Free Men All*, 145–46.
17.	Ibid., 166.
18.	Ibid., 167–68.
19.	James S. Pike, ed., *First Blows of the Civil War* (New York: American News Company, 1879), 278.
20.	Charles Warren, *The Supreme Court in United States History*, vol. 2 (Boston: Little Brown, 1922), 539.

21.   Morris, *Free Men All*, 173–80.

22.   Finkelman, *An Imperfect Union*, 11, 238.

23.   Paul Finkelman, *Dred Scott v. Sandford: A Brief History with Documents* (Boston: Bedford Books, 1997), 34–35.

24.   Ethan Greenberg, *Dred Scott and the Dangers of a Political Court* (Lanham, MD: Lexington Books, 2010), 222.

25.   Abraham Lincoln, "A House Divided," quoted in Finkelman, *Dred Scott v. Sandford*, 185–95.

26.   Powell, *Nullification and Secession*, 350.

27.   Finkelman, *An Imperfect Union*, 239.

28.   Ibid., 318.

29.   Jeffrey Rosen, "The First Hundred Years," *The Supreme Court*, http://www.pbs.org/wnet/supremecourt/antebellum/print/history.html.

30.   "The Question of States' Rights: The Constitution and American Federalism (An Introduction)," *Exploring Constitutional Law*, http://law2.umkc.edu/faculty/projects/ftrials/conlaw/statesrights.html.

31.   Robert Fanuzzi, *Abolition's Public Sphere* (Minneapolis: University of Minnesota Press, 2003), 76–78.

32.   Bill Kauffman, *Bye Bye, Miss American Empire* (White River Junction, VT: Chelsea Green Publishing, 2010), 30.

33.   Michael Perman, *Pursuit of Unity: A Political History of the American South* (Chapel Hill: University of North Carolina Press, 2009), 65–66.

34.   Edward L. Ayers, "The Causes of the Civil War, 2.0," *New York Times*, April 28, 2011.

35.   "Confederate States of America—Georgia Secession," *The Avalon Project*, Yale Law School, http://avalon.law.yale.edu/19th_century/csa_geosec.asp.

36.   Finkelman, *Imperfect Union*, 20–21.

37.   Herbert Croly, *The Promise of American Life* (New York: Macmillan, 1911), 152.

Chapter 4: Progressives Give Birth to a Nation

1.   John Joseph Wallis and Wallace E. Oates, "The Impact of the New Deal on American Federalism," in *The Defining Moment: The Great Depression and the American Economy in the Twentieth Century*, eds. Michael D. Bordo et al. (Chicago: University of Chicago Press, 1998).

2.   Richard Epstein, *How Progressives Rewrote the Constitution* (Washington, DC: Cato Institute, 2006), 2.

3.   Jeanne Boydston et al., *Making a Nation: The United States and Its People* (New York: Pearson Education, 2004), 502.

4.   James West Davidson et al., *Nation of Nations: A Narrative History of the American Republic* (New York: McGraw-Hill, 2007), 620.

5.   W. E. B. DuBois, "Another Open Letter to President Wilson," Septem-

ber 1913, teachingamericanhistory.org/library/document/another-open-letter-to-president-wilson/.

6. William Loren Katz, *Eyewitness: The Negro in American History* (New York: Pitman Publishing Corporation, 1967), 389–90.

7. Epstein, *How Progressives Rewrote*, 101.

8. Gary Gerstle, "Federalism in America: Beyond the Tea Partiers," *Dissent*, Fall 2010.

9. Bill Kauffman, *Bye Bye, Miss American Empire* (White River Junction, VT: Chelsea Green Publishing, 2010), 32.

10. William Archibald Dunning, *Essays on the Civil War and Reconstruction* (New York: Macmillan, 1904), 60.

11. Kurt T. Lash, "The Lost Jurisprudence of the Ninth Amendment," *Texas Law Review* 83, no. 3 (February 2005): 653–54.

12. Edward Hamilton, *A Federal Union, Not a Nation* (Boston: Lee and Shepard, 1880), 6.

13. Ibid., 30.

14. Edward Bellamy, *Looking Backward, 2000–1887* (Boston: Ticknor and Company, 1888), Kindle edition, chapter 19.

15. Arthur Lipow, *Authoritarian Socialism in America: Edward Bellamy and the Nationalist Movement* (Berkeley: University of California Press, 1982), 30.

16. Kauffman, *American Empire*, 40–41.

17. Herbert Croly, *The Promise of American Life* (New York: Macmillan, 1911), 276.

18. Frank Strong, "Cooperative Federalism," *Iowa Law Review* 23, no. 4 (May 1938): 478–79.

19. Randy Barnett, "The Original Meaning of the Commerce Clause," *University of Chicago Law Review* 68, no. 1 (Winter 2001): 101.

20. Croly, *The Promise of American Life*, 351.

21. Henry Litchfield West, *Federal Power: Its Growth and Necessity* (New York: George H. Doran, 1918), 71.

22. Croly, *The Promise of American Life*, 276.

23. James T. Young, *The New American Government and Its Work* (New York: Macmillan, 1920), 279.

24. Edward S. Corwin, *National Supremacy* (New York: Henry Holt, 1913), 41.

25. Edward S. Corwin, *John Marshall and the Constitution* (New Haven, CT: Yale University Press, 1920).

26. Charles W. Pierson, *Our Changing Constitution* (New York: Doubleday, Page and Company, 1922), 28.

27. Gerstle, "Beyond the Tea Partiers."

28. Strong, "Cooperative Federalism," 472.

29. "The Progressive Presidents," AP US History Notes, StudyNotes, www.apstudynotes.org/us-history/topics/the-progressive-presidents/ (accessed June 28, 2013).

30. Strong, "Cooperative Federalism," 479–82.

31. West, *Federal Power*, 66
32. Strong, "Cooperative Federalism," 476–83.
33. "About the ULC," http://www.uniformlaws.org/Narrative.aspx?title= Frequently Asked Questions.
34. West, *Federal Power*, 61.
35. Raoul Berger, *Government by Judiciary: The Transformation of the Fourteenth Amendment* (Indianapolis: Liberty Fund, 1997).
36. Stephen Gardbaum, "New Deal Constitutionalism and the Unshackling of the States," *University of Chicago Law Review* 64, no. 2 (Spring 1997).
37. Stephen Gardbaum, "The Nature of Preemption," *Cornell Law Review* 79, no. 4 (May 1994): 801.
38. Strong, "Cooperative Federalism," 477.
39. West, *Federal Power*, 123.
40. "Child Labor in U.S. History," Child Labor Public Education Project, www.continuetolearn.uiowa.edu/laborctr/child_labor/about/us_ history.html.
41. Sharron Solomon-McCarthy, "The History of Child Labor in the United States: Hammer v. Dagenhart," Yale–New Haven Teachers Institute, curriculum unit 04.01.08, www.yale.edu/ynhti/curriculum/ units/2004/1/04.01.08.x.html#e.
42. Pierson, *Our Changing Constitution*, 59.
43. Epstein, *How Progressives Rewrote*, 61.
44. Pierson, *Our Changing Constitution*, 147.
45. Michael S. Greve, *The Upside-Down Constitution* (Cambridge, MA: Harvard University Press, 2012), Kindle edition, chapter 11.

Chapter 5: FDR Creates Satellite States

1. Franklin D. Roosevelt, "Radio Address on States' Rights," March 2, 1930, in *The Public Papers and Addresses of Franklin D. Roosevelt*, vol. 1 (New York: Random House, 1938), 569.
2. John Steele Gordon, "Justice Brandeis, Call Your Office," *Commentary*, January 4, 2010.
3. Amity Shlaes, *The Forgotten Man: A New History of the Great Depression* (New York: Harper Perennial, 2008); Jim Powell, *FDR's Folly: How Roosevelt and His New Deal Prolonged the Great Depression* (New York: Three Rivers Press, 2004).
4. Chris Edwards, *Downsizing Government* (Washington, DC: Cato Institute, 2005), 149–50.
5. Marion Elizabeth Rodgers, *Mencken: The American Iconoclast* (New York: Oxford University Press, 2005), 408.
6. Susan Stein-Roggenbuck, "A Contest for Local Control: Emergency Relief in Depression-Era Michigan," *Michigan Historical Review* 26, no. 2 (Fall 2000): 90–125.

7. Ira Katznelson, *Fear Itself* (New York: Liveright, 2013), 92–94.
8. John P. Diggins, *Mussolini and Fascism: The View from America* (Princeton, NJ: Princeton University Press, 1972), 279.
9. Franklin D. Roosevelt, Inaugural Address, March 4, 1933, as published in Samuel Rosenman, ed., *The Public Papers of Franklin D. Roosevelt,* vol. 2: *The Year of Crisis, 1933* (New York: Random House, 1938), 11–16.
10. James Q. Whitman, "Of Corporatism, Fascism, and the First New Deal," *American Journal of Comparative Law* 39, no. 4 (Autumn 1991): 747–78.
11. Gary D. Best, *Pride, Prejudice and Politics: Roosevelt vs. Recovery, 1933–1938* (New York: Praeger, 1991).
12. *Korematsu v. United States*, 323 U.S. 214, 230 (1944) (dissenting opinion).
13. Edwards, *Downsizing Government*, 153.
14. James Patterson, "The New Deal and the States," *American Historical Review* 73, no. 1 (October 1967): 75.
15. Katznelson, *Fear Itself*, 92–94.
16. Patterson, "The New Deal and the States," 75.
17. Delbert Clark, "Nine Groups Instead of 48 States," *New York Times Magazine*, April 21, 1935, SM5.
18. A. Christopher Bryant, "The Third Death of Federalism," *Cornell Journal of Law and Public Policy* 17, no. 1 (Fall 2007): 115–19.
19. Edward G. White, *The Constitution and the New Deal* (Cambridge, MA: Harvard University Press, 2000), 206.
20. "Annotation 44—Article I," Findlaw, http://constitution.findlaw.com/article1/annotation44.html.
21. Robert G. Natelson, "The Agency Law Origins of the Necessary and Proper Clause," *Case Western Law Review* 55, no. 2 (Winter 2004): 243–322.
22. John Joseph Wallis and Wallace E. Oates, "The Impact of the New Deal on American Federalism," in *The Defining Moment: The Great Depression and the American Economy in the Twentieth Century*, eds. Michael D. Bordo et al. (Chicago: University of Chicago Press, 1998), 167.
23. Gary Gerstle, "Federalism in America: Beyond the Tea Partiers," *Dissent*, Fall 2010.
24. Strong, "Cooperative Federalism," 514.
25. Wallis and Oates, "Impact of the New Deal," 165.
26. Paul Krugman, "Barack Must Be Good," *New York Times*, December 25, 2008.
27. Gavin Wright, "The Political Economy of New Deal Spending: An Econometric Analysis," *Review of Economics and Statistics* 56, no. 1 (February 1974): 30-38.
28. Robert Caro, *The Power Broker* (New York: Vintage, 1975), 426–41.
29. Michael S. Greve, *The Upside-Down Constitution* (Cambridge, MA: Harvard University Press, 2012), Kindle edition, chapter 8.
30. Ibid., chapter 11.

31. Ibid., chapter 9.
32. Stein-Roggenbuck, "A Contest for Local Control," 90.
33. Patterson, "The New Deal and the States," 78.
34. Greve, *Upside-Down*, chapter 8.

Chapter 6: Big Brother Comes of Age

1. Todd Wallack, "US Targets Hub Signs," *Boston Globe*, March 2, 2011, www.boston.com/realestate/news/articles/2011/03/02/us_says_high_profile_boston_signs_violate_rules/.
2. Federal Highway Administration and Massachusetts Department of Transportation Highway Division, Right of Way Bureau, "Office of Outdoor Advertising Process Review," undated.
3. Paul Robinson, "National Interstate and Defense Highways Act," in *Encyclopedia of American History: Postwar United States, 1946–1968*, revised edition, eds. Adam Winkler et al. (New York: Facts on File, 2010).
4. John Joseph Wallis and Wallace E. Oates, "The Impact of the New Deal on American Federalism," in *The Defining Moment: The Great Depression and the American Economy in the Twentieth Century*, eds. Michael D. Bordo et al. (Chicago: University of Chicago Press, 1998), 172.
5. See http://www.fhwa.dot.gov/infrastructure/beauty.cfm.
6. *The Status of Federalism in America: A Report of the Working Group on Federalism of the Domestic Policy Council* (Washington, DC: US Department of Justice, 1986), 32–33.
7. John Kincaid, "State-Federal Relations: Revolt Against Coercive Federalism?," in *The Book of the States 2012* (Lexington, KY: Council of State Governments, 2012), 45.
8. Gary Gerstle, "Federalism in America: Beyond the Tea Partiers," *Dissent*, Fall 2010.
9. Chris Edwards, *Federal Aid to the States: Historical Causes of Government Growth and Bureaucracy*, Cato Policy Analysis no. 593, May 22, 2007, p. 8.
10. *State of North Carolina v. Califano*, 445 F.Supp. 532 (E.D.N.C. 1977). See *The Status of Federalism in America*, n. 136.
11. Chris Edwards, *Downsizing Government* (Washington, DC: Cato Institute, 2005), 106–16.
12. Peter Ferrara, "Block Grants for All: Liberating the Poor and Taxpayers Alike," *Heartland Institute Policy Brief*, May 2014, p. 14.
13. Daniel Sutter, *Welfare Block Grants as a Guide to Medicaid Reform*, Mercatus Center Working Paper 13-07, George Mason University, April 2013.
14. Ron Haskins, *Work over Welfare: The Inside Story of the 1996 Welfare Reform Law* (Washington, DC: Brookings Institution, 2006), 336.
15. Pietro S. Nivola, "Last Rites for States Rights?," Brookings Institution, *Reform Watch*, no. 1 (June 2000).
16. *Jim C. v. US*, 235 F.3d 1079, 1081–82 (8th Cir. 2000).

17. John Kincaid, interview with the author, March 13, 2013.
18. Congressional Research Service, *Unfunded Mandates Reform Act: History, Impact and Issues*, December 6, 2012 ("CRS UMRA Report"), 2.
19. Nivola, "Last Rites?"
20. *Federally Induced Costs Affecting State and Local Governments*, US Advisory Commission on Intergovernmental Relations, Washington, DC, September 1994.
21. Edward Koch, "The Mandate Millstone," *Public Interest*, no. 61 (Fall 1980): 42–57.
22. CRS UMRA Report, 36.
23. David A. Super, "Rethinking Fiscal Federalism," *Harvard Law Review* 118, no. 8 (June 2005): 2581.
24. CRS UMRA Report, 7–9.
25. Richard A. Epstein and Mario Loyola, "The United State of America," *Atlantic*, July 2014, www.theatlantic.com/politics/archive/2014/07/the-united-state-of-america/375270.
26. "The Clean Water Act at 30," *New York Times*, October 22, 2002.
27. Jonathan Adler, "Fables of the Cuyahoga: Reconstructing a History of Environmental Protection," *Fordham Environmental Law Journal* 14, no. 1 (Fall 2002): 89–146.
28. Peter Schuck, *Why Government Fails So Often and How It Can Do Better* (Princeton, NJ: Princeton University Press, 2014), 246.
29. Jonathan Adler, "Let Fifty Flowers Bloom: Transforming the States into Laboratories of Environmental Policy," American Enterprise Institute Federalism Project, Roundtable on Federalism and Environmentalism, September 20, 2001.
30. William O. Douglas, "The Bill of Rights Is Not Enough," *New York University Law Review* 38, no. 2 (April 1963): 219.
31. Brian Young, "Life Before Roe: A Brief Survey of US Abortion Law Before the 1973 Decision" (Stafford, VA: American Life League, 1995).
32. Lino A. Graglia, "The Supreme Court's Perversion of the 1964 Civil Rights Act," *Harvard Journal of Law and Public Policy* 37, no. 1 (Winter 2014): 103.
33. William H. Riker, *Federalism: Origin, Operation, Significance* (Boston: Little, Brown, 1964), 155.
34. James E. Ferguson II, "Preview of 1995 Court Term: Racial Equality," ACLU.org, September 27, 1995, www.aclu.org/racial-justice/preview-1995-court-term-racial-equality.
35. James B. Meriwether and Michael Millgate, eds., *Lion in the Garden: Interviews with William Faulkner, 1926–1962* (New York: Random House, 1968), 60.
36. Jeremy Bailey, "Richard Weaver's Untraditional Case for Federalism," *Publius* 34, no. 4 (September 2004): 33–50.
37. E. J. Dionne, *Why Americans Hate Politics* (New York: Touchstone, 1992), chapter 2.

38. Edwin Meese III, "Big Brother on the Beat: The Expanding Federalization of Crime," *Texas Review of Law and Politics* 1, no. 1 (Spring 1997).

39. Julie Rose O'Sullivan, "The Federal Criminal 'Code': Return of Over-federalization," *Harvard Journal of Law and Public Policy* 37, no. 1 (Winter 2014): 57–67.

40. Brannon Denning and Glenn Reynolds, "Rulings and Resistance: The New Commerce Clause Jurisprudence Encounters the Lower Courts," *Arkansas Law Review* 55, no. 4 (Winter 2003): 1253.

41. David Morris, "The Sainted Clause," *AlterNet*, June 15, 2005, www.alter net.org/story/22221.

42. "The Court and Marijuana," *New York Times*, June 8, 2005, http://www .nytimes.com/2005/06/08/opinion/08wed2.html?_r=0

43. William Van Alstyne, "The Second Death of Federalism," *Michigan Law Review* 83, no. 7 (June 1985): 1712.

44. Raoul Berger, *Federalism: The Founders' Design* (Norman: University of Oklahoma Press, 1987), 8.

45. Brian Bailey, "Federalism: An Antidote to Congress's Separation of Powers Anxiety and Executive Order 13,083," *Indiana Law Review* 75, no. 1 (Winter 2000): 333.

46. Nina A. Mendelson, "A Presumption against Agency Preemption," *Northwestern University Law Review* 102, no. 2 (Spring 2008): 695–725.

47. "Lawyers/Law Firms: Background," OpenSecrets.org, Center for Responsive Politics, April 2010, www.opensecrets.org/industries/back ground.php?cycle=2014&ind=K01.

48. Mendelson, "Presumption," 695–725.

49. William Funk et al., *Limiting Federal Agency Preemption: Recommendations for a New Federalism Executive Order*, Center for Progressive Reform, White Paper 809 (November 2008): 3.

50. *Hearing Before the Subcommittee on Commerce, Trade, and Consumer Protection of the Committee on Energy and Commerce, US House of Representatives*, 111th Cong. (May 6, 2010), www.gpo.gov/fdsys/pkg/CHRG-111hhrg76575/ html/CHRG-111hhrg76575.htm.

51. *Arizona v. United States*, 132 S. Ct. 2492 (2012).

52. Catherine M. Sharkey, "Inside Agency Preemption," *Michigan Law Review* 110, no. 4 (February 2012): 556.

53. William Yeatman, *The U.S. Environmental Agency's Assault on State Sovereignty* (Arlington, VA: American Legislative Exchange Council, 2013).

54. Mario Loyola, "Cooperation or Coercion: Is the EPA Trying to Deputize the States?," Federalist Society Teleforum, July 28, 2014.

55. David B. Rivkin Jr. and Adam Doverspike, "Do Sue and Settle Practices Undermine Congressional Intent for Cooperative Federalism on Environmental Matters?," *Engage* 15, no. 2 (July 2014).

56. Yeatman, *Assault on State Sovereignty*.

57. Linda Greenhouse, "The Nation: Long Term; For a Supreme Court Gray-

beard, States' Rights Can Do No Wrong," *New York Times*, March 16, 2003, http://www.nytimes.com/2003/03/16/weekinreview/the-nation-long-term-for-a-supreme-court-graybeard-states-rights-can-do-no-wrong.html.

58.   "Inching Closer to States' Rights," *New York Times*, May 29, 2011, http://www.nytimes.com/2011/05/30/opinion/30mon1.html.

Chapter 7: The Blessings of Liberty

1.   Alex Newman, "Poll: Most Americans View Feds as Threat to Liberty," *New American*, May 4, 2014, www.thenewamerican.com/usnews/politics/item/18188-poll-most-americans-view-feds-as-threat-to-liberty.

2.   Peter Schuck, *Why Government Fails So Often and How It Can Do Better* (Princeton, NJ: Princeton University Press, 2014), 2.

3.   William Greider, "The Right's Grand Ambition: Rolling Back the 20th Century," *Nation*, May 12, 2003.

4.   Lily Dane, "Tea Party Leader Is Harassed While Testifying about Being Harassed by IRS," *Daily Sheeple*, February 10, 2014, www.thedailysheeple.com/tea-party-leader-is-harassed-while-testifying-about-being-harassed-by-the-irs_022014.

5.   Debra Heine, "ATF Director B. Todd Jones Has No Idea Why His Agents Hounded Catherine Engelbrecht in 2012 & 2013," Breitbart.com, April 3, 2014, www.breitbart.com/InstaBlog/2014/04/03/ATF-Director-B-Todd-Jones-Has-No-Idea-Why-His-Agents-Hounded-Catherine-Engelbrecht-in-2012-2013.

6.   Stan Veuger, "Yes, IRS Harassment Blunted the Tea Party Ground Game," *Real Clear Markets*, June 20, 2013, www.realclearmarkets.com/articles/2013/06/20/yes_irs_harassment_blunted_the_tea_party_ground_game_100412.html.

7.   Nicholas Quinn Rosenkranz, "Targeting the Constitution," *Volokh Conspiracy* (blog), *Washington Post*, September 23, 2014, www.washingtonpost.com/news/volokh-conspiracy/wp/2014/09/23/targeting-the-constitution/.

8.   *Bond v. United States*, 131 S. Ct. 2355 (2011).

9.   *Gregory v. Ashcroft*, 501 US 452 (1990).

10. See, e.g., C. William Michaels, *No Greater Threat: America after September 11 and the Rise of a National Security State* (New York: Algora, 2002); Nancy Chang, *Silencing Political Dissent* (New York: Seven Stories, 2002).

11. Ann Althouse, "The Vigor of the Anti-Commandeering Doctrine in Times of Terror," *Brooklyn Law Review* 69, no. 4 (Summer 2004): 1254–56.

12. Ernst A. Young, "Welcome to the Dark Side: Liberals Rediscover Federalism in the Wake of the War on Terror," *Brooklyn Law Review* 69, no. 4 (Summer 2004): 1283.

13. Macon Phillips, "Facts Are Stubborn Things," White House blog, August 4, 2009, www.whitehouse.gov/blog/Facts-Are-Stubborn-Things.
14. "Stockman Asks for Probe of Alleged Audits of Citizens Reported to White House Email Address," press release, May 14, 2013, http://www.guidrynews.com/story.aspx?id=1000052146.
15. Young, "Dark Side," 1285.
16. Barton Gellman and Ashkan Soltani, "NSA Tracking Cellphone Locations Worldwide, Snowden Documents Show," *Washington Post*, December 4, 2013.
17. John Shiffman and Kristina Cooke, "U.S. Directs Agents to Cover Up Programs Used to Investigate Americans," Reuters, August 5, 2013.
18. Frederic Paul, "The Week NSA Surveillance Finally Jumped the Shark," *Network World*, December 10, 2013, http://www.networkworld.com/article/2225975/security/the-week-nsa-surveillance-finally-jumped-the-shark.html.
19. Robert McMillan, "Why Does the NSA Want to Keep Its Water Bill Secret?," *Wired*, March 19, 2014, www.wired.com/2014/03/nsa-water/.
20. Tony Semerad, "Bluffdale Ordered to Release NSA Water Records," *Salt Lake Tribune*, March 19, 2014.
21. George Will, "Blowing the Whistle on Leviathan," *Washington Post*, July 27, 2012.
22. Virginia Hennessy, "Marine Biologist Nancy Black Fined $12,500 for Violating Marine Mammal Protection Act," *Monterey Herald*, January 13, 2014.
23. Julie Rose O'Sullivan, "The Federal Criminal 'Code': Return of Overfederalization," *Harvard Journal of Law and Public Policy* 37, no. 1 (Winter 2014): 57.
24. Brian A. Reaves, *Federal Law Enforcement Officers, 2008* (Washington, DC: US Department of Justice, Bureau of Justice Statistics, June 2012).
25. "Guns in Schools Policy Summary," Law Center to Prevent Gun Violence, http://smartgunlaws.org/guns-in-schools-policy-summary/#state.
26. O'Sullivan, "Return of Overfederalization," 57.
27. Harvey Silverglate, "What the 'Wall Street Journal' Missed about False Statements Made to the FBI," Forbes.com, April 18, 2012, www.forbes.com/sites/harveysilverglate/2012/04/18/what-the-wall-street-journal-missed-about-false-statements-made-to-the-fbi/.
28. Vikrant Reddy, "King v. United States and the Overfederalization of Criminal Law," *Right on Crime* (blog), Texas Public Policy Foundation, July 20, 2012, www.rightoncrime.com/2012/07/king-v-united-states-and-the-overfederalization-of-criminal-law/.
29. John Enshwiller and Gary Fields, "For Feds, 'Lying' Is a Handy Charge," *Wall Street Journal*, April 9, 2012.
30. Derek Cohen, "Civil Asset Forfeiture Abuse," *Belltowers*, March 5, 2014, http://thebelltowers.com/2014/03/05/civil-asset-forfeiture-abuse/.

31. Dick Carpenter, Larry Salzman, and Lisa Knepper, *Inequitable Justice: How Federal "Equitable Sharing" Encourages Local Police and Prosecutors to Evade State Civil Forfeiture Law for Financial Gain* (Washington, DC: Institute for Justice, 2011).

32. Ross Marchand, "The Felonization of America," *Right on Crime* (blog), Texas Public Policy Foundation, January 31, 2014, www.rightoncrime .com/2014/01/the-felonization-of-america/.

33. *Smart Reform Is Possible: States Reducing Incarceration Rates and Costs While Protecting Communities* (New York: American Civil Liberties Union, August 2011).

34. Susan Klein and Ingrid Grobey, "Debunking Claims of Overfederalization of Criminal Law," *Emory Law Journal* 62, no. 1 (September 2012): 1.

35. Harvey Silverglate, "Federal Criminal Law: Punishing Benign Intentions," in *In the Name of Justice*, ed. Timothy Lynch (Washington, DC: Cato Institute, 2009).

36. Pete Kennedy, "Dan Allgyer, Pennsylvania," A Campaign for Real Milk, February 3, 2012, www.realmilk.com/case-updates/dan-allgyer/.

37. Young, "Dark Side," 1290.

38. Bradley A. Smith, "Connecting the Dots in the IRS Scandal," *Wall Street Journal*, February 26, 2014.

39. Ajit Pai, "The FCC Wades into the Newsroom," *Wall Street Journal*, February 10, 2014.

Chapter 8: Democracy, for a Change

1. Ann O'Neill, "Showdown at the H20 Corral," CNN.com, May 10, 2012, http://cnn.com/2012/05/10/us/tombstone-water-fight.

2. "Tombstone v. United States," Goldwater Institute, February 17, 2012, http://goldwaterinstitute.org/article/tombstone-v-united-states.

3. Holly Fretwell, *Bringing Local Knowledge to Federal Lands*, R Street Policy Study no. 18, February 2014.

4. Erik Olin Wright and Joel Rogers, *American Society: How It Really Works* (New York: Norton, 2010).

5. Hans von Spakovsky, "Government's Shocking Interference in Rancher's Life," *Daily Signal*, June 11, 2013, http://dailysignal.com/2013/06/11/court-rebuffs-government-overreach-in-nevada/.

6. "Memorandum on Genuine Autonomy for the Tibetan People," International Campaign for Tibet, http://savetibet.org/policy-center/memorandum-on-genuine-autonomy-for-the-tibetan-people/.

7. Fretwell, "Local Knowledge."

8. Henry Litchfield West, *Federal Power: Its Growth and Necessity* (New York: George H. Doran, 1918), 96.

9. James Bennett, "True to Form, Clinton Shifts Energies Back to U.S. Focus," *New York Times*, July 5, 1998.

10. Testimony of John Jones, *Legislative Hearing on H.R. 250, H.R. 382, H.R. 432, H.R. 758, H.R. 1512, H.R. 1434, H.R. 1439, H.R. 1459, and H.R. 885, Subcommittee on Public Lands and Environmental Regulation*, 113 Cong. (April 16, 2013), www.gpo.gov/fdsys/pkg/CHRG-113hhrg80524/pdf/CHRG-113hhrg80524.pdf.

11. Catherine M. Sharkey, "Inside Agency Preemption," *Michigan Law Review* 110, no. 4 (February 2012): 556.

12. Bill Kauffman, *Bye Bye, Miss American Empire* (White River Junction, VT: Chelsea Green Publishing, 2010), Kindle edition, Introduction.

13. Brian Bailey, "Federalism: An Antidote to Congress's Separation of Powers Anxiety and Executive Order 13,083," *Indiana Law Review* 75, no. 1 (Winter 2000): 349.

14. Steven G. Calabresi, "A Government of Limited and Enumerated Powers: In Defense of *United States v. Lopez*," *Michigan Law Review* 94, no. 3 (December 1995): 795–96.

15. Jennifer Maloney, "From New York's 'Mr. Mayor,' Quips Even in Crisis," *Wall Street Journal*, February 2–3, 2013.

16. Neal McCluskey, "LEARNing about something good in Washington," *Cato at Liberty* (blog), Cato Institute, May 21, 2010, www.cato.org/blog/learning-about-something-good-washington.

17. Richard A. Epstein and Mario Loyola, "The United State of America," *Atlantic*, July 2014, www.theatlantic.com/politics/archive/2014/07/the-united-state-of-america/375270.

18. John Kincaid, interview with the author, March 13, 2013.

19. Michael Greve, "Interposition Now," *Library of Law and Liberty*, December 6, 2012, www.libertylawsite.org/2012/12/06/interposition-now/.

20. Mike Shields, "The ABCs of Medicaid Block Grants," *KHI News Service*, May, 2011, http://www.khi.org/news/2011/may/02/abcs-medicaid-block-grants/.

21. Peter Schuck, *Why Government Fails So Often and How It Can Do Better* (Princeton, NJ: Princeton University Press, 2014), 196.

Chapter 9: Real Diversity

1. "Diversity and Inclusion," US Office of Personnel and Management, www.opm.gov/policy-data-oversight/diversity-and-inclusion/.

2. Bill Kauffman, *Bye Bye, Miss American Empire* (White River Junction, VT: Chelsea Green Publishing, 2010).

3. Tom Fox, "Treating Citizens like Customers," *On Leadership* (blog), *Washington Post*, September 17, 2014, www.washingtonpost.com/blogs/on-leadership/wp/2014/09/17/treating-citizens-like-customers/.

4. Richard A. Epstein and Mario Loyola, "The United State of America," *Atlantic*, July 2014, www.theatlantic.com/politics/archive/2014/07/the-united-state-of-america/375270.

5. Heather Gerken, "A New Progressive Federalism," *Democracy*, March 2011.
6. Maya Rhodan, "States Lead the Way on Sentencing Reform," *Time*, February 14, 2014.
7. Barbara Gottlieb, "States Lead the Action for Toxics Policy Reform," Physicians for Social Responsibility, May 1, 2013, www.psr.org/environment-and-health/environmental-health-policy-institute/responses/states-lead-the-action.html.
8. Pietro S. Nivola, "Rediscovering Federalism," *Issues in Governance Studies*, Brookings Institution, July 2007, p. 3.
9. Andrew Coulson, "The Impact of Federal Involvement in America's Classrooms," Congressional testimony, February 10, 2011, www.cato .org/publications/congressional-testimony/impact-federal-involvement-americas-classrooms.
10. John Kincaid, "State-Federal Relations: Revolt Against Coercive Federalism?," in *The Book of the States 2012* (Lexington, KY: Council of State Governments, 2012).
11. Coulson, "Impact."
12. Richard Whitmire, "Tennessee and DC Lead Education Reform," *USA Today*, November 7, 2013.
13. "Gold Standard Studies," Friedman Foundation for Educational Choice, http://www.edchoice.org/Research/Gold-Standard-Studies.
14. Ted Rebarber and Alison Consoletti Zgainer, eds., *Survey of America's Charter Schools 2014* (Washington, DC: Center for Education Reform, 2014).
15. John Kincaid, interview with the author, March 13, 2013.
16. The Hon. Rob Bishop, interview with the author, April 12, 2013.
17. Dinan, *Talk Back,* 6–8.
18. Neal McCluskey, "Education Experts Also Oppose Core," *Albany Times Union*, October 30, 2013.
19. Jessica Michele Herring, "Immigration Reform 2014: New Jersey, Pennsylvania, Lead Immigration Reform by Enacting DREAM Act Legislation," *Latino Post*, January 14, 2014, www.latinopost .com/articles/3113/20140114/immigration-reform-2014-new-jersey-pennsylvania-lead-immigration-reform-by-enacting-dream-act-legislation.htm.
20. Gabriel Roth, "Federal Highway Funding," Downsizing the Federal Government, Cato Institute, June 2010, www.downsizinggovernment .org/transportation/federal-highway-funding.
21. Don Jeffrey, "Vermont Fights Ruling It Can't Shut Entergy Nuclear Plant," Bloomberg.com, January 14, 2013, www.bloomberg.com/news/2013-01-14/vermont-fights-ruling-it-can-t-shut-entergy-nuclear-plant.html.
22. Jonathan Turley, "Fighting Pot with Water," *USA Today*, July 7, 2014.
23. Tim Dickinson, "Jerry Brown's Tough-Love California Miracle," *Rolling Stone*, August 29, 2013.
24. Turley, "Fighting Pot."

25. Jill E. Fisch, "The New Federal Regulation of Corporate Governance," *Harvard Journal of Law and Public Policy* 28, no. 1 (Fall 2004): 39.
26. Frank Easterbrook, "Federalism and Commerce," *Harvard Journal of Law and Public Policy* 36, no. 3 (Summer 2013), 937–39.
27. Ibid.
28. Michael Memoli, "Democratic Governors Join Obama in Push for Higher Minimum Wage," *Los Angeles Times*, February 21, 2014.
29. Conor Friedersdorf, "Role-Reversal in Debate over States' Rights?," *Orange County Register*, January 7, 2014.
30. "Tea Party's 'States' Rights' Constitutional Amendment," *Daily Kos*, January 2, 2011, www.dailykos.com/story/2011/01/02/932988/-Tea-Party-s-States-Rights-Constitutional-Amendment.
31. Indur Goklany, *Clearing the Air: The Real Story of the War on Air Pollution* (Washington, DC: Cato Institute, 1999), 3, 91–96.
32. Jonathan Adler, "Let Fifty Flowers Bloom: Transforming the States into Laboratories of Environmental Policy," American Enterprise Institute Federalism Project, Roundtable on Federalism and Environmentalism, September 20, 2001.
33. Richard Revesz, "Federalism and Environmental Regulation: A Normative Critique," in *The New Federalism: Can the States Be Trusted?*, eds. John Ferejohn and Barry Weingast (Stanford, CA: Hoover Institution, 1997).
34. James Buckley, *Freedom at Risk* (New York: Encounter, 2010).
35. Peter Applebome, "A Vision of a Nation No Longer in the U.S.," *New York Times*, October 18, 2007.
36. *Thomas More Law Center v. Obama*, 651 F.3d 529 (6th Cir. 2011).
37. E. Fuller Torrey, *How to Bring Sanity to Our Mental Health System*, Heritage Foundation, Center for Policy Innovation Discussion Paper No. 2, December 19, 2011, 9.
38. E. Fuller Torrey, "Fifty Years of Failing America's Mentally Ill," *Wall Street Journal*, February 5, 2013, A15.
39. Fuller, *Sanity*, 9.
40. Herbert Storing, *What the Anti-Federalists Were For* (Chicago: University of Chicago Press, 1981), Kindle edition, chapter 3.
41. Brutus I, 2.9.16, in Storing, *What the Anti-Federalists Were For*.
42. Jason Crook, "Towards a More 'Perfect' Union: The Untimely Demise of Federalism and the Rise of a Homogeneous Political Culture," *University of Dayton Law Review* 34, no. 1 (Fall 2008): 47.

Chapter 10: A More Competent Government

1. Sharon Begley, "As ObamaCare Tech Woes Mounted, Contractor Payment Soared," Reuters, October 17, 2013.
2. Michael D. Shear, "Boehner Calls for More Action on V.A. Scandal," *New York Times*, June 4, 2014.

3. Peter Schuck, *Why Government Fails So Often and How It Can Do Better* (Princeton, NJ: Princeton University Press, 2014), 190.
4. Marshall J. Breger and Gary J. Edles, "Established by Practice: The Theory and Operation of Independent Federal Agencies," *Administrative Law Review* 52, no. 4 (Fall 2000): 1131.
5. Chris Edwards, *Downsizing Government* (Washington, DC: Cato Institute, 2005), 74.
6. Al Gore, *Creating a Government That Works Better and Costs Less: Report of the National Performance Review* (Darby, PA: Diane Publishing, 1993), 93.
7. John Samples and Emily Ekins, *Public Attitudes toward Federalism*, Cato Policy Analysis no. 759, September 23, 2014, p. 23.
8. Schuck, *Why Government Fails*, 166–67.
9. Daniel P. Moynihan, "Quadragesimo Anno," in *The Federal Budget and the States*, 24th edition (Cambridge, MA: Taubman Center, 2000), 14.
10. Pietro S. Nivola, "Rediscovering Federalism," *Issues in Governance Studies*, Brookings Institution, July 2007, pp. 2–3.
11. Michael Waddoups and David Clark, "A Modest Proposal to the Federal Government: Let Utah Do It," *Washington Post*, February 19, 2010.
12. Chris Edwards, "Fiscal Federalism," Downsizing the Federal Government, Cato Institute, June 2013, www.downsizing government.org/fiscal-federalism.
13. Edwards, *Downsizing Government*, 114.
14. Ibid., 111–14.
15. Beryl H. Davis, "Improper Payments: Remaining Challenges and Strategies for Government Reduction Efforts," *Testimony Before the Subcommittee on Federal Financial Management, Government Information, Federal Services, and International Security, Committee on Homeland Security and Governmental Affairs, US Senate* (Washington, DC: Government Accountability Office, March 2012).
16. "OMB Issues Instructions to Agencies and States for Combating Waste, Fraud, and Abuse in Federal Programs," Office of Management and Budget, news release, June 19, 2003, www.whitehouse.gov/sites/default/files/omb/assets/omb/pubpress/2003-22.pdf.
17. *Reporting Improper Payments: A Report Card on Agencies' Progress, Hearing Before the Federal Financial Management, Government Information, and International Security Subcommittee of the Committee on Homeland Security and Governmental Affairs, United States Senate*, 109th Cong. (March 9, 2006), www.gpo.gov/fdsys/pkg/CHRG-109shrg27749/pdf/CHRG-109shrg27749.pdf.
18. Davis, "Improper Payments."
19. Schuck, *Why Government Fails*, 192.
20. Timothy Male, "U.S. Is Overspending to Save Salmon, *Seattle Times*, March 19, 2014, http://seattletimes.com/html/opinion/2023155976_timothymaleopedendangeredspecies18xml.html./.

21. Paul C. Light, "Has the National Government Become an 'Awful Spectacle'?," *Public Administration Review* 71, issue supplement s1 (December 2011): S155.
22. William Stanbury and Fred Thompson, "Toward a Political Economy of Government Waste: First Step, Definitions," *Public Administration Review* 55, no. 5 (September/October 1995): 418.
23. John Shannon, "Federalism's 'Invisible Regulator'—Interjurisdictional Competition," in *Competition Among States and Local Governments*, eds. Daphne Kenyon and John Kincaid (Washington, DC: Urban Institute Press 1991).
24. Ferrara, "Block Grants for All."
25. Ibid.
26. Edwards, *Downsizing Government*, 108–10.
27. Nora Gordon, "Do Federal Grants Boost School Spending? Evidence from Title I," *Journal of Public Economics* 88, nos. 9–10 (August 2004): 1771–92.
28. Robert B. Helms, *Medicaid: The Forgotten Issue in Health Reform*, American Enterprise Institute Health Policy Outlook no. 14, November 2009.
29. Stanbury and Thompson, "Government Waste," 418.
30. John Ydstie, "Sen. Burns Scrutinized for Earmark Tied to Abramoff," National Public Radio, March 27, 2006, www.npr.org/templates/story/story.php?storyId=5299944.
31. Ronald D. Utt, *President's Plan to Consolidate Federal Economic Development Programs Is Long Overdue*, Heritage Foundation Web Memo #656 on Federal Budget, February 7, 2005.
32. Rick Newman, "Why Federal Government Trumps the States," *U.S. News & World Report*, September 23, 2011.
33. *Federal Assistance: Grant System Continues to Be Highly Fragmented* (GAO-03-718T), Government Accountability Office, Washington, DC, April 29, 2003, www.gao.gov/assets/110/109870.pdf.
34. Edwards, *Downsizing Government*, 57.
35. Light, "Awful Spectacle."
36. David Fahrenthold, "What Does Rural Mean: Feds Have 15 Answers," *Washington Post*, June 9, 2013, A1.
37. Edwards, *Downsizing Government*, 57.
38. Schuck, *Why Government Fails*, 190.
39. Lennard G. Kruger, *Staffing for Adequate Fire and Emergency Response: The SAFER Grant Program*, Congressional Research Service, Washington, DC, January 23, 2014.
40. Edwards, *Downsizing Government*, 115.
41. *Message of the President of the United States Transmitting the Reports of the Commission on Economy and Efficiency*, House of Representatives Document 1252, Washington, DC, 1913.
42. Edwards, *Downsizing Government*, 52–53.
43. Paul C. Light, *A Government Ill Executed* (Cambridge, MA: Harvard University Press, 2008), 168.

44. Waddoups and Clark, "Modest Proposal."
45. John Kincaid, interview with the author, March 13, 2013.
46. Schuck, *Why Government Fails*, 169.
47. Organisation for Economic Co-operation and Development, *Government at a Glance 2013: Switzerland*, www.oecd.org/gov/GAAG2013_CFS_CHE.pdf.

Chapter 11: A Lasting Peace

1. "160 Tennessee National Guardsmen Deployed to Afghanistan," News Channel 5, Nashville, March 16, 2014, www.jrn.com/newschannel5/news/250551911.html.
2. Maya Schenwar, "States Push to Take Back National Guard," *Truthout*, February 11, 2009, http://truth-out.org/archive/component/k2/item/82486:states-push-to-take-back-national-guard.
3. Ibid.
4. *2015 National Guard Bureau Posture Statement* (Washington, DC: National Guard Bureau), www.nationalguard.mil/portals/31/Documents/Posture Statements/2015%20National%20Guard%20Bureau%20Posture%20Statement.pdf.
5. Schenwar, "States Push."
6. John R. Vile, *The Constitutional Convention of 1787*, vol. 1 (Denver: ABC-CLIO, 2005), 320.
7. *2015 National Guard Bureau Posture Statement*.
8. Jerry Cooper, *The Rise of the National Guard* (Lincoln: University of Nebraska Press, 1997), 9.
9. *Houston v. Moore*, 18 US 1 (1820).
10. James Biser Whisker, "The Citizen-Soldier under Federal and State Law," *West Virginia Law Review* 94, no. 4 (Summer 1992): 967–68.
11. Cooper, *Rise of the National Guard*, 9.
12. John R. Brinkerhoff, "Restore the Militia for Homeland Security," *Journal of Homeland Security*, November 2001, available at www.constitution.org/mil/cmt/brinkerhoff_nov01.htm.
13. Peter A. Fish, "The Constitution and the Training of National Guardsmen," *Journal of Law and Politics* 4, no. 3 (Winter 1988): 597.
14. Ibid., 630–31.
15. *Perpich v. Department of Defense*, 880 F.2d 11 (8th Cir. 1989), *aff'd* 110 S.Ct. 2418 (1990).
16. Akhil Amar, "Of Sovereignty and Federalism," *Yale Law Journal* 96, no. 7 (June 1987): 1425.
17. Josh Hicks, "National Guard Is New Gay Rights Battleground as Four States Refuse to Handle Federal Benefits," *Washington Post*, September 21, 2013.
18. National Governors Association, "America Wins: The Struggle for Con-

trol of the National Guard," State-Federal Brief, undated, www.nga.org/files/live/sites/NGA/files/pdf/1210NationalGuardAmericaWins.pdf.

19. Ken Picard, "Leahy to Reverse White House 'Power Grab' of National Guard," *Seven Days*, June 27, 2007.

20. Alfonso Chardy, "Reagan Aides and the Secret Government," *Miami Herald*, July 5, 1987.

21. Christian Smith, *Resisting Reagan: The U.S. Central America Peace Movement* (Chicago: University of Chicago Press, 1996).

22. Walter Pincus, "National Guard Association, Vets Groups, Know How to Win at Defense Fiscal Football," *Washington Post*, May 26, 2014.

23. Chris Johnson, "How Will Obama Handle National Guard Units Disobeying Federal Directive?," *Washington Blade*, September 30, 2013.

24. Hicks, "Battleground."

25. Benson Scotch, "Memo to the Wisconsin Assembly Committee on Veterans and Military Affairs," March 13, 2010, *Democracy Square*, http://democracycharter.com/publications-talks/scotch-legal-memo-wisconsin-safeguard-guard-act.

26. Jessica Zuckerman et al., "Why More States Should Establish State Defense Forces," Heritage Foundation, *Backgrounder*, no. 2655, February 28, 2012.

27. State Guard Association of the United States, http://www.sgaus.org.

Chapter 12: An Action Plan

1. Amy Vickers, "The Energy Policy Act: Assessing Its Impact on Utilities," *Journal of the American Water Works Association* 85, no. 8 (August 1993): 56.

2. Doug Bandow, *Demonizing Drugmakers: The Political Assault on the Pharmaceutical Industry*, Cato Policy Analysis no. 475, May 8, 2003, pp. 32–35.

3. Jon Harper, "Senator: More Than 1,000 Veterans May Have Died as a Result of VA Misconduct," *Stars and Stripes*, June 24, 2014.

4. John W. Dawson and John J. Seater, "Federal Regulation and Aggregate Economic Growth," *Journal of Economic Growth* 18, no. 2 (June 2013): 137–77.

5. Ernst A. Young, "Welcome to the Dark Side: Liberals Rediscover Federalism in the Wake of the War on Terror," *Brooklyn Law Review* 69, no. 4 (Summer 2004): 1302.

6. Daniel P. Moynihan, "Quadragesimo Anno," in *The Federal Budget and the States*, 24th edition (Cambridge, MA: Taubman Center, 2000).

7. Ronald D. Utt, "'Turn Back' Transportation to the States," Heritage Foundation, *Backgrounder* no. 2651 (February 6, 2012).

8. Ibid.

9. Ibid.

10. "54% Say States Should Be Able to Opt Out of Federal Programs," Rasmussen Reports, August 26, 2011.

11. Charles Murray, "Tax Withholding Is Bad for Democracy," *Wall Street Journal*, August 13, 2009, http://online.wsj.com/articles/SB10001424052 9702043136045743282735726737 30.

12. Peter Ferrara, "Block Grants for All: Liberating the Poor and Taxpayers Alike," *Heartland Institute Policy Brief*, May 2014, p. 19.

13. Lindsey Burke, "How the A-PLUS Act Can Rein In the Government's Education Power Grab," Heritage Foundation, *Backgrounder*, no. 2858 on Education, November 14, 2013.

14. *The Path to Prosperity: Fiscal Year 2015 Budget Resolution* (Washington, DC: House Budget Committee, April 2014).

15. Paul Ryan, *Expanding Opportunity in America: A Discussion Draft from the House Budget Committee* (Washington, DC: House Budget Committee Majority Staff, July 24, 2014).

16. Linda Bilmes and Shelby Chodos, "Want to Stimulate the Economy? Let's Hand Cash Directly to the States," *Washington Post*, June 29, 2012.

17. John Kincaid, interview with the author, March 13, 2013.

18. See the website of the Firearms Freedom Act at http://firearmsfreedom act.com.

19. Justine McDaniel, Robby Korth, and Jessica Boehm, "In States, a Legislative Rush to Nullify Federal Gun Laws," *GovBeat* (blog), *Washington Post*, August 29, 2014, www.washingtonpost.com/blogs/govbeat/wp/2014/08/29/in-states-a-legislative-rush-to-nullify-federal-gun-laws/.

20. Ibid.; Kathleen S. Callahan, Lisa M. Lindemenn, and Barak Y. Orbach, "Arming States' Rights: Federalism, Private Lawmakers, and the Battering Ram Strategy," *Arizona Law Review* 52, no. 4 (Winter 2010): 1161–1206.

21. "State Marijuana Laws Map," *Governing*, no date, www.governing.com/gov-data/state-marijuana-laws-map-medical-recreational.html.

22. "4th Amendment Protection Act," Tenth Amendment Center, no date, http://tenthamendmentcenter.com/legislation/4th-amendment-pro tection-act/.

23. Michael Maharrey, "Utah Legislator Introduces Bill to Cut Off NSA's Water Supply," Tenth Amendment Center, February 12, 2014, http://tenthamendmentcenter.com/2014/02/12/utah-legislator-introduces-bill-to-cut-of-nsa-data-centers-water-supply/.

24. Michael Greve, "Cooperation or Coercion: Is the EPA Trying to Deputize the States?" Federalist Society Teleforum, July 28, 2014.

25. Ted Cruz and Mario Loyola, *Reclaiming the Constitution: An Agenda for State Action* (Austin: Texas Public Policy Foundation, November 2010), 16.

26. Nina A. Mendelson, "A Presumption against Agency Preemption," *Northwestern University Law Review* 102, no. 2 (Spring 2008): 695–725.

27. Catherine M. Sharkey, "Federalism Accountability: 'Agency-Forcing' Measures," *Duke Law Journal* 58, no. 8 (May 2009): 2174–6.

28. Catherine M. Sharkey, "Inside Agency Preemption," *Michigan Law Review* 110, no. 4 (February 2012): 584.

29. Vikrant Reddy, "You Don't Have to Make a Federal Case out of It," *USA Today*, December 9, 2012.

30. "States Cut Both Crime and Imprisonment," Pew Charitable Trust, Public Safety Performance Project, December 19, 2013, www.pewtrusts.org/en/multimedia/data-visualizations/2013/states-cut-both-crime-and-imprisonment.

31. Akhil Amar, "Of Sovereignty and Federalism," *Yale Law Journal* 96, no. 7 (June 1987): 1425.

32. John J. Gibbons, "The Eleventh Amendment and State Sovereign Immunity: A Reinterpretation," *Columbia Law Review* 83, no. 8 (December 1983): 1943, n. 296.

33. William Duker, *A Constitutional History of Habeas Corpus* (Westport, CT: Greenwood Press, 1980), 126–80.

34. Amar, "Of Sovereignty and Federalism," 1517.

35. McDaniel, Korth, and Boehm, "Legislative Rush."

36. Owen J. Roberts, "Fortifying the Supreme Court's Independence," *American Bar Association Journal* 35, no. 1 (January 1935), 4.

37. Wayne A. Logan, "Constitutional Cacophony: Federal Circuit Splits and the Fourth Amendment," *Vanderbilt Law Review* 65, no. 5 (October 2012).

38. "Federal Control of the East v. West," presentation by the Hon. Rob Bishop, available at http://energystates.org/wp/wp-content/uploads/2012/12/RepBishopEPSCPresentation-.pdf.

39. Michelle L. Price, "Feds Miss Public Lands Deadline as Utah Gears Up for a Fight," *Standard Examiner*, January 3, 2015, http://www.standard.net/Government/2015/01/03/Utah-gears-up-for-lands-fight-as-deadline-passes-1.

40. "Utah Transfer of Public Lands Act," Utah Sierran, https://utah.sierraclub.org/content/utah-transfer-public-lands-act.

41. Colby Frazier, "With GOP Support, Utah Wilderness Act Clears Committee," *City Weekly*, March 4, 2014.

42. Alex Newman, "Western States Want Feds to Surrender 'Federal Land,'" *New American*, April 22, 2014.

43. "Federal Control of East v. West."

44. Jonathan Adler, "Let Fifty Flowers Bloom: Transforming the States into Laboratories of Environmental Policy," American Enterprise Institute Federalism Project, Roundtable on Federalism and Environmentalism, September 20, 2001.

45. Paul R. Portney, "Environmental Policy in the Next Century," in *Setting National Priorities: The 2000 Election and Beyond*, eds. Henry J. Aaron and Robert D. Reischauer (Washington, DC: Brookings Institution Press, 1999), 379.

46. Adler, "Fifty Flowers."
47. Pietro S. Nivola, "Last Rites for States Rights?," Brookings Institution, *Reform Watch*, no. 1 (June 2000).
48. Fred Lucas, "Obama Calls for Palestinian Self-Determination in Israel Speech," Cnsnews.com, March 21, 2013, http://cnsnews.com/news/article/obama-calls-palestinian-self-determination-israel-speech.

Index

About the Author

Adam Freedman is one of America's leading commentators on law, and holds degrees from Yale, Oxford, and the University of Chicago. He is also the author of *The Naked Constitution: What the Founders Said and Why It Still Matters*. A former columnist for the *New York Law Journal*, he covers legal affairs for Ricochet.com and is a regular contributor to *City Journal*. He lives in Brooklyn, New York, with his wife and two daughters.